THE DOBE JU/'HOANSI

RICHARD B. LEE

University of Toronto

First edition published as
THE DOBE !KUNG

WADSWORTH

™

THOMSON LEARNING

Australia • Canada • Mexico • Singapore • Spain
United Kingdom • United States

Anthropology Editor: Lin Marshall
Assistant Editor: Reilly O'Neill
Editorial Assistant: Danette Cross
Marketing Manager: Diane McOscar
Project Manager, Editorial Production: Angela Williams Urquhart
Print/Media Buyer: Kristine Waller/Jessica Reed

Production Service: Carlisle Publishers Services
Text Designer: Carlisle Publishers Services
Copy Editor: Robert Marcum
Cover Designer: Carlisle Publishers Services
Cover Printer: Lehigh Press
Compositor: Carlisle Publishers Services
Printer: R.R. Donnelley & Sons

Printed in the United States of America
1 2 3 4 5 6 7 05 04 03 02 01

For more information about our products, contact us at:
Thomson Learning Academic Resource Center
1-800-423-0563
For permission to use material from this text, contact us by:
Phone: 1-800-730-2214
Fax: 1-800-730-2215
Web: http://www.thomsonrights.com

Library of Congress Cataloging-in-Publication Data
Lee, Richard B.
  The Dobe Ju/'hoansi / Richard B. Lee.—3rd ed.
  p. cm.— (Case studies in cultural anthropology)
  Includes bibliographical references and index.
  ISBN 0-15-506333-2
  1. !Kung (African people) 2. San (African people) I. Title. II. Series.

DT1058.K86 L44 2002
306'.089'961—dc21   2001055911

Asia
Thomson Learning
60 Albert Street, #15-01
Albert Complex
Singapore 189969

Australia
Nelson Thomson Learning
102 Dodds Street
South Melbourne, Victoria 3205
Australia

Canada
Nelson Thomson Learning
1120 Birchmount Road
Toronto, Ontario M1K 5G4
Canada

Europe/Middle East/Africa
Thomson Learning
Berkshire House
168-173 High Holborn
London WC1 V7AA
United Kingdom

Latin America
Thomson Learning
Seneca, 53
Colonia Polanco
11560 Mexico D.F.
Mexico

Spain
Paraninfo Thomson Learning
Calle/Magallanes, 25
28015 Madrid, Spain

Foreword

ABOUT THE SERIES

These case studies in cultural anthropology are designed for students in beginning and intermediate courses in the social sciences, to bring them insights into the richness and complexity of human life as it is lived in different ways, in different places. The authors are men and women who have lived in the societies they write about and who are professionally trained as observers and interpreters of human behavior. Also, the authors are teachers; in their writing, the needs of the student reader remain foremost. It is our belief that when an understanding of ways of life very different from one's own is gained, abstractions and generalizations about the human condition become meaningful.

The scope and character of the series has changed constantly since we published the first case studies in 1960, in keeping with our intention to represent anthropology as it is. We are concerned with the ways in which human groups and communities are coping with the massive changes wrought in their physical and sociopolitical environments in recent decades. We are also concerned with the ways in which established cultures have solved life's problems. And we want to include representation of the various modes of communication and emphasis that are being formed and reformed as anthropology itself changes.

We think of this series as an instructional series, intended for use in the classroom. We, the editors, have always used case studies in our teaching, whether for beginning students or advanced graduate students. We start with case studies, whether from our own series or from elsewhere, and weave our way into theory, and then turn again to cases. For us, they are the grounding of our discipline.

ABOUT THE AUTHOR

Richard Lee was born in New York City and grew up in Toronto, Canada, where he was educated in the Toronto school system. At the University of Toronto he studied anthropology, philosophy, and sciences, receiving his B.A. in 1959 and his M.A. in 1961. Moving to the University of California at Berkeley for doctoral research, he embarked on a multidisciplinary study of the Ju/'hoansi/!Kung San in Botswana and Namibia in collaboration with Irven DeVore.

With DeVore he is the cofounder of the Kalahari Research Group, an informal consortium of scholars from a number of fields who have done research with the San. Lee has made nine trips to the Ju/'hoansi, totaling about forty-eight months of fieldwork. Hunter-gatherer research also has taken him to Tanzania, Alaska, and northern Russia, as well as the Yukon, Labrador, and other points in the Canadian sub-arctic.

Currently he is a University Professor of Social/Cultural Anthropology and Past-Chair of the African Studies Programme at the University of Toronto. He has also taught at Harvard, Rutgers, and Columbia, and has held research positions at the Center for Advanced Study in the Behavioral Sciences at Stanford University and at the Center for African Studies, Kyoto, Japan. He has lectured at more than fifty institutions in the United States, Canada, Europe, and Africa.

His books include *Man the Hunter* and *Kalahari Hunter-Gatherers* (with Irven DeVore), *Politics and History in Band Societies* (with Eleanor Leacock), *The !Kung San: Men, Women, and Work in a Foraging Society* and *The Cambridge Encyclopedia of Hunters and Gatherers.* He has also been involved in the BBC television series *The Making of Mankind* with Richard Leakey, the CBC/PBS television series *Planet for the Taking* with David Suzuki and the television documentary *Distant Echoes* with Yo Yo Ma.

In addition to his work on foraging peoples, Lee has written on the political struggles of indigenous peoples, on the origins of the state, on the CETI Problem, on critical Marxist theory, and on problems of interpretation in African history. Lee is a past-president of the Canadian Anthropology Society and a Fellow of the Royal Society of Canada. In 1990, he was awarded an honorary doctor of letters degree from the University of Alaska, Fairbanks, for his research and advocacy on foraging peoples. Richard Lee has three children, all of whom have been adopted into the Ju/'hoansi kinship system.

ABOUT THE CASE STUDY

This third edition contains new information and insights that enhance the status of this valuable and useful case study. Of particular importance is a new Chapter 7, "Complaint Discourse, Aging, and Caregiving among the Ju/'hoansi," by Harriet Rosenberg. Her participation in the project is of long standing, and she is married to the author. In this chapter she answers the questions, "How do Ju/'hoansi care for elders and what is the language through which care is negotiated?" Suffice it to say here that both the language and the care are representative of the core of Ju/'hoansi society and culture and help us to understand that core.

The Kalahari Debate about the origins of Ju/'hoan culture has animated the pages of leading anthropology journals for over a decade. In the new Appendix B, "The Kalahari Debate: Ju/'hoan Images of The Colonial Encounters," the terms of this controversy are laid out for the reader. Revisionists take the view that Ju/'hoansi culture is the result of their being long-term servants of cattle keepers and at the bottom of the social hierarchy. Their notable traits of sharing and egalitarianism are thought of in the revisionist view as the result of their history of servitude. Lee and his associates, by contrast, see these traits rather as the result of a long-standing free and independent hunting and gathering life. Lee went to the people themselves, something no one else had apparently considered, and asked them about their past. The evidence of oral history together with evidence from archeology and from early explorers' accounts makes a convincing case for the argument centering on independence and autonomy.

Added to Chapter 12 are new materials on a central problem of our times: the survival of indigenous peoples in a globalizing world. In the section, "Ju/'hoansi at the Millennium: Progress and Poverty," positive aspects of change are described, including the development of schools and education and the establishment of wildlife conservancies, combining eco-tourism, controlled hunting, and wildlife conservation.

The small and hard-won gains of recent decades are threatened by the onsweep of the HIV/AIDS, pandemic that reaches staggering proportions in southern Africa (an estimated 35.8% of adults in Botswana are carrying the virus). Though reliable figures are lacking, there is strong evidence the Ju/'hoansi are not nearly as affected as most other Botswana groups. Lee examines causes of these lower rates, notably that Ju/'hoansi women are in a different position vis à vis sexual encounters than most southern African women: they are more independent and can insist on the use of condoms or refuse sexual advances.

This case study is enhanced by these new additions and provides valuable insights into the changing circumstances of one of the best known hunting and gathering populations on the face of the earth. Instead of collapsing, the Ju/'hoansi show remarkable resilience in the face of rapid change. Also enhanced is our understanding of anthropological interpretation in the areas of gender and aging, the symbolic order in history and prehistory, and in theories of "modernization." Each of these are of great value to students approaching anthropology from a variety of perspectives.

George Spindler
Ethnographics
1274 Alice St. Davis, CA, 95616

Preface

PREFACE TO THE THIRD EDITION

Since the publication of the Second Edition I have returned to the area almost every year, most recently in July 2001. This edition of *The Dobe Ju/'hoansi* offers several new elements. In addition to updating the entire book, three new sections have been added. The new Chapter 7, entitled, "Complaint Discourse: Aging and Caregiving among the Ju/'hoansi," contributed by Dr. Harriet Rosenberg, discusses aging among the Ju and compares it to the situation of the elderly in North America. The new chapter contributes in two ways. First, it adds a dimension on aging and the life cycle that had been missing from earlier editions. Rosenberg also offers a basic insight of interest to all students of the Ju/'hoansi, an insight into the core dynamic of Ju life: how through humor and complaint they are able to live rich lives under conditions that many readers would find harsh and impoverished.

The second major addition springs from a lively controversy that developed within anthropology in the 1980s and 1990s over the historical status of the Ju/'hoansi. This argument, which came to be known as the Kalahari Debate or Kalahari revisionism, concerns the question of who the Ju/'hoansi were historically: independent foragers with a long tradition of hunting and gathering, or in the views of some critics (the "revisionists"), not hunter-gatherers at all but long-term servants of Bantu overlords, dominated by outsiders. Archaeological and historical evidence was marshaled by both sides of the controversy. Curiously, in the debate neither side had asked in any detail what the Ju/'hoansi themselves thought about these issues. In Appendix B, "The Kalahari Debate: Ju/'Hoan Images of the Colonial Encounter," Ju/'hoan elders tell their oral histories of pre-colonial life. Some of the answers were surprising to both sides of the debate. The essay also reviews the evidence from two other sources: European explorers' accounts and what the archaeological record has revealed. We present here only a fraction of a larger body of work; therefore an extensive bibliography offers suggestions for additional reading.

A third section, "Ju/'hoansi at the Millennium: Progress and Poverty" (at the end of Chapter 12) brings the Ju/'hoan story up to the present. Readers are always curious about how successfully the Ju have been in moving away from the hunting and gathering way of life. How are the Ju/'hoansi coping with the stresses of "development" as they enter the fourth decade of rapid social change? This section tells a complex story of successes and failures. Regionally the people of Dobe have witnessed remarkable changes in the 1990s: the end of apartheid and the coming to power of Nelson Mandela's ANC government in South Africa. And the Botswana nation, formerly one of the world's poorest, has prospered through its booming diamond and tourism industries. Locally however, the Dobe people have suffered drought and cattle disease, and setbacks in their efforts to secure their land base. There is new material on all of these issues.

Most important, however, the people of Dobe find themselves at the epicenter of what many consider the most important historical development of the new millennium. The crisis of HIV/AIDS is the worst epidemic to afflict humankind since the Middle Ages. Botswana, despite its prosperity and economic success (or perhaps because of it), has not escaped the catastrophe. In a June 2000 survey by UNAIDS, Botswana's rate of HIV-positive people ages 15–49 was estimated at 35.8 percent, recognized by the UN and WHO as *the highest rates of HIV/AIDS in the world.* Living far from the population centers, how have the people of Dobe fared along with their cousins in Nyae Nyae, Namibia? Have they succumbed to the tragedy of AIDS or have the people of Dobe successfully fought off the full impact of the disease? This story is addressed in the second-last chapter of the book.

In addition to this new material the third edition contains many new photos and over 30 new references, as well as information on the new Kalahari Peoples Fund website that when fully operational will offer up-to-date bulletins about the situation in the Kalahari and links to many other related websites about Africa and indigenous peoples. As with earlier editions, a portion of the book's royalties goes to the ongoing development work of the Kalahari Peoples Fund. I hope you enjoy the book.

R.B.L
Toronto, July 2001

PREFACE TO THE SECOND EDITION

Two images epitomize the long journey travelled by the subjects of this book. In the first it is the early 1960s, somewhere in southern Africa. Night has fallen. Under a vast and starlit sky of breathtaking beauty, the silence is all-encompassing. Gradually, groups of leather-clad hunter-gatherers can be discerned sitting in front of grass huts at flickering fires and the sound of their laughter can be heard. They trade stories of hunts failed and successful, the arrival of visitors bearing gifts from the West, the expected marriage of a young girl, the foolish antics of an old man of the neighboring pastoralists, and the passing of a government vehicle from the distant capital, the first such sighting in six weeks. To one side, a young anthropologist fiddles with a portable radio—the only one within 50 miles—listening in shock as news comes in of the violent death of a great leader in a distant country. The anthropologist is bursting with the news, but explaining it to the people proves a problem: Only a few had heard of "America" or the "United States" and no one could name the name of America's great chief. The anthropologist is left alone with his thoughts.

In the second image, the setting is the same but the scene shifts to the 1990s: The cloudless night sky is still vast and the stars brilliantly clear; the camp fires flicker as before, but in important ways the scene is different. Cows are lowing in the background; bicycles and ploughs are parked behind mud-walled houses; and dressed in store-bought shirts, pants, dresses , and sweaters—some of it purchased that day from one of several passing peddlers—the people of each household are glued to their radios, as hourly bulletins come in on the upheaval in another far-off country and the fate of its president. This time people discuss these events with animation. All except the very oldest know there is a place called Russia, and the name of its great chief is on everyone's lips.

Scene one, of course, took place at the time of John F. Kennedy's assassination in November 1963; scene two, at the time of the attempted overthrow of Mikhail Gorbachev in Moscow in August 1991. The place? Dobe, a waterhole in northwestern Botswana, southern Africa. The people are the !Kung or Ju/'hoansi, a San-speaking people who had lived as hunter-gatherers into the latter third of the twentieth century.

The years 1963 to 1991 are less than three decades apart yet so much had changed, in the world at large, and particularly in the Dobe area itself. In that span of years the people of the Dobe area had experienced the arrival of stores, clinics, schools, and airstrips. They had gone from an existence based largely on hunting and gathering to one in which farming, herding, cash work, and welfare were as important as foraging.

One more image may bring home just how dramatic have been the changes between the 1960s, and the 1980s and 1990s. In the standard reference work on Botswana (Sillery, 1952), the area around Dobe was considered the least known and most isolated part of the whole territory. This was borne out by my 1963–64 field work. During that time only one vehicle every four to six weeks came to the Dobe area: a total of about a dozen per year. But during my 1986–87 field work, I counted a motor vehicle *every four to six hours,* or some 1400–2200 per year, a 120-fold increase. These vehicles brought a constant stream of visitors: traders, government officials, veterinarians, medical staff, agricultural demonstrators, and tourists.

But as I wrote earlier, think of this: If an observer had arrived in the Dobe area in 1993 instead of 1963, she would not have seen daily hunting with poisoned arrows, full-time gathering of the rich mongongo nut harvest, the weekly healing dances in which powerful healers spiritually defended the !Kung against illness and misfortune. By the 1980s and 1990s, bow and arrow hunting had declined drastically, cultivated grains and food relief were now the staples of the diet, and penicillin rivalled *n/um* as the main defense against illness.

So much has happened as well in *our* world that we are in danger of losing sight of the fact that the !Kung and many people like them have, even in our lifetimes, lived good lives without the benefit of wage labor, bank accounts, credit cards, or supermarkets. They have raised generations of children and taught them dignity, self-respect, and the skills of life without schools, television, or Nintendo, and have cared for their elderly without pension plans or "old folks" homes. Perhaps more remarkable, they have been able to do all this while living lightly on the land in a degree of harmony with their natural environment, in what might be termed the oldest example of sustainable development. In short, even in this hard-bitten age of social and ecological crisis, of wars and economic depression, the !Kung San show us that other ways of being are possible. This book is about letting the !Kung tell their story against the backdrop of these decades of change.

At the same time it would be a serious error to romanticize the !Kung and to make them into the paragons of all virtue, noble remnants of the Stone Age. The !Kung have all the human failings that characterize people everywhere: conflict, violence, stupidity, prejudice are not absent—to take one example, before they settled the !Kung had a homicide rate that was high even by U.S. urban standards. And whatever success they enjoyed as hunter-gatherers has been seriously compromised by the tensions that accompany rapid change.

Telling the !Kung story is the first goal; but something else must be added. It would be all too easy to tell a "just-so story" to make them into the polar opposites of upward-striving urbanites, to give them all the desirable qualities that we lack (or think we lack). This can be avoided only if the observer is prepared to test hunches or suppositions against empirical evidence, and to throw out even cherished views if the data don't support them. For a variety of reasons "science" has become a dirty word in many university courses, and science-bashing a popular sport. But without some commitment to test the merits of competing explanations against the evidence, what we write will have more in common with fiction than with ethnography. And that would be too bad since wishful thinking is no substitute for understanding.

This book is an account of how one anthropologist has tried to peel off the layers of myth and misunderstanding surrounding the San and gradually sloughed off his own misconceptions to arrive at a clearer sense of how the !Kung have been able to survive as a people with so much aplomb and zest for living.

One major change in this second edition of the *The Dobe !Kung* concerns terminology. For many years the term "!Kung San" has been in common use, especially among anthropologists, even though it is not a term used by the people themselves. This new edition documents the !Kung people's coming to political consciousness and their emerging determination to take hold of their own destiny, to assert their political rights and revitalize their communities. In this respect the !Kung people are following the paths charted by aboriginal peoples in Canada, the United States, Australia, Russia, and elsewhere; if the appellation "First Nations" or "First Peoples" fits the indigenous peoples of North America, Australia, and elsewhere, then surely it cannot be denied to the !Kung of Botswana and Namibia.

The !Kung call themselves—and always have—Ju/'hoansi (pronounced "zhut-wasi"), meaning "real people". To acknowledge their new sense of empowerment, it is appropriate that anthropologists and students change our old habits and adopt this term of self-appellation. The sound "Ju" has no equivalent in English, but is common in many other languages, and is similar to the French "jamais" or "je."

Out of respect for the people and their new-found consciousness, this edition of *The Dobe !Kung* has been retitled *The Dobe Ju/'hoansi* (pronounced "doebay zhut-wasi"). Throughout the text, "!Kung" has been changed to "Ju/'hoansi" in contexts where their full name seems appropriate, to "Ju/'hoan" as an adjective, and to "Ju" ("person" or "people") where a less formal reference is needed. It is worth noting that the spelling "Ju/'hoansi" was chosen (over variants such as "Ju/wasi" or "Zhu/twasi") by a group of Ju people themselves, working in conjunction with linguist Patrick Dickens (Dickens et al. 1990).

One implication of the new usage is that in the course of events the older terms "!Kung" and "San" will take their place alongside "Bushmen" (and "Eskimo" and "Indian") on the shelf of terms whose time has passed. However, the terminology is in flux and old habits die hard; don't be surprised if the older terms appear here from time to time. Eventually the process of self-naming will be fully in the hands of the people themselves.

Since the publication of the first edition, I have returned to the region four times (1985, 1986, 1987, 1993) and have witnessed some of the events that are shaping the lives of the Ju/'hoansi. Through the wonders of long-distance telephone calls and fax machines, I also have been able to maintain close contact with people there. Of particular importance has been ongoing contact with several literate Ju/'hoansi whose education had been facilitated by the Kalahari Peoples Fund, and with whom I now keep in touch by mail. The frequent movement of graduate students and colleagues from North America to Namibia and Botswana and back has provided another source of constantly updated information.

There have been a number of important changes in the Dobe area and on the larger world stage. Of greatest local impact has been the successful freeing of neighboring Namibia from South African rule and its achievement of independence under United Nations auspices in March 1990. The fate of the Namibian Ju/'hoansi has strongly affected people in the Dobe area, as have trends in the Dobe area itself. These trends, visible in the early 1980s, have intensified and have created new crises (and opportunities) for the Dobe people.

For this new edition, every page of the original text has been reviewed and updated when necessary. The historical section of Chapter 2 has been expanded considerably and updated to address several issues raised by critics of earlier !Kung research. The most visible changes for this edition are the addition of two new chapters: Chapter 11, which details the events of the last decade in Botswana and Namibia and their impact on the Ju/'hoansi; and Chapter 12, which reviews some of the changes in anthropological theory and practice brought about by the articulation of the Ju/'hoansi with the world economy and their entrance onto the world stage through films and other media. Chapter 12 also offers some reflections on the lessons of the Ju/'hoansi and other indigenous peoples for an age which has seen the end of the Cold War and the emergence of environmental and economic crises as the most pressing issues in the world today.

R.B.L.
Toronto, Canada 1993

PREFACE TO THE FIRST EDITION

This is a book about the !Kung San, a remarkable people whom I have been privileged to know since the 1960s. It describes their ways of making a living, their social organization, their politics, sexual and nonsexual, and their world view and religious beliefs.

What it can only suggest to the reader is the !Kung spirit: that peculiar combination of humor and malice, of anger and fun that characterizes their sense of themselves as a special people. These are elusive qualities, and I can only hope you catch a glimpse of them here and there, in between the more concrete accounts of work effort, caloric intake, marriage patterns, and kinship behavior.

A book like this one can also only hint at the fragility of this quality of life as it attempts to adapt in the face of onrushing change. Working with a people like the !Kung is like a race against time: only four years after my arrival the first trading store opened, six years later a school and a clinic were built. By the 1980s, transistor radios and Western clothing were everywhere. I was able to observe a foraging mode of life during the last decades of its existence. If our work had begun in 1983 instead of 1963, we would not have seen daily hunting with poisoned arrows, full-time gathering of the rich mongongo harvest, and weekly healing dances in which powerful healers spiritually defended the !Kung against illness and misfortune. Today, bow-and-arrow hunting has almost ceased, cultivated grains are now the staples of the diet, and penicillin, not *n/um,* is the main defense against illness. Livestock, cash reserves, and material wealth have replaced social relationships as the main source of security for the !Kung. Game meat, once freely given, is now bought and sold.

And yet, even today much remains: a vital culture, a language with over 15,000 speakers, and a people with a continuing sense of humor and self-esteem. The !Kung, in a word, are survivors, not in the pejorative sense of relics from the distant past, but in the best modern sense—a physically hardy people with inner resources of spirit. They still retain a healthy skepticism about the good intentions of those outsiders who would "develop" them, and, as of this writing, have not forgotten how to hunt and gather. If the rest of us went away tomorrow they would be none the worse for it.

/Twi!gum, a thoughtful !Kangwa man with a keen sense of the absurd, put it all into perspective. Seeing that every !Kung household owned or had access to a store-bought iron cooking pot, I recently asked /Twi, "What did the !Kung do in the old days before they had iron cooking pots to cook in?" /Twi looked at me gravely and pondered my question. After a long, meaningful silence, he finally replied tongue firmly in cheek, "Everyone knows that people can't live without iron cooking pots, so we must have died."

It is to /Twi, his wife N!uhka, and the !Kung of the twenty-first century that I dedicate this book.

R.B.L.
Toronto, Canada 1983

A Note on the Ju Language

The San languages are characterized by unusual sounds called clicks. These are produced when the tongue is drawn sharply away from various points of articulation on the roof of the mouth. The four clicks used in Ju/'hoansi appear as follows:

/   Dental click, as in Ju/'hoansi */Xai/ xai, /Du/ da* (in spoken English this sound denotes a mild reproach, written "tsk, tsk").

≠   Alveolar click, as in *≠Toma.*

!   Alveopalatal click as in *!Kung, n!ore.*

//   Lateral click, as in *// gangwa* (in spoken English this sound is used in some dialects to urge on a horse).

Other features of the San orthography that should be noted include:

~   Nasalization as in */twã.*

"   Glottal flap as in *//"xa* (mongongo) or *K"au.*

j   Pronounced as the "j" in French "jamais" or "je;" example: Ju/'hoansi
     (alternate spelling "Zhu/wasi")

For the nonlinguist, San words may be pronounced by simply dropping the
click. For example, for // *gangwa* read *gangwa,* and for ≠*Toma//ˌgwe* read *Toma
gwe. Dobe* rhymes with *Toby.*

Acknowledgments

The !Kung research was conceived at the University of California at Berkeley, was centered for many years at Harvard University, and since 1972 has branched out to a number of different institutions. I am particularly indebted to the University of Toronto for the continuing support it has provided in innumerable ways. Funding for the research has come from several sources: the National Science Foundation, the National Institute of Health, the Wenner-Gren Foundation, the Canada Council, the Social Sciences and Humanities Research Council of Canada, and the Connaught Fund of the University of Toronto. Part of this manuscript was produced during my tenure as a Connaught Senior Fellow in the Social Sciences.

I also want to thank the government of Botswana, whose officials have made a major contribution to the success of the !Kung research. The people of Botswana have been unfailingly courteous and have made us feel welcome time and time again. I hope that this study, and others like it, will repay in a small way the many debts owed to them. A portion of the proceeds from this book is earmarked for the Kalahari Peoples Fund, a nonprofit foundation supporting development projects in Botswana.

Thanks are also due to the members of the Kalahari Research Group for valuable suggestions and criticisms, and for many good times over the years. Though not all of us agree on all issues, I continue to respect their individual and collective views.

For help in reading portions of the manuscript, I want to thank Megan Biesele, Harriet Rosenberg, Jane Schneider, and the late Marjorie Shostak, critics who are in no way responsible for any errors this book may contain. Sheryl Adam produced the index for the second edition.

For the second and third editions, several colleagues and friends have been particularly helpful with information and advice: Megan Biesele, Alec Campbell, Mathias Guenther, Robert Hitchcock, and Jacqueline Solway. Chapters 12 and 13 are drawn in part from a joint manuscript with Dr. Biesele, and I would thank Dr. Biesele for permission to use portions of that manuscript here. For updates on the Dobe and Nyae Nyae areas and other assistance, thanks go to Andrea Brandle, Henry Harpending, Scholastika Iipinge, Trefor Jenkins, Richard Katz, Jeffrey Kurland, Brigit Lau, John Marshall, Lorna Marshall, Jeanette Peterson, Claire Ritchie, Verna St. Dennis, Paul Sheller, Marjorie Shostak, Andrew Smith, Ida Susser, Renée Sylvain, and Polly Wiessner. Research Assistants from regional universities made important contributions to our 1980s field work: Makgolo Makgolo, Dorothy Molokomme, Leonard Ramotakwane, Pombili Ipinge, Karen Neshaya, and particularly Nandi Ngcongco. I also want to thank Royal /Too/to, Chiqo Nxaue, and Benjamin Xishe for their ongoing correspondence since 1986.

A special vote of thanks goes to Harriet, David, Miriam, and Louise, whose good humor and emotional support continue to sustain me.

Finally, my deepest debt is to the Ju people of Botswana.

i !ha weyshi // kau ge: May you live in health and peace always.

Contents

!Kung at the mouth of Twihaba caves.

1/The Ju/'hoansi

INTRODUCTION: A VOYAGE OF DISCOVERY

The inhabitants of these parts are a much finer race of Bushmen than we had generally met with. Freedom and the enjoyment of their own game for food and the skins for clothing are the main causes. They acknowledge no chief and are in the habit of defending themselves against oppressors and intruders either from Lake Ngami or the Namaqua region: in former times they have often combined to resist marauding parties sent out by the Batuana and other tribes. Their minds are free from apprehension of human plunderers, and the life they lead is a comparatively fearless one. The population is numerous, and they are more attached to each other than in other parts.

James Chapman (1868)

Not far from the border of South West Africa . . . is a group of caves . . . visited by few white people. The journey involves a long and arduous trek across sandy country through which no road passes and a competent guide is essential. . . . The country in the vicinity of these caves is probably the least known in the whole Protectorate and Bushmen and the wild animals have it to themselves.

Anthony Sillery (1952)

Chapman in the 1860s and Sillery almost a century later were referring to the same fabled people—the !Kung San of the Kalahari Desert, fierce and independent, unknown to the outside world until recently. And I was going out to find them. The !Kung, or Ju/'hoansi (pronounced Ju/wasi) as they call themselves, were virtually unknown to scientists until the 1950s, and now, in October 1963, I was on my way to !Goshe, a waterhole in northwestern Bechuanaland, to make a year-long study of them.

I had traveled a long way from North America: by plane from Berkeley, California to my home in Toronto; from there to Nairobi, Kenya, where I met my friends and collaborators Irven and Nancy DeVore and their family. We then traveled by Land Rover over half the African continent, arriving in Botswana in August. Irven DeVore and I, along with Adam Kuper, surveyed the northwestern Kalahari for two weeks looking for a suitable study site, without success. Then, after the DeVores had returned to Harvard, I came back to the Kalahari with two Land Rovers and two African assistants, determined to find the elusive !Kung. The area west of !Goshe appeared to offer our last hope for success.

Hour after hour, our Land Rover ground slowly in four-wheel drive through the deep sand. On the threshold of a great adventure, I retraced in my mind the steps that had brought me to this place. In the early 1960s there had been a renaissance in evolutionary studies in anthropology. Fueled by the Leakeys' fossil discoveries in East Africa, by new dating techniques, by archeological finds and nonhuman primate field research, and by the rediscovery of long-disregarded nineteenth-century classics in evolutionary social anthropology, there was a new and growing interest in studies of the evolution of human behavior. I was part of the generation of anthropology graduate students excited by the prospects of a new interdisciplinary synthesis in anthropology, a new view of humanity's beginnings based on the firm data of archeology, physical anthropology, and ethnography.

What particular circumstances had brought me to the Kalahari? The piece of research that had captured *my* imagination was the study of contemporary hunting and gathering peoples. Few people live this way today, but 12,000 years ago, foraging for wild game and plant foods had been the universal mode of human subsistence. (The term *foragers* or *foraging peoples* is a convenient shorthand for groups with this kind of adaptation.) Our ancestors evolved as foragers, and all basic human institutions—language, marriage, kinship, family, exchange, and human nature itself—were formed during the two- to four-million-year period when we lived by hunting and gathering. Thus the study of the surviving foragers—the San, Inuit (Eskimo), Australian aborigines, and others—had much to teach us.[1]

---

[1]Although the preceding paragraph accurately reflects the view about foragers and human evolution prevalent in the 1960s, today I would be much more cautious on what this material can and cannot teach us about our species' distant past. Some of these changing perspectives are set out in Chapter 13.

On the road to the Dobe area.

But in order to be able to learn their lessons, we have to exercise the utmost caution. In dealing with a people as exotic as the !Kung, we have to be careful to avoid the twin pitfalls of racism and romanticism. First, foragers like the !Kung are not "missing links"; they are as human as we are, and their histories are as long as the histories of any other human group. And second, nowhere will we find foragers today living in Pleistocene conditions, that is, as hunters living in a world of hunters. All foragers have been in some contact with nonforaging peoples, some for a very long time. There are no "lost" continents or lost tribes (Wolf, 1982), and even the Ju/'hoansi whom I was on my way to visit had been known to exist and had been named in the nineteenth century.[2]

If one takes these pitfalls carefully into account, there is still much to be learned from contemporary foragers. In fact, it is their very humanity that has made people like the Ju/'hoansi and other foragers so important for science. These peoples, despite their cultural and geographic diversity, have a core of features in common, and this core of features represents the basic human adaptation stripped of the accretions and complications brought about by agriculture, urbanization, advanced technology, and national and class conflict—all of the "advances" of the last few thousand years.

How do they make a living? How do they organize their communities? How are they able to settle conflicts in the absence of chiefs? These central questions could be studied directly if (and it is a big if) I could find the right people—leading independent lives, getting their own food, and settling their own quarrels. In the 1860s all interior Ju/'hoansi had lived this way. Even by the 1950s there were still many who did. But this was 1963, and the winds of change were sweeping Africa. Could such an adaptation survive in the jet age?

After many hours of driving we suddenly came upon signs of human settlement, and at sundown we pulled into !Goshe, a row of mud huts that stretched for a mile along a sand ridge. A dozen men, women, and children came out to greet us. The San people of !Goshe were friendly and open. I stammered a few words of greeting in Ju/'hoansi and passed out tobacco, which they eagerly accepted. However, as I soon learned, most of the !Goshe Ju worked for their Bantu-speaking neighbors, herding their goats and cattle. They dined on milk and meat, and politically they were subject to their overlords, the aristocratic Tswana. Were there any waterholes, I asked, where Ju people lived without Blacks and cattle? There was one, they told me, about a full day's travel to the west at a place called Dobe, near the beacon that marked the border with South West Africa. My assistants, Enoch Tabiso and Onesimus Mbombo, and I decided to go to Dobe first thing the next morning.

A WATERHOLE CALLED DOBE

October is the hottest month of the Kalahari year, and by nine a.m. the sun was already a hot disc high in the sky as we drove our Land Rover into the dry pan of Dobe, cut the engine, and waited in the pool of shade by the truck. After ten minutes a cluster

---

[2]In 1971, a Philippine millionaire claimed to have found a lost tribe of foragers living out of touch with the rest of the world for 500 years. The "gentle Tasaday" became the world's most famous foragers, with TV specials and *National Geographic* spreads, until a 1986 expedition exposed crucial aspects of their story as a fraud (Berreman, 1992; Lee, 1992c). The irony is that over a dozen authentic southeast Asian hunter-gatherers had been ignored by the media, probably because they wore blue jeans, had transistor radios, and regularly interacted with their agricultural neighbors.

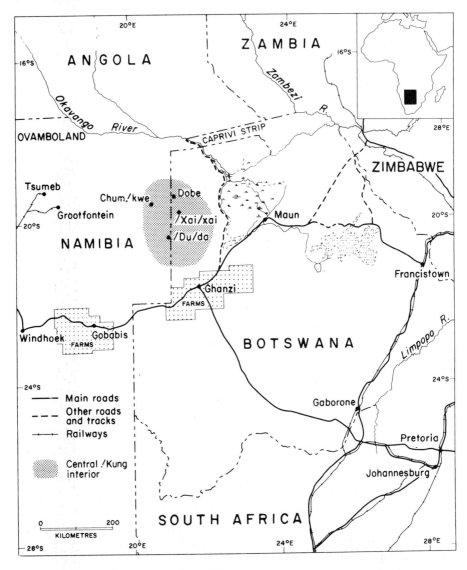

Figure 1–1. The Dobe area in southern Africa.

of brown figures dressed in leather appeared 100 years away and stopped in the shade at the pan's edge, waiting silently. We approached them, and I warily sized them up. They were all short, the men about five foot two, the women well under five feet. Their brown skins were deeply seamed with lines from exposure to the sun. They were dressed in sueded leather, the men in tight-fitting breechclouts, the women in beaded aprons and soft skins. Both sexes were naked above the waist. The women were handsomely adorned with necklaces, arm bands, and hair ornaments of beads made from ostrich eggshells. Both sexes wore their densely curled hair close cropped, and as I observed them more closely I saw that their high foreheads and cheekbones were etched with geometric lines of tattooing that showed up blue under their golden skins. Each of the men wore a bow and quiver in a sling over his shoulder, and two of them had spears in their hands, but on the whole they seemed friendly enough. After a few minutes, Onesimus broke the silence with greetings in Tswana. Then, in my one sentence of !Kung, I asked *"a !ku re o a juwe?"* (What is your name?) of each in turn.

"Mi o ≠Toma," responded the first, a small, wizened man in his sixties with a sardine can key hanging from his ear.

"Mi o ≠Toma," said a handsome young man in his thirties wearing a shredded western cloth cap.

"Mi o N!eishi," replied a barrel-chested man in his late fifties whose deep-set eyes smiled in a sea of wrinkles.

"Mi o Tin!ay," a handsome middle-aged woman with full lips spoke next.

"Mi o //Koka," said a very old and spry woman in a leather *kaross* that seemed too big for her.

"Mi o //Gumin!a," said a tiny, dignified old woman with a twinkle in her eye.

Finally a young woman with a baby at her breast and a four-year-old at her side said, *"Mi n/ a o Sa// gai."*

The nine people who came out to meet us were core members of the Dobe camp, a strongly independent group of people who, we later learned, had been associated with the waterhole for over 30 years and who preferred to live on their own in the "bush" rather than share a waterhole with cattle and goats.

≠Toma// gwe and the men of Dobe.

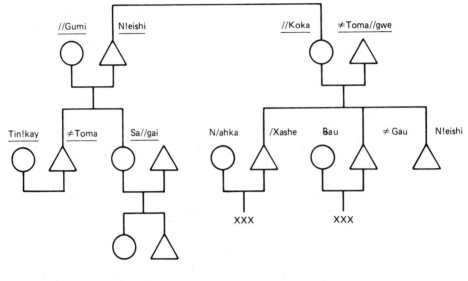

Key

Underlined names = people met on Day 1 .

⌐▔▔⌐ indicates marriage

⌐▔▔▔ indicates siblingship

△   male

◯   female

Figure 1–2. The core of the Dobe Camp.

They were related to one another as follows (Figure 1–2).

//Koka and her younger brother N!eishi were core "owners" of Dobe along with their spouses—the formidable old ≠Toma// gwe (≠Toma sourplum) and the diminutive //Gumin!a (Old//Gumi). ≠Toma// gwe and //Koka had three married sons in their thirties who were away hunting with their wives and children, while //Gumi and N!eishi had a married son and a married daughter—the younger ≠Toma and Sa// gai, who were present to greet us.

I asked them if I could come and stay with them and learn their language, and after much discussion they agreed. Would they be interested in learning English in return? This question, when it passed through the interpreters, was greeted with gales of laughter. ≠Toma// gwe chortled no, that the sounds the Europeans made were much too difficult for him. I replied that *we* found their click sounds impossible to pronounce. This was met with puzzled but sympathetic looks. Imagine anyone finding clicks difficult, they seemed to be saying!

As the tension eased //Gumin!a asked for *shoro,* the Ju word for tobacco, and the others joined in. When we gave them some of the strong leaf tobacco they favored they pulled out what appeared to be Western-style commercial briar pipes, which they lit with flint and steel kits. The pipes, in fact, turned out to be home-made replicas of our pipes, complete to the last detail, including a contrasting mouthpiece carved in black wood.

As the odor of strong tobacco swirled around us, we talked and talked—of where I was to camp, where to draw water, where the wild foods were—and passed pipefuls

//Koka cooking meat.

of tobacco around at frequent intervals as the sun rose in the sky. Finally, when the details were settled and we were about to disperse, ≠Toma// gwe indicated to the interpreter that he had one more thing to say.

"Some years ago," he began in a voice that was both warm and scolding, "a man called Mashtalo, his wife Norna, and his children came to live at a place called /Gausha to the west.[3] Many good things happened," he continued, "to the people of /Gausha as a result of Mashalo being there: blankets, clothes, pots, knives, beads all came their way. But none of this good fortune reached us in Dobe. We were sad and just lived. Now that you have come, our hearts are glad. Now we have a White man of our own. We waited so long. It's about time that you've come. We expect good things from you, so don't disappoint us. And another thing," his voice was rising in pitch, "if you have anything to give away, give everything to us, not to those other people." His hand gesture indicated points east, west, and south, covering most of the known !Kung villages.

I was floored by this last speech. With extraordinary aplomb, the old man had managed to welcome me while criticizing me for not coming sooner; and admonish *me* to be generous while baldly stating that *he* for his part was going to keep everything for himself!

Stunned, I got back into the truck and headed off to pitch camp. Clearly this fieldwork was not going to be a piece of cake. The people were friendly, but not pushovers, and they seemed to have at least some of the personality quirks that afflicted people in urban society. ≠Toma certainly lived up to his nickname: the sourplum. Yet there was something likable about ≠Toma's frankness. I thought to myself, I'm going to like it here.

In the evening I reflected on the day's events. So these were the Ju/'hoansi-!Kung of fable and legend. Now, brought face to face with an all-too-human reality, it was a conscious effort for me to conjure up the grand theories of human evolution that had set my odyssey in motion. The Dobe !Kung seemed so familiar. ≠Toma// gwe, with

---

[3]A reference to the family of Laurence and Lorna Marshall, who had conducted fieldwork at Nyae Nyae in the 1950s (see Ch. 2, pp. 11–14).

Sa// gai and her son ≠Toma.

his sardine-key earring, infectious laugh, and rudeness, reminded me of a crotchety great-uncle of mine back in Toronto; and N!eishi with the broad shoulders and deep chest reminded me of my own father (much later, in fact, N!eishi adopted me as his son).

It became clear that an enormous task lay before me—to make sense of the thriving contemporary !Kung culture with all its complexities and contradictions. I had to count the people, learn their language, find out what they ate and what ate them (both physically and spiritually), and make sense, if possible, of the paradoxes of generosity and selfishness that seemed to lurk beneath the surface of their lives. The building of evolutionary theories would have to wait for the time being, on the back burner.

I was to spend the better part of the next three decades trying to unravel these and other paradoxes the !Kung presented. But for the moment I turned to the immediate task of pitching a tent to protect us from the onrushing heat of the October Kalahari.

2/The People of the Dobe Area

When Dutch explorers reached the Cape of Good Hope in the seventeenth century, they found two kinds of people living there. First were the numerous cattle- and goat-herding peoples, whom the Dutch named the *Hottentots,* a term that mimics their strange (to the Dutch) click-filled language. These people called themselves *Khoi* ("people"), the term they are known by today. Second were the nonherding peoples, similar in language and appearance to the Khoi, but who kept no livestock, instead living on wild plants, animals, and shellfish. The Khoi called them *Sonqua,* or *San,* a Khoi term that means "aborigines" or "settlers proper." Because they were elusive and shy and lived in much smaller groups than the Khoi, the Dutch named them *Bosjesmans,* that is, people of the bush—*Bushmen*—a term by which they were known until recently to the rest of the world. Although widely used, the term *Bushman* has both racist and sexist connotations. Recognizing these problems, many researchers have agreed to call them the *San,* and I would urge my readers to do the same.[1]

For thousands of years the Khoi and the San occupied most of southern Africa west of the Bantu-speaking peoples in the Eastern Cape. But as White settlement expanded north in the eighteenth century, bitter conflicts arose with the native peoples, conflicts that escalated into genocidal warfare against the San. By the late nineteenth century the San had been virtually exterminated within the boundaries of the present-day Republic of South Africa, and most writers of the day spoke of them as a dying race. As exploration pushed farther north, however, the grim obituary on the San proved, happily, to be premature. In the security of the Kalahari Desert, thousands of San continued to live as hunter-gatherers in relatively peaceful proximity to a variety of neighboring Black herders and farmers. By the mid-1950s, physical anthropologists, linguists, and archeologists had begun to map out the numbers and distribution of the living San. They are now estimated to number more than 100,000, a figure that appears to be on the increase (Table 2–1, Figure 2–1).

---

[1]The term *San* is not without problems of its own. Some point to this Nama term's negative connotations, meaning "worthless" or "no account." And the term *Bushman* has its advocates among anthropologists and others. *San* leaders themselves are divided over the term *Bushmen.* At a recent meeting reported by Megan Biesele, one said he never wanted to hear the term used again in post-apartheid Namibia. Another argued that the term could be ennobled by the way in which they themselves now chose to use it. However, as *Pan-San* or *Pan-Bushman* political consciousness grows in southern Africa, we assume a general term will emerge. By the late 1990s, San had come into general use by the San people themselves.

TABLE 2–1   ESTIMATED NUMBERS OF CONTEMPORARY SAN BY COUNTRY
AND LANGUAGE FAMILY IN 2001.

Country	Central	Northern	Southern	Country Totals
Angola	5,000	5,200	—	10,200
Botswana	40,000	11,000	2,500	53,500
Namibia	8,000	28,000	4,200	40,200
South Africa	2,000	1,500	1,500	5,000
Zambia	1,700	—	—	1,700
Zimbabwe	1,400	—	—	1,400
Total	58,100	45,700	8,200	112,000

Based on estimates provided in part by Dr. Robert Hitchcock for January 2001.

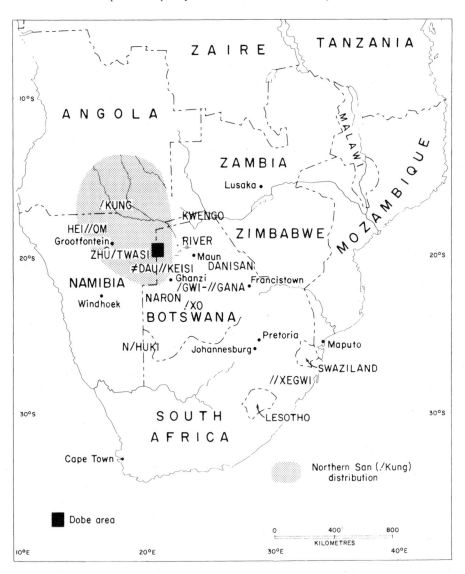

Figure 2–1. The Distribution of the San in Africa.

WHO ARE THE SAN?

The San are a cluster of indigenous peoples in southern Africa who speak a click language and who have a tradition of living by hunting and gathering. They are to be distinguished from the Khoi, whom they resemble physically, by the Khoi's possession of livestock, and from the Bantu by marked physical, linguistic, and cultural differences.

San come in a variety of shapes and sizes. Many are short and pale-skinned, while others are tall and dark-skinned like their Bantu-speaking neighbors. This variability has prompted a rough division of the San on physical grounds into the "Yellow" and "Black" San.

The Black San include peoples in southeastern Angola, western Zambia, and eastern Botswana who speak languages of the *Tshu-Khwe* group and whose economy is based on mixed herding, farming, foraging, and wage labor. It also includes the Nama- and (formerly) !Kung-speaking Hei//kum in northern Namibia. The Black San are genetically indistinguishable from surrounding Bantu populations, and it is likely that their gene pools have been augmented by the influx of Bantu-speaking refugees from the colonial wars and raiding of the nineteenth century.

The Yellow San are found in southern Angola, western and central Botswana, and northern and eastern Namibia. They speak languages of three different language families: the Northern !Kung, the Central Tshu-Khwe, and the Southern! Xo, (A fourth language family—the //Xam—were believed to be virtually extinct in South Africa, but in the aftermath of apartheid hundreds of //Xam speakers have re-emerged.[2] Linguistically diverse, they are physically similar to one another: short, pale-skinned, deep-chested, with straight foreheads and small, almost delicate faces and jaws. The latter are the distinctive features of *neotony*—the retention of infantile traits into adult life—a trend that is found to some extent in all modern populations of *Homo sapiens*. Economically, the Yellow San include full-time gatherer-hunters (increasingly rare), mixed farmers and herders, and since the 1960s, a growing number of farm and migrant laborers.

The numbers and distribution of the contemporary San are shown in Table 2–1, updated for this edition.

STUDIES OF THE SAN

Modern *ethnographic* studies of the San begin with the expeditions of Laurence and Lorna Marshall and their family to the !Kung of Nyae Nyae in 1951. Their many field trips since 1952 have produced a distinguished series of books (see L. Marshall, 1976, 1999; and E. M. Thomas, 1959) and films by John Marshall (see film guide, pp. 161–64). The more southerly /Gwi San of the Central Kalahari have been studied by Silberbauer (1965, 1981), Tanaka (1980, 1991), Cashdan (1977, 1983, 1987, 1990), and Kent (1989a, 1989b), while the southernmost of the contemporary San, the !Xo, have been studied by Heinz (1966, 1972), Eibl-Eibesfeldt (1972), and Sbrzesny (1976). The Naron (Nharo), a populous, settled group living on farms and cattle-posts have been studied by Bleek (1928), Guenther (1979, 1986), and Barnard (1976, 1978). Research on !Xo linguistics has been done by Traill (1974). Vierich (1982) and Hitchcock (1982) have done detailed

---

[2]The !Kung language group in turn has three subdivisions: northernmost are the !Kung proper, found mainly in northern Namibia and Angola, also known as the Vasekela; centrally located are the Ju/'hoansi (Zhu/twasi) of Namibia and Botswana, the subjects of this book; and southernmost are the ≠Dau//keisi or MaKowkow (literally, "northside people," a reference to their position relative to the populous Nharo, located in the Ghanzi and Gobabis districts (see Figure 2–1).

TABLE 2–2   THE HARVARD KALAHARI RESEARCH GROUP

Name	Affiliation	Research Interests
Megan Biesele	Texas A&M U.	folklore, ecology, development
Alison Brooks	George Washington U.	prehistory, anthropological theory
Nicholas Blurton Jones	UCLA	ethology, evolutionary ecology
Irven DeVore	Harvard U.	ecology, evolutionary theory
Nancy DeVore	Harvard U., Anthrophoto	photography
Patricia Draper	U. Nebraska	child behavior, aging, evolutionary ecology
John Hansen	Witwatersrand U., Johannesburg, S.A.	pediatrics
Henry Harpending	U. Utah	demography, physical anthropology, Ju, Herero
Nancy Howell	U. of Toronto	demography, evolutionary ecology
Richard Katz	Saskatchewan Federated Indian Colleges, Saskatoon, Sask.	ritual, healing, change
Melvin Konner	Emory U.	infancy, evolutionary theory
Richard Lee	U. of Toronto	ecology, social organization, AIDS, history, anth. of development
Marjorie Shostak	Emory U.	life history, gender studies
Stewart Truswell	Sydney U., Australia	medicine, health and nutrition
John Yellen	National Science Foundation, Washington, D.C.	ethno-archaeology, prehistory

studies of San economic change in the eastern Kalahari. A comprehensive overview of studies of all the San and Khoi peoples has been published by Barnard (1992a).

The most extensively studied San group has been the Ju/'hoansi–!Kung of the Dobe area. Starting in 1963 with a two-person team consisting of Irven DeVore and myself, the Kalahari Research Project has grown to include well over a dozen specialists in many fields.

Today the Dobe !Kung are probably the world's best-documented foraging society. There have been book-length studies published on ecology and society by Lee (1979), on ethnoarchaeology (Yellen, 1977), on demography (Howell, 1979, 2000), and on healing (Katz, 1982; Katz, Biesele, and St. Dennis, 1997). The late Marjorie Shostak has published a superb autobiography of Nisa, a Dobe !Kung woman (1981, 1983) and a follow-up study (2000). Studies of all these subjects, plus genetics, health, folklore, child rearing, and other topics have been published in a collection of papers edited by Lee and DeVore (1976). (See also Lee and DeVore, 1968; Konner, 1983; Eaton, Shostak, and Konner, 1988; Lee and Daly, 1999). Both branches of Ju/'hoansi scholarship have been commemorated in an exhibition entitled "Ju/wasi: Bushmen of the Kalahari" curated by Irven DeVore at the Peabody Museum of Anthropology at Harvard University (Lord, 1991).

In addition, Ju/'hoansi economics and exchange systems have been studied by Wiessner (1977, 1982, 1986, 1990). Wilmsen has written on Ju archeology, ethnohistory, ecology, and political economy (1978b, 1981, 1989; Wilmsen and Denbow, 1990). Table 2–2 lists the members of the original Kalahari Research Project, while Table 2–3 lists the members of the Marshall group and other researchers.

TABLE 2–3   THE MARSHALL GROUP AND OTHER KALAHARI RESEARCHERS

Name	Affiliation	Research Interests, Ethnic Group(s)
Marshall Group:		
Laurence Marshall	private, Cambridge, Mass.	general anthropology, Ju/'hoansi, etc.
Lorna Marshall	private, Cambridge, Mass.	ethnography, Ju/'hoansi, /Gwi
John Marshall	Documentary Educational Resources, Watertown, Mass.	film, anthropology of development, Ju/'hoansi, /Gwi
Elizabeth Marshall Thomas	private, Peterborough, New Hampshire	ethnography, literature, Ju/'hoansi, /Gwi
Claire Ritchie	private, England	development, film
Other Scholars:		
Alan Barnard	Edinburgh U.	social anthropology, Naron
Alec Campbell	Botswana Society, Gaborone, Bot.	archeology, rock art, ethnography, development
Elizabeth Cashdan	U. of Utah	history, behavioral ecology, /Gwi-//Gana
James Denbow	U. of Texas	Iron Age archeology, Botswana, Zaire
James Ebert	James Ebert Associates, Albuquerque, New Mexico	archeology, ecology, remote sensing, Botswana
I. Eibl-Eibesfeldt	Max Planck Inst., Seeweissen, Germany	human ethology, !Xo
Robert Gordon	U. of Vermont	history, politics, media
Mathias Guenther	Wilfrid Laurier U., Waterloo, Ontario	social anthropology, change, folklore, art, Naron
H. J. Heinz	private, Maun, Botswana	social anthropology, parasitology, change, !Xo
Robert Hitchcock	U. of Nebraska	development anthropology, ecology, archeology, history, Eastern Basarwa, Botswana, Namibia, etc.
Trefor Jenkins	South African Inst. for Medical Research	genetics, medical research, nutrition, Botswana, Namibia, Zimbabwe, South Africa
Susan Kent	Old Dominion U., Virginia	ecology, archeology, nutrition, settlement patterns, theory, !Xo, /Gwi
Harriet Rosenberg	York U; Toronto	social anthropology, aging
George Silberbauer	Monash U., Australia	social anthropology, ecology, /Gwi
Jacqueline Solway	Trent U., Peterborough, Ont.	social anthropology, development anthropology, kinship, gender, Bakgalagadi
Kazuyoshi Sugawara	Kyoto U., Japan	gender, kinship, worldview
Renée Sylvain	Dalhousie U.	gender, political economy, Omaheke
Jiro Tanaka	Kyoto U., Japan	ecology, ethnography, change, /Gwi
Helga Vierich	U. of Alberta, Canada	ecology, social change, development anthropology, Eastern /Twa
Pauline Wiessner	U. of Utah	archeology, ethnoarcheology, exchange systems, Ju/'hoansi
Thomas Widlok	Max Planck Inst., Halle, Germany	Hei//om, social change
Edwin Wilmsen	U. of Texas	archeology, political economy, nutrition, history, theory, Ju/'hoansi, Herero

Although this book is based largely on my own field research, I will frequently draw on the published research of these other specialists.

THE DOBE AREA

What sort of place is the Dobe area, scene of so many studies of Ju/'hoansi life? In 1963 it consisted of a cluster of 10 waterholes north and south of the Aha Hills in the northwest Kalahari Desert. The area can be conveniently divided into three divisions. The more northern waterholes are strung out along the length of the !Kangwa Molapo, a 100-kilometer-long dry river valley that has its source in the Nyae Nyae area of Namibia and wends its way eastward through Botswana before disappearing in the desert west of the Okavango swamps. Unlike the rest of the sandy Kalahari, the !Kangwa Molapo traverses an area of limestone and granite outcrops. The Ju/'hoansi name for the area, *N!umsi,* meaning "the region of rocks or stones," reflects this geological oddity. In addition to the permanent waterpoints, the !Kangwa valley has a hinterland of gathering and hunting areas to the north, east, and west of about 3000 square kilometers.

South of the Ahas a smaller dry river valley, the /Xai/ xai Molapo, forms the main axis of settlement, with its one major waterhole at /Xai/ xai Pan and a hinterland containing many smaller seasonal waterpoints to the west, south, and east.

In the center are the Aha Hills themselves, consisting of several scattered ranges of low hills 100 meters above the surrounding plain.

About 70 percent of the Ju live in N!umsi, while the remainder live at /Xai/ xai. The Aha Hills, because of lack of surface water, contained no permanent settlements until recently. About one-third of the Dobe area lies across the border in Namibia. Since the building of a border fence by South Africa in 1965, this western portion of the area has been cut off to the gathering and hunting Ju.

Together, the three regions of the Dobe area in both Botswana and Namibia comprise an area of about 8000 square kilometers (3000 square miles). The area's features and its waterholes are shown in Figure 2–2.

EXPLORING THE DOBE AREA

After my initial contacts with ≠Toma //gwe and his kin, I built a camp at Dobe. The Ju suggested several spots that didn't appeal to me, and so I picked a pleasant grove of trees on the edge of a stony pan. All was well until the first rains came. We woke up one morning ankle-deep in water, with the Ju standing at the door of my tent laughing until the tears came to their eyes.

Packing quickly, we moved our camp with its sodden bedding to a better-drained location, and I proceeded with my work. The first order of business was to get a sense of the immediate area. On foot, by truck, and, later on, donkeyback, I spent the better part of two months visiting each waterhole in turn, counting the people and getting a sense of the economic basis of each locale.

The !Kung population in 1964 stood at 466, with 379 residents and 87 seasonal visitors. There were also some 340 Blacks with their cattle residing in the area (Table 2–4). Although Ju/'hoansi occupied all the waterholes, each grouping had its own distinctive features.

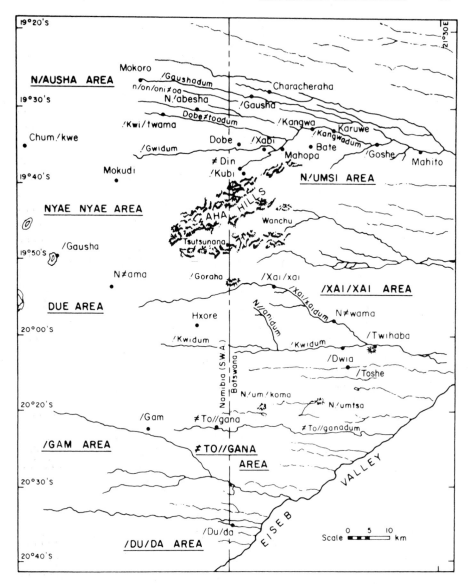

Figure 2–2. The Dobe area and surrounding regions. Namibia is on the left, Botswana on the right.

!Goshe was the easternmost settlement in the area. With a population of 75 Ju and 30 Blacks, !Goshe was also the most acculturated of all the Ju settlements. The Ju had lived with and worked for the Blacks for decades, herding their cattle and tending their fields. Some !Goshe families had acquired herds of their own, and a substantial portion of their diet now consists of milk, meat, eggs, and grains. When I arrived they were already relatively sedentary, having occupied the same villages for over five years. Their relative wealth set ! Goshe people somewhat apart from other Ju/'hoansi. They tended to marry amongst themselves, yet they still participated in reciprocal

TABLE 2–4   POPULATION OF THE DOBE AREA BY WATERHOLE, 1964

	San & Resident	Marginal	Total	Blacks
!Goshe	75	0	75	30
!Kangwa Matse	9	0	9	—
!Kangwa	36	0	36	72
Bate	41	3	44	29
Mahopa	33	10	43	65
!Xabi	10	0	10	12
!Kubi	23	25	48	65
/ Xai/ xai	117	30	147	67
Dobe	35	0	35	0
Other	0	19	19	0
	379	87	466	340

exchanges with other Ju who visited them, often giving a bag of grain in exchange for a wild product. Among the Ju and Blacks alike, !Goshe was famous as a center of ritual and medicine. Healing dances were held frequently (almost daily at times), and a !Goshe woman named /Twan!a pioneered the introduction of the important women's healing dance–!*Gwahtsi* (see Chapter 9).

Traveling west up the !Kangwa Valley for eleven kilometers (seven miles) one arrived at the waterhole of !Kangwa *ma tse*—small !Kangwa. With a population of nine !Kung and a few Blacks, it was little more than a cattle-post suburb of !Kangwa.

Five kilometers farther to the west was !Kangwa, the major settlement in the !Kangwa valley. The community takes its name from the !Kangwa Rock Spring, an abundant and perennial source of clear, cool water. !Kangwa was the administrative center or *kgotla* of the District, the headquarters of the Tribal Headman and the Tax Collector. At !Kangwa the 72 Blacks outnumbered San, and the Ju/'hoan population of 36 subsisted by a combination of working for the Tswana headman, herding the Blacks' cattle, and gathering and hunting.

Eight kilometers south of !Kangwa, at the base of the Aha mountains, were the Bate villages, home of 41 Ju and 29 Blacks. The Ju kinship links were to !Kangwa and Mahopa, and many relatives liked to visit Bate in the fall to eat the delicious Marula nuts for which Bate was famous.

Three separate waterpoints constituted the Mahopa waterhole, strung out in the bed of the !Kangwa River. With a population of 65 Blacks and 2000 cattle, Mahopa was a major center for Ju employment as herders for the Blacks. The 33 Mahopa Ju had close ties to Bate, !Kangwa, and Dobe, and the camps saw a constant stream of visitors from west and east. Subsistence was based on about 75 percent gathered and hunted foods and about 25 percent grains and milk. Mahopa people also had attempted to plant their own crops, with varying degrees of success.

A crossroads, !Xabi was a small waterhole three miles east of Dobe, occupied principally by the family of the Tswana Headman, his Herero wife, and his Ju clients: population 10 !Kung, 12 Blacks.

South of !Xabi was !Kubi, a populous waterhole in the forests at the base of the Aha Hills. The population of 65 Herero provided employment for the 23 Ju/'hoan residents. These Herero arrived after 1954 as a result of a major shift of population

Lee exploring the Dobe area on donkeyback.

in the western fringes of the Okavango swamps. !Kubi, it turned out, has been the site of hunter-gatherer life for tens of thousands of years. The Middle Stone Age prehistoric site of ≠Gi, excavated by John Yellen and Alison Brooks, lies only a kilometer from !Kubi Pan (Brooks and Yellen, 1979; Yellen and Brooks, 1988). In the early 1960s the !Kubi Ju maintained close ties with the Ju of Nyae Nyae and had extensively intermarried with them. The !Kubi waterhole was also famous locally for its Marula nuts, and it was and is the only source of Baobab fruit and Tsin beans in the northern Dobe area.

The most interesting of all the waterholes for me was /Xai/ xai, which lay 28 kilometers (17 miles) south of !Kubi across the Aha Hills. The 117 Ju and 67 Blacks were dispersed in ten villages around the perimeter of the /Xai/ xai pan. Each of these villages had access to a hinterland for gathering and hunting. In general, villages on the east side of /Xai/ xai pan gathered to the east, villages on the north side had a northern hinterland, and so on. Not far from /Xai/ xai to the east were the legendary caves of /Twihaba, one of the geological wonders of Botswana that Sillery spoke about with such awe (see Chapter 1).

/Xai/ xai had been a meeting place for well over a century, and probably much longer. Bands from the four corners of the Ju/'hoan world traditionally gathered there in the dry season to trade, dance, and arrange marriages. Today this history is reflected in the far-reaching ties that /Xai/ xai Ju maintain with Ju to the north, west, south, and east. Later in my stay with the Ju/'hoansi I was to live at /Xai/ xai for fourteen months.

My tour of the area brought me back to Dobe, my spiritual home for the first fifteen months of my fieldwork. I named the region the Dobe area in honor of my adopted waterhole. A small, inaccessible spring deep in a rock cleft provided the sole source of water for the 35 Ju of Dobe, the one waterhole in the 1960s with no non-!Kung or livestock resident. Centered around the families of 70-year-old //Kokan/a and her younger brother N!eishi, the Dobe camps consisted largely of more traditional Ju who preferred to live on their own rather than herd cattle for Blacks. They remained on good terms with Blacks at Mahopa, where they frequently visited to ask for some milk, the staple of the Herero diet. These handouts supplemented a diet that, during the 1960s, varied from 85 to 100 percent gathered-and-hunted foods. Vast mongongo forests lie within a day's walk north and west of Dobe (see Chapter 4).

A HISTORY OF CONTACT

As my work continued, I began to get a sense of the recent history of the Dobe area. Later, archeologists added information on a much deeper time scale.

From the archeological record, the Dobe area has been a hunting and gathering stronghold for literally thousands of years. Middle Stone Age materials 20–40,000 years old have been found at ≠Gi and elsewhere (Yellen and Brooks, 1988; Brooks and Yellen, 1992). The Later Stone Age of the Dobe area shows remarkable continuity from at least 3000 B.C., and probably as early as 18,000 B.C. Yellen and Brooks have reported unbroken deposits of Later Stone Age materials underlying or close to contemporary Ju/'hoansi villages. The Dobe area Ju/'hoansi themselves have no tradition of being refugees from other areas.

Throughout this period, hunters and gatherers pursued their way of life with no evidence of agriculture and minimal evidence of domesticated animals. Some recent writing, however, has argued that the Dobe area !Kung, far from being hunters and gatherers in the past, were pastoralists and tribute-paying subjects to Bantu-speaking, Iron Age overlords. A lively and sometimes acrimonious debate has sprung up around these opposing viewpoints (see Appendix B for a more extended discussion).

While the issues are complex, it should be possible to resolve the question one way or another. For example, if such a history of domination and alternative subsistence existed, it should be expressed archeologically through the presence of Iron Age sites within the Dobe area or a strong element of Iron Age trade goods such as iron and/or ceramics on the Later Stone Age sites. Despite considerable efforts to find such sites, there is simply no evidence of Iron Age occupation of the Dobe area before the twentieth century (Yellen and Brooks, 1988; Brooks and Yellen, 1992).

However, it is true that after about 500–800 A.D., potsherds and iron fragments are found on Dobe area sites; does this denote overlordship by outsiders? The problem is the quantities of these exotic goods are minute; at one excavation (Wilmsen, 1978b), of the 384 potsherds found only 32 were sub-surface finds, all of them thumbnail-sized. Similarly only eight fragments of iron were found in subsurface

The main Dobe camp, spring 1964.

contexts spanning a period of over 1000 years. This handful of potsherds and iron fragments in stratigraphic contexts contrasts with the finding of several thousand stone tools on the same site. The paucity of Iron Age material can hardly be taken to denote Iron Age domination of the area. Rather than domination, the picture is consistent with a pattern of hunters and gatherers going about their business and engaging in intermittent long-distance trade with distant Iron Age peoples. Such trade is noted in Ju/'hoansi oral histories in which desert products such as furs and ivory were exchanged for iron, (later) tobacco, and possibly agricultural products (Solway and Lee, 1990; Lee, 1991).[3] The oral traditions of both Dobe and Nyae Nyae Ju/'hoansi state that iron arrowheads only came into general use during the lifetimes of the grandparents of the present generation (Marshall, 1976:146; Lee, 1979:133). This view is corroborated by historical evidence: the German explorer Schinz found Ju/'hoansi not far from Nyae Nyae still using bone arrowheads in 1886 (Schinz, 1891:357):

> The area seemed to be very thinly settled. Nevertheless from time to time we did meet scattered Bushmen hordes. . . . The people who visited us at this occasion called themselves the !Kun San. . . . The entire dress of these poor root diggers consists of nothing more than two small furs to cover their private parts and buttocks, and instead of ostrich egg-shell beads their arms and legs are adorned with grass ornaments.
>
> The weapons consisted of a hefty throwing stick, [and] a medium-sized bow with arrows made of thin Phragmites reed, *the poisoned tips of which were made not of iron, but of carefully worked bone splinters, which in this part of South West Africa was frequently made of eland antelope* (Schinz, 1891:357; emphasis added).[4]

---

[3]On this point, see also comments by Jacobson (1990:131) and Wiessner (1990:135–36).

[4]Translated from the original German by Mathias Guenther. The Ju/'hoan bone arrowheads that Schinz collected can be found in the collections of the Basle Museum, Switzerland.

Similarly, the argument that the Dobe area residents were pastoralists in the distant past also does not bear up under scrutiny. Only one "cow" bone has ever been found in an undisturbed Dobe area context, a bovine maxilla (upper jaw) fragment at a depth of 63 centimeters, /Xai/ xai (Wilmsen, 1978b). Surely if they had been pastoralists in the past, evidence of more than a single bone would have been found, and in loose sands such items can move up or down relatively rapidly, making historical inference strictly on the basis of depth extremely chancy (Yellen and Brooks, 1988; Ebert, 1989). Furthermore, archaeozoologists who study faunal remains note that it is hard to distinguish domestic cows' teeth from the teeth of African Cape Buffalo, which also occurs in the region (Yellen, 1990c:516).[5] So on archeological as well as historical grounds, the case for the pre-colonial Ju/'hoansi as autonomous foragers is holding up remarkably well (see also Lee and Guenther, 1993).

What is the Ju/'hoansi's view of their own history? As detailed in Appendix B, contrary to these views, the Dobe San were convinced that their ancestors were a distinct people who lived on their own by hunting and gathering. When the area was opened up after 1870, Blacks and Whites arrived within a few years of one another, but Ju/'hoan elders insisted that when outsiders finally came to their area in the nineteenth-century *it was Whites who came first and the Blacks only came after.* When told of the views of Wilmsen and Denbow (1990)—that their ancestors had been herders and serfs for centuries—the Ju/'hoansi were offended. In response, the elders characteristically posed a rhetorical question: how could their ancestors, they wondered, be portrayed as long-time serfs of Black masters when these same Blacks only arrived within the last three generations (Lee, 1998; Smith and Lee, 1997).

Another contention of recent writing is that the Dobe Ju/'hoansi were early victims of colonialism. The reason they are hunters and gatherers today is because nineteenth-century European hunters and traders swept through their area, taking everything of value and reducing them to penury.[6] Their position as egalitarian hunters in the twentieth century, in this view, is a product of their poverty and the inroads of capitalism, and not a tradition traceable to their own indigenous past. But contrary to this view, the historical evidence shows that Dobe lay far off the beaten paths of nineteenth-century mercantile activity. Almost all the known explorers consistently bypassed the area as they crisscrossed the continent in search of wealth (Lee and Guenther, 1993). It enjoyed a brief period of prosperity in the late 1870s—when White hunters decimated the elephant herds—and then resumed its marginal status which it held well into the twentieth century.

Distance, isolation, and the reputation for fierceness of the Ju/'hoansi themselves probably account in equal measure for the profound ignorance of the Nyae Nyae-Dobe areas prior to the present century. Here and there intriguing glimpses are found. The explorer and trader James Chapman, who went toward the Dobe area in the 1860s but never reached it, characterized the Ju/'hoansi–!Kung as "a fierce and independent people who possess no cattle" (Chapman, 1868 II:13). Writing of the southern

---

[5]Given the importance attached to this piece of bone, it would be desirable to examine it more closely. Unfortunately, through no fault of the original excavators, the specimen in question was lost in a lab fire.
[6]A position spelled out in Wilmsen (1989) and Wilmsen and Denbow (1990). See also Schrire (1984) and Gordon (1984). The counter-case for the historical integrity and autonomy of the Ju/'hoansi–!Kung has been made in Solway and Lee (1990), Lee (1990b: 510–12), Lee and Guenther (1991, 1993, and in this book in Appendix B). Readers interested in the debate are encouraged to consult this literature.

Ju/'hoan speakers of the Ghanzi area (known as the MaKowkow), Chapman presents this very positive image of the mid-nineteenth century !Kung, noting that the !Kung's military prowess kept invaders at bay:

> The inhabitants of these parts are a much finer race of Bushmen than we had generally met with. Freedom and the enjoyment of their own game for food and the skins for clothing are the main causes. They acknowledge no chief and are in the habit of defending themselves against oppressors and intruders either from Lake Ngami or the Namaqua region: in former times they have often combined to resist marauding parties sent out by the Batuana and other tribes. Their minds are free from apprehension of human plunderers, and the life they lead is a comparatively fearless. The population is numerous, and they are more attached to each other than in other parts (Chapman, 1868[1971] Vol. 1:165).

The first non-San to penetrate the area (in modern times) were European hunters and Tswana herders. From the 1870s on, the herders came to trade, hunt, and graze their cattle. After some initial shyness, the Ju were quickly incorporated into the Tswana tributary system. The Ju acted as trackers for the Tswana and helped butcher the meat, and when the summer had passed they acted as porters, carrying the season's take of their new overlords back to the east. A Ju/'hoan man describes this period:

> The type of work that we !Kung entered then was called *n/ i // wana !ha* ["shoulder the meat-carrying yoke"]. The country was teeming with game, and the Tswanas came up on horseback with guns. They put us under the carrying yoke. We had to carry the meat that they shot from the kill sites back to the camps; and then at the end of the summer hunting season, a line of porters would carry bales of *biltong* [dried meat strips] back to Tsau. Then there they would be paid off in balls of *shoro* [tobacco], which they carried back to the West. We !Kung also did our own hunting, and brought the hides and *biltong* in for tobacco.

From the late 1870s, European hunters from the south also came to the Dobe area to seek the rich resources of ivory, rhino horn, and fur-bearing animals. Some men had affairs with Ju women, and the descendants of these unions today live at !Kubi. (It was not until the 1950s that the first Europeans lived for any length of time in the interior.) In Ju/'hoan oral history the period 1870–1920 is sometimes called the time of *Koloi* (Tswana-wagons), a reference to the oxwagons that the Tswana later brought with them on their annual trips.

The largest number of non-Ju in the Dobe area today are members of the Herero people. The Herero are southwestern Bantu-speakers who have a long history in the territory of Namibia. During the tragic war of 1904–1907, thousands of Herero were slaughtered by the Germans. Several thousand Herero escaped across the desert and were given asylum in the then-British colony of Bechuanaland (Botswana). After 1920 the ruling Tswana gave a few families of Herero permission to settle in the Dobe area, and this event marked the beginning of a new era for the Dobe Ju. These contacts are discussed in Chapter 10.

European presence in the Dobe area, apart from the early hunters, occurred at an even later date. The first government patrol to reach Dobe from Bechuanaland dates from 1934. The area really became known to outsiders when the Marshall family began their studies of the adjacent Nyae Nyae area in 1951. Even after the Nyae Nyae Ju/'hoansi had been settled on a government station at Chum!kwe (now spelled

Tjum!kui) in 1960, the Dobe people continued to live in relative isolation. During my first year in the field only about one truck every six weeks reached the Dobe area. Although the Ju/'hoansi of Dobe had seen many Whites, I was the first to live in their area, and this fact created a certain bond between us.[7] The major changes that occurred after 1970, after my main fieldwork was completed, are detailed in Chapters 11 and 12.

---

[7]Strictly speaking, I was not the first White. A man named Venter (called Fendare by the !Kung) lived with his Nama wife at !Kubi for some years after 1927. Also, although a number of anthropologists worked in the Dobe area after 1964, for the first year I was there on my own. Irven and Nancy DeVore rejoined me at Dobe only after October 1964.

3/Environment and Settlement

The Dobe area quickly began to captivate my senses. The October days were fiercely hot and drowsy, with the smells of countless aromatic shrubs and trees hanging heavily in the air. Bird calls were a constant background to the day's activities. There were the staccato rhythms of the woodpeckers, the cooing of the turtle doves, the sharp, high-pitched cries of the plovers, and the characteristic *kooweeei* of the grey loerie that the local English called the go-away bird. The giant dung beetles and other exotic insects went about their daily business. Swarms of stingless bees hovered about the waterhole. Wildlife was abundant. Antelope and warthog tracks were everywhere, as well as leopard and hyena. At night, lions could be heard grunting to each other as they fed on their kills.

At midday, the land was a furnace. Since walking in the sun could consume a quart of body water per hour through sweat, during the hottest part of the day the people rested. At dusk the burning heat broke its grip on the land and life became animated. Firewood was gathered, nuts were roasted, and food was cooked in iron pots. As night fell the firelight rose in intensity to cast an orange glow over people, dogs, huts, and trees.

But my favorite time was after dark. In the cool I could sit in front of my tent on a canvas folding chair and observe the heavens. On moonlit nights the light was incredibly bright, light enough to read by. And when the moon set I saw a heavenly display the likes of which I didn't know existed. The sky became a dense mass of points of light. Literally thousands of stars were visible, not the paltry few hundred that the reflected city lights allow us in the northern sky. The Ju/'hoansi call the Milky Way *!gu !ko!kemi,* "the backbone of the sky," and the ridge of stars overhead with dozens of patches of interstellar dust does look like a vertebral column.

The habitat intrigued me. I resolved to learn as much about it as I could, and wherever I went in those first few months I was constantly peppering the Ju with questions. "What kind of plant is this? What soil does it grow on? Do you eat it? What animals eat it? Does it have any use to you?" The !Kung enjoyed this kind of work. They were superb botanists and could read the landscape like a road map. My knowledge of the environment grew by the day.

The Dobe area is part of a vast basin 1000 to 1200 meters above sea level, bisected by the Botswana-Namibia border on the northern fringe of the Kalahari Desert. The first impression of a traveler to this region is an immense flatness, where the sky dominates the landscape. The Aha Hills rise only 100 meters above the surrounding plain, and from their top one sees what seem to be endless vistas of brush and savannah stretching to the horizon in every direction. Thus the observer is surprised to find in the Ju/'hoan, language of travel a rich vocabulary of climbing and descending as they discuss trips from one waterhole to another. For example, a trip to Nokaneng is always referred to as *kowa // hai* (literally, "to descend to the east"). As one gains familiarity with the area, one realizes that the Ju/'hoansi are right: there are slight elevation differences from place to place, and I soon came to appreciate how important these differences are in the structuring of drainage, vegetation zones, and key plant resources.

At several points in the landscape the sandy plain is broken by dry river courses like the !Kangwa and the /Xai/ xai. Some of these river courses can be traced for 100 kilometers. They rarely hold flowing water, perhaps twice in a decade, but when they do the flow of water can be considerable. In a few localities the underlying rock formations are exposed. These rocks form an important source of subsurface water. Some areas are riddled with sinkholes and caves, such as the extensive underground network of caves at /Twihaba (known as Drodsky's Caves), which are mentioned in Chapter 1.

The upper reaches of the !Kangwa Valley are extremely flat. When one reaches !Kangwa, however, the relief becomes much sharper. By !Goshe the riverbed is a seven-meter-deep miniature canyon between vertical banks. Here the down-cutting of the river has exposed deposits of high-quality chert, a rich source of prehistoric tools, and in recent years, of flints for the flint-and-steel fire-making kits used by the !Kung. In fact, the lower !Kangwa descends so steeply that after a heavy rainfall the river bed becomes a raging torrent for a few hours, with cascades to challenge a white-water canoeist.

THE DUNE AND *MOLAPO* SYSTEM

Apart from hills and dry rivers, the main feature of the Dobe area is a system of fixed longitudinal dunes running parallel to each other and oriented roughly east–west. The dune crests and flanks have deep, loose, red and white sands. The *melapo* (river courses, in Setswana) between the dunes and in the more deeply incised river valleys are characterized by compacted, fine-grained gray soils. Each supports a distinctive association of trees and shrubs with a distinctive array of edible species.

The Ju themselves distinguish four kinds of habitats: (1) dunes, (2) flats, (3) *melapo,* and (4) hardpan and river valleys.

Dunes Unlike the moving dunes of the Namib and southern Kalahari deserts, the dunes of the northern Kalahari are fixed by vegetation. Ricinodendron rautanenii (the mongongo nut), the major plant food of the Dobe-area !Kung, is found only on the crests of the fixed dunes. The mongongo provides a protein-rich nut meat and a nutritious fruit, and the tree's hollow interior traps rainwater for drinking.

Flats Intermediate in elevation between the dunes and the melapo are plains of buff-to-white compacted sands. The flats provide extensive groves of Grewia berry bushes, the vegetable ivory palm with its tasty fruit, and a number of other edible species.

Melapo Two subtypes can be distinguished here. The smaller melapo have compacted soils of light gray or buff. Here are found dense thickets of small trees verging on forests. Well-defined melapo, with gray, compacted, silty soils and occasional beds of hardpan, support many species of Acacia with their edible gums.

Hardpan The soils here consist of patches of bare rock alternating with patches of sand or mud. The baobab tree with its fruit and seed is the most important food found here.

!Kangwa spring in the dry season.

The same view during a heavy rainy season.

Water Sources

The northern Kalahari is a semidesert, and water scarcity is a major problem. The Ju rely on a hierarchy of water sources ranked in order of abundance. First are the permanent waterholes found in the main river bottoms where the bedrock is exposed. Most of these waterholes are natural, but all have been improved and maintained either by the San themselves or, more recently, by the Blacks. Second are the seasonal waters that exist for one to six months a year: these are found in the *melapo* between the dunes, where local drainage patterns produce a depression. These vary from small depressions 15 feet in diameter and ankle deep, holding water for a few weeks after heavy rains, to great ponds up to 300 feet long, holding water for months or even year-round in years of high rainfall.

Third in importance are the small quantities of water found in the hollow interiors of mongongo and other trees. And finally, there are several species of water-bearing root, which may be dug up and used in emergencies. With these sources the Ju plan their annual round, spending the winter season close to the permanent waters and the summer months ranging widely at the secondary and lesser water sources.

FAUNA

Despite recent changes, the Dobe area still harbors an impressive array of African plains game. With over 50 resident mammal species, the area can still provide the Ju/'hoansi with a solid hunting subsistence base. At the same time, the Ju hunters have

A seasonal pan during the rainy season.

to compete for their prey with representatives of all the major predator species: lions, leopards, and others. In addition to the mammals, 90 species of birds, 25 species of reptiles and amphibians, and up to 90 species of invertebrates are also known to the Ju, making a total of about 260 named species in their animal universe.

Ungulates (hoofed mammals) are the main game animals of the Ju. Most prominent are kudu, wildebeest, and gemsbok. Giraffe, eland, roan antelope, and hartebeest are also present. The nonmigratory warthog, steenbok, and duiker are extremely plentiful and are the most frequently killed of the ungulates.

Lion, leopard, cheetah, hyena (two species), wild dog, and a dozen smaller forms of carnivores are all found in the Dobe area. Their kills and tracks are frequently encountered on gathering trips, yet the Ju do not seem to be afraid of these predators. The Ju sleep in the open without fires when necessary and make no provision to protect or fortify their living sites (but see fn 3).

Of other mammals, the elephant is the only large nonungulate regularly seen in the Dobe area. A few pass through the area each rainy season. In an exceptionally wet year, such as 1973–1974, a dozen might be seen. Many more are seen on the Namibian side. Buffalo and sometimes hippo are also summer visitors. Of the small- to medium-sized mammals, four are important in the diet: ant bear, porcupine, springhare, and scrub hare. The pangolin (scaly anteater) is less common but is also eaten. Completing the list of mammals are one shrew, two species of squirrel, three species of bat, and 14 species of mouse and gerbil. None of these small mammals are eaten by the Ju. Finally, there are three primates, also not eaten: the tiny galago, the vervet monkey, and the baboon; the latter two are rarely seen. A summary of the mammals is found in Table 3–1.

Considering the dryness of the area, birdlife is surprisingly abundant. About 100 species of birds are resident in the Dobe area, and another 40 are summer migrants. Of these, the Ju have identified at least 90 species. The abundant ostrich, though rarely hunted for food, is prized for its eggs. They are emptied, their contents eaten, and the shells cleaned and used for water canteens and in bead making. Other important game birds include the very abundant guinea fowl and francolin, as well as ducks, korhaan, sandgrouse, quail, and dove.

Twenty-five species of reptiles and amphibians have been recorded, including snakes, lizards, tortoises, chameleons, and frogs. The six kinds of poisonous snakes loom large in the lives of the Ju/'hoansi. Although snakebites are rare (only three cases occurred in 10 years, none fatal), the !Kung take precautions to clear their campsites of brush that would conceal a snake, and whenever they find a poisonous snake, they kill it with a club or digging stick. (Women appear to be as proficient as men at killing snakes.)

Fish are not present in the Dobe area, but aquatic species such as terrapin, leeches, clams, and snails are found in isolated waterholes, indicating a time in the past when the area was connected to a river system by flowing water.

Of the countless invertebrates in the Dobe area, about 85 to 90 species are known to the San, including an abundance of scorpions, spiders, ticks, millipedes, and centipedes, and some 70 species of insects. Few insects are eaten. Wild honey is a superb delicacy but highly subject to seasonal fluctuation. No honey was seen in 1963–1964, but it was fairly common and highly prized in 1967–1969. The most important of the insects for subsistence are the species of *chrysomelid* beetles used by

TABLE 3–1   MAMMALS OF THE DOBE AREA

Animal	Occurrence*	Animal	Occurrence
Ungulates	*Other*		
Buffalo	R	Ant bear	C
Duiker	VC	Baboon	VR
Eland	U	Bat (3 species)	C
Gemsbok	C	Elephant	R
Giraffe	U	Galago	C
Hartebeest	U	Scrub hare	VC
Impala	VR	Mouse (12 species)	VC
Kudu	C	Pangolin	C
Roan antelope	U	Porcupine	C
Steenbok	VC	Shrew	C
Warthog	VC	Springhare	VC
Wildebeest	C	Bush squirrel	U
Zebra	R	Ground squirrel	C
		Vervet	R
Carnivores			
Aardwolf	C		
Bat-eared fox	C		
Caracal	U		
Cheetah	C		
Genet	C		
Honey badger	C		
Brown hyena	VR		
Spotted hyena	C		
Black-backed Jackal	C		
Leopard	U		
Lion	C		
Banded mongoose	C		
Slender mongoose	C		
Yellow mongoose	C		
Serval	VR		
Wild cat	C		
Wild dog	C		
Zorilla	C		

*VC = very common, daily sights of tracks
C = common, weekly sightings of tracks
U = uncommon, monthly sightings of tracks
R = rare, few sightings per year or less
VR = very rare, one or two sightings in a decade

the Ju for poisoning their hunting arrows. The grubs produce a slow-acting but highly effective poison, which when applied to arrows can kill a wounded animal in 6 to 24 hours.

CLIMATE

With a mean elevation of 1100 meters above sea level, the Dobe area lies within the summer rainfall zone of southern Africa. The area experiences hot summers with a four-to-six-month rainy season and moderate-to-cool winters without rainfall. The

BARA	≠TOBE	/GUM	/GAA	/HUMA
Summer	Autumn	Winter	Early Spring	Spring Rains
HOT RAINY	COOLER DRYING	COOL VERY DRY	HOT DRY	HOT DRY/WET

D   J   F   M   A   M   J   J   A   S   O   N

Figure 3–1. Seasons of the !Kung.

hottest months of the year are October to February, when temperatures average 30 to 40 degrees Centigrade (86 to 104 degrees Fahrenheit). In June and July, the coldest months of the year, night temperatures fall to freezing or near freezing, but they rise during the day to a comfortable 24 to 27 degrees Centigrade (75 to 80 degrees Fahrenheit). Temperatures are fairly consistent from year to year, but this is not the case with rainfall. The annual precipitation may vary from year to year by as much as 500 percent.

The Seasonal Round

The !Kung accurately divide the year into five seasons (Figure 3–1).

!Huma (spring rains)   Their year begins with the first rains in October and November. These are light thundershowers that often fall on one area and miss other areas entirely. This is a spectacular area for lightning. According to the United States Weather Service, Botswana has one of the highest incidences of lightning in the world. Brilliant displays light the Dobe sky at this time of year. The first rains also have the effect of triggering growth in plants and reproduction in animals, and overnight the parched landscape is transformed into one of lush greenery.

Bara (main summer rains)   From December to March the heaviest rains fall, bringing with them a season of plenty. Migratory ducks, geese, and other waterfowl flock to the seasonal pans in great numbers. Elephant and buffalo may migrate from the Okavango swamps. The major summer plant foods—fruits, berries, melons, and leafy greens—also make their appearance, and the Ju camps are widely distributed at seasonal waterpoints in the hinterland.

±Tobe (autumn)   A brief autumn occurs in April or May after the rains have ceased but before the onset of the really cold weather. The seasonal pans shrink and dry out at this time of year, and the !Kung may converge on the larger summer pans that still hold water. Food is abundant, with plenty of the summer berries and melons still available. The April mongongo nut harvest puts a major new food into the diet.

!Gum (winter)   The cool dry season extends from the end of May through August. It is heralded by a sharp drop in nightly temperatures, with the peak cold in late June. In 1968 and 1987, Dobe experienced a month or more of freezing and near-freezing nights. The !Kung winter camps, usually around a permanent waterhole, are well stocked with firewood to burn through the cold nights. Fortunately, the days are crisp,

Filling ostrich eggshells from a small summer waterhole, 1968.

clear, and warm. The diet is varied during the winter months. Mongongo fruit and nut, baobab, and many species of roots and bulbs provide the staples. The clear, pleasant days are ideal for walking; winter is a time for visiting relatives at distant camps. The good tracking conditions encourage more hunting and the setting up of snarelines. As the season passes, plant foods become increasingly scarce as foods are eaten up in wider and wider radii around the permanent waterholes.

!Gaa (spring dry season)   The final season of the !Kung year begins in late August with a rapid increase in daily temperatures and ends in October or early November with the onset of the first rains. This is the least attractive time of year. Although humidity remains low, the days are exceedingly hot, with highs from 33 to 43 degrees Centigrade (92 to 110 degrees Fahrenheit) in the shade. Work is difficult, and the better foods may be available only at distances from camp. It is in this season that the !Kung make use of the widest variety of plant foods. Fibrous roots, ignored at other times, may be dug and eaten without enthusiasm. Hunting, however, can be very good at this time of year due to the weakness of the animals. The !Kung eagerly await the onset of the next rainfall and the new season of plenty.

Rainfall is concentrated in the hot summer months (October to May), and from June to September the Dobe area is completely dry. The most striking fact, however, is the enormous yearly variation in amount and distribution of rainfall. Figure 3–2 shows the rainfall at Dobe for two rainy seasons and most of a third. Rainfall varied from 239 millimeters in the drought of 1963–1964 to 597 millimeters in the good year of 1967–1968, a swing of 250 percent (from 10 to 24 inches). Month-to-month and place-to-place variations further increase the uncertainty of precipitation.

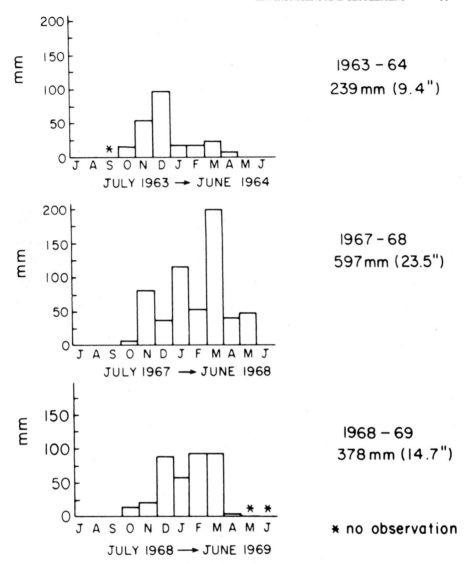

Figure 3–2. Rainfall at Dobe for three years.

Droughts are frequent. At Maun (the nearest weather station to Dobe with long-term records), drought occurs two years out of every five, and severe drought occurs about one year in four.[1] With a lower average rainfall, the situation at Dobe would be, if not worse, at least no better than the situation at Maun (Lee, 1972). In the rainy season of 1991–1992, the rains failed almost totally, precipitating what is widely regarded as the worst drought of the century over much of southern Africa.

Too *much* rainfall can also present a problem. Superrecord rains fell in 1973–1974 (1184 millimeters or 47 inches at Maun) and seriously reduced the mongongo crop,

---

[1]Severe drought occurs when annual rainfall is less than 70 percent of average.

although the crop recovered the following year. Too much rain occurred again in the rainy season of 1999–2000.

The message of the foregoing discussion is clear. There is no such thing as a typical rainfall year for the Ju/'hoansi. They must continuously adapt their subsistence strategy to high-rainfall years, to low-rainfall years, and to marked local variability. Theirs is long-term adaptation to the problem of living: the ethnographer sees only a small segment of the overall pattern in a given year of fieldwork. This theme will crop up again as we explore the !Kung way of life in more depth (for example, see Chapter 8 on *Hxaro* Exchange).

SETTLEMENT PATTERNS

The Ju/'hoan word for village or camp, *chu/o,* means literally "the face of the huts." The *chu/o* symbolizes for the Ju the safety, comfort, and companionship of the group, and the term is contrasted in their thought with the term *t'si,* meaning "bush" or wilderness. *Chu/o* is tamed space, cultural space; *t'si* is untamed or natural space.[2]

A typical Ju/'hoan camp is a rough circle of grass huts some 10 to 30 meters (30 to 100 feet) in diameter, arranged around a central clearing. This section discusses the settlement patterns of the Ju during the 1960s, under the following headings:

1. Village Types
2. The Layout of the Camp
3. Hut and Shelter Construction
4. Ethnoarcheology

Village Types

Mobility is the essence of the Ju adaptation. This factor strongly influences the settlement pattern. Ju villages are easily established and moved frequently. Habitations are built in a few hours or a few days, and camp sites are rarely occupied for more than a few months before being abandoned. In all, five types of villages and camps can be usefully distinguished.

A. Dry season villages   These sites, occupied for three to six months from May or June to September or October, are fairly large, often containing 8 to 15 huts and 20 to 50 people. They are always located near permanent water sources and, because of their accessibility (to outsiders) and their long duration, are by far the most thoroughly studied of all the Ju/'hoan village types. Dry season huts tend to be well constructed; the site is cleared with care, and large middens of garbage accumulate before the site is abandoned. As a result, the archeological visibility of the dry season camps is highest of all the settlement types.

B. Rainy season villages   These are located near major seasonal water and food sources. They are highly variable in size (from 3 to 20 huts) and are usually occupied for periods of three weeks to three months. The site is casually cleared, and the huts

---

[2]Unlike the Mbuti pygmies, who revere the forest, the !Kung do not express reverence or even much affection for the semi-arid savannah that surrounds them. They know it intimately, derive all their economic needs from it, and are comfortable traveling through it, but they do not deify it or attribute any supernatural powers to the land *per se* (see Chapter 9).

A rainy season camp in the mongongo groves.

are hastily constructed, though thickly thatched in order to provide shelter from the rains. When these are abandoned, the saplings used in hut construction may be moved to the next locale. A group may occupy as many as six sites in the course of a single rainy season.

C. Spring and fall camps   These are called camps rather than villages; because of the dry weather no huts are built, and they are rarely occupied for more than two or three weeks. Under certain circumstances similar short-term camps may also be established in summer when the group is moving from one foraging area to another, or in the winter when a group is taking advantage of a still-available seasonal water source.

D. Overnight stops   These are what the name implies. Only a fire is built, and the site is abandoned the next morning. Overnight stops occur in all seasons.

E. Cattle post villages   These new-style villages have become increasingly common since 1970. They involve solid, carefully constructed huts, usually built on sites close to an Herero or Tswana village. The size of these villages varies from 1 to 20 huts, but common to all is a crescent-shaped (not circular) layout around a central cattle kraal, with hut mouths facing the cattle compound rather than each other. This shift in layout sums up a key symbolic shift in social orientation. Whereas the older camps were circular so that the Ju could look at each other, the cattle-post Ju now look to the livestock for their survival. Another prominent feature of these villages is their long duration; some are still occupied 18 to 20 years after being built.

The Layout of the Camp

Choosing a site is not a great problem for the Ju/'hoansi. They look for good shade trees in an area that has not been too recently occupied. They do not return again and

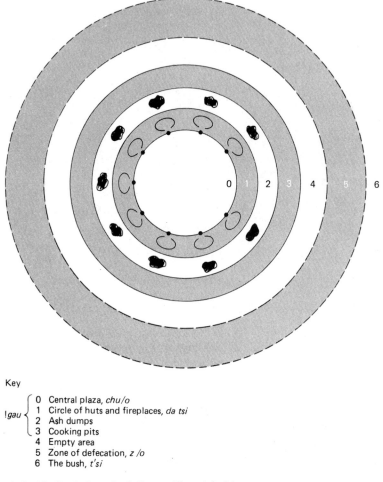

Key

!gau {
  0 Central plaza, *chu/o*
  1 Circle of huts and fireplaces, *da tsi*
  2 Ash dumps
  3 Cooking pits
  4 Empty area
  5 Zone of defecation, *z /o*
  6 The bush, *t'si*

Figure 3–3. Idealized plan of a Ju/'hoan village (chu/o).

again to the same spot, so there is not much opportunity for a great residue of artifacts to build up. They live lightly on the land.

The village site itself can be seen as consisting of five concentric circles, each with a different function (Figure 3–3). In the center lies the village's public space, a cleared "plaza" from 5 to 25 meters (15 to 75 feet) in diameter where children play and people may gather, and where in the evening healing dances are held. Around the central area is the most important part of the village, the ring of huts—*chu tsi*—and hearths—*da tsi*-. Each woman builds her hut with a space of three to five meters from those of her neighbors. Directly in front of the hut mouth is the family fire, at which all the food is cooked, where people socialize in the evening, and around which the family sleeps at night. The space immediately around the hut and fire is carefully cleared of all grass and low shrubs so that people can move about easily day or night, without fear of poisonous snakes or scorpions.

Most villages exhibit a symbolic order, with the most senior household situated on the side of the village from which its ancestors were said to have come and with its married children's huts strung out to the right and left. Other senior households and in-law segments usually situate themselves opposite the most senior couple, with their offspring strung out to their right and left, and thus a circle is constituted (see also Marshall, 1960).

The next ring, about five meters deep immediately behind the huts, is the zone of ash heaps and garbage dumps. Every 10 days or so women clean out their hearths and dump the ashes and nutshells behind their huts. In a six-month camp, middens up to half a meter (20 inches) in height will accumulate and the fireplace in turn may be scooped out so that it gradually sinks a foot below grade.

The third ring, about 25 meters (80 feet) deep, is the zone where cooking pits or earth ovens are dug. Whenever a large animal is killed, the head is cooked separately by digging a two-foot-deep pit, filling it with burning wood, placing the head on top of the fire, then adding more embers and wood, and covering it with sand. After two hours of cooking, the meat is served. Butchery of large animals and emptying and cleaning of entrails is also carried out here.

The last ring in the cultural space is the area of defecation, *z/o*. Depending on the size of the camp, this zone can be from 100 to 300 meters (350 to 1000 feet) in depth. !Kung have no latrines or privies, and they distribute themselves widely when carrying out their toilet. The abundant Kalahari dung beetles that roll into balls and quickly carry away and bury human and animal feces help to keep the *z/o* relatively clean and odor-free.

Beyond this outer perimeter, paths radiate outward into the *t'si* itself, the wild lands of subsistence into which the foragers venture.

Despite the !Kung imagery of the *t'si* as wilderness, and in spite of the real dangers that lurk in *t'si,* it is extremely interesting and significant that the traditional Ju did not attempt to fortify or stockade their village sites in any way.[3] They sleep in the open, protected only by their sleeping fires, which keep the carnivores at bay, and by their mutual trust of and peaceful relations with their human neighbors.

Hut and Shelter Construction

A !Kung rainy season hut can be constructed in a day. A dry season hut, to last for several months, takes three or four days to build. First, 10 to 12 saplings are cut, and each is dug in vertically in a circle with an opening for the mouth. The tops are tied together to form a dome, and the frame is strengthened horizontally with pliable branches. Then bundles of grass are cut and transported back to the site, where handfuls of thatch are carefully woven into the frame to form the walls. In the rainy season the top of the hut is heavily thatched to protect against the elements. In the dry season the dome of the hut is left open to catch the warming sun. People do not live in their huts, which are only 2 to 2.5 meters (6 to 8 feet) wide and less than 2 meters (6.5 feet) high. They use them as a place to store their belongings, as a windbreak and a place for an afternoon nap, and as a symbolic element to structure the living space. Since they are composed of organic materials, huts quickly become infested with bugs and are not particularly pleasant places to be in.

Three other kinds of structures are built in !Kung villages: tree storage areas, storage platforms, and meat-drying racks. For the first, a nest of branches and thatch is

---

[3]Only since the arrival of cattle have some villages put up a rough stockade to keep the animals from eating their thatching and other articles (see Chapter 10).

built at chest height in the crotch of a convenient tree. Men store their arrow poison out of reach of children, dried strips of *biltong* out of reach of dogs, and other valuables out of sight of the inquisitive eyes of neighbors.

The storage platform, built on four poles, serves the same function, with the additional advantage of casting a pool of shade for conversation. The drying rack is built if a large kill provides more meat than can be locally consumed.

In recent years the Ju/'hoansi have been abandoning their beehive-shaped grass huts in favor of the more substantial Tswana-style house with a vertical pole and mud walls, a mud floor, and a separate thatched roof. These huts take weeks or months to build, and when one is completed its owner is not likely to want to leave it soon. Many of these new-style huts are occupied continuously for years and mark the dramatic transition to sedentary life.

Ethnoarcheology

Until recently, Ju/'hoan life in the Dobe area constituted an endless cycle of seasonal movement, with each group building and abandoning three to six villages each year. These abandoned villages—// *gung/ osi*—form an important part of the social landscape. Each permanent waterhole is surrounded by dozens of them, and most adults can point to the campsites of their childhood. With the passing of the generations, gradually the campsites fade from human memory, become buried in the sand, and are converted into archeological sites.

The fact that Ju village sites of the 1960s strongly resemble the village sites of prehistoric foragers 100 to 500 years old or more offers us two kinds of important data. First, it shows us the continuity of the living cultures of the Dobe area with those of the past, and second, it offers us the chance to use the behaviors of the living as an aid to the interpretation of the past. The new science of *ethnoarcheology* does precisely this: the foraging behavior of living people is observed and then the material residues of that behavior are plotted. The residues produced by known behaviors are then compared with archeological residues for which the behaviors are not known.

Underlying ethnoarcheology is an assumption of uniformitarianism.[4] The same processes that produce the campsites of contemporary !Kung are postulated to have been instrumental in producing the campsites of prehistoric foragers. For example, if a group of 20 occupies a camp for 14 days and leaves a residue of 2.0 cubic meters of nutshells, and the same group's occupation of 28 days leaves 4.0 cubic meters, what length of stay would we expect to find for a residue of 6.0 cubic meters, of 1.0 cubic meter, and so on? This is one kind of question that ethnoarcheology seeks to answer.[5]

John Yellen, Alison Brooks, Polly Wiessner, and others have been doing ethnoarcheology research on the !Kung for over 20 years. Readers wishing to find out more about this approach are encouraged to consult their work (Yellen, 1977, 1990c; Brooks, Gelburd, and Yellen, 1981; Wiessner, 1982, 1986).

---

[4]A term coined by the great nineteenth-century geologist and friend of Darwin, Charles Lyell (1793–1867).

[5]If you answered 42 days and 7 days, you were correct. Of course the same volume of residue could be produced by a larger group staying for a shorter period; for example, a residue of 6.0 cubic meters could be produced by a group of 42 staying 20 days.

4/Subsistence: Foraging for a Living

The morning after I arrived in Dobe and before I had even set up my camp, my new-found neighbors came to me with a proposition. N!eishi and his son ≠Toma approached me and said, "There is no food in our camp and we are hungry, would the bearded White man take us in his truck to get some food?"

"Isn't there any food around here?" I asked through the interpreter.

"There is some," the answer came back. "A few bitter roots and berries. But we want to show you a place where the food is good and there is plenty."

"But what kind of food?" I asked, reaching for my notebook.

"// gxa," ≠Toma said. "The Tswanas call it mongongo."

I had heard about mongongo, from reading the Marshall research (they called it *mangetti,* the Herero name for it), and the Dobe camp was littered with mounds of empty nutshells. I was keen to see what the trees looked like. A trip there would also put me on good terms with my neighbors.

"How far is it?" I asked, not wanting to get involved in a wild-goose chase.

"Oh, it's not far," N!eishi and ≠Toma assured me. "We'll be there in no time."

Just as the truck started, six women from Dobe camp rushed forward and asked if they could come too. They hopped onto the back, and as we set out they broke out in a song, a rousing chorus with a pleasant melody sung in complex rhythms. I later learned that this was the truck song (*dotsi*), sung whenever the Ju/'hoansi got a lift on one. The joyous words to celebrate the luxury of high-speed transportation go something like this: "*do si bereka, moseliseliyana*" (while the truck does the work we sit around and get fat).

I also liked the lyric to another verse that went "Those who work for a living, that's their problem!" Despite the song, the travel was anything but high-speed, and our destination was anything but near. We ground along for hours in four-wheel drive at a walking pace where no truck had ever been before, swerving to avoid ant bear holes and circumventing fallen trees.

At several points along the way I spotted trees that looked familiar.

"Isn't that a mongongo tree?" I asked. "And what are those little nuts lying on the ground?"

"Yes, that's mongongo, all right," ≠Toma replied, "but those groves are almost finished. Keep going."

It was noon before ≠Toma signaled that we had reached our destination. It was worth waiting for. We stood on the top of the dune in the middle of a large grove of mongongo trees that stretched east and west to the horizon. The fallen nuts densely covered the ground. This was a fresh grove, unpicked this season. I reckoned we were about 10 miles north of Dobe.

Without ceremony, the women fanned out and started to pick. Grabbing my camera, stopwatch, and notebook, I hastened to follow them. They bent from the waist with a smooth and effortless motion and picked five or six nuts each time and popped them in their *karosses,* one-piece garments-*cum*-carrying-bags. Every 10 minutes or so, each would return to the truck to spill out her load on the spot she had picked out. The individual piles began to accumulate rapidly. The men were collecting too, using smaller bags than those of the women. I sampled how rapidly the women were able to pick. They were gathering at the rate of 40 to 60 nuts per minute, or 2000 to 3000 nuts per hour. By two o'clock everyone was finished; they dumped their final few onto the piles, which looked enormous to me. The women took off their *karosses* and laid them flat. After piling all their nuts into the middle of the *karosses,* they made manageable bundles of them by bringing the four corners together and sewing the edges together with bark stripped from a nearby tree. Some women used pieces of store-bought cloth to make their bundles. Some stopped to crack a few nuts with stones they found nearby and eat them as they waited for the others to finish.

The bundles were loaded on the truck, which, with the eight people, was riding dangerously low. We set off on our return journey, arriving home before nightfall.

I was curious to see just how much food had been gathered in the short time we had been in the groves. A simple fisherman's scale gave a rough-and-ready answer. The women's loads weighed 30 to 50 pounds each, and the men's 15 to

Tin!kay packing mongongo nuts at !Gausha.

25 pounds each. That worked out to about 23,000 calories of food for each woman collector, and 12,000 for each man. Each woman had gathered enough to feed a person for 10 days and each man enough for 5 days. Not at all a bad haul for two hours' work![1]

My first full day of fieldwork had already taught me to question one popular view of hunter-gatherer subsistence: that life among these people was precarious, a constant struggle for existence. My later studies were to show that the !Kung in fact enjoyed a rather good diet and that they didn't have to work very hard to get it. As we will see, even without the aid of an anthropologist's truck, the !Kung had to work only 20 hours a week in subsistence. But what about the fact that N!eishi had come to me that morning saying that they were hungry and that there was no food nearby? Strictly speaking, N!eishi spoke the truth. October is one of the harder months of the year, at the end of the dry season, and the more desirable foods had been eaten out close to Dobe. What N!eishi did not say was that a little farther away food *was* available, and, if not plentiful, there was enough to see them

---

[1]Of course being on the truck saved the collectors about six hours walking time, and these hours would have to be factored in to get a more accurate idea of the actual work involved.

The mongongo.

through until the rains came. When N!eishi came to me with his proposition, he was making an intelligent use of his resources, social and otherwise. Why hike in the hot sun for a small meal, when the bearded White man might take you in his truck for 10 large ones?

The security of Ju/'hoan life is attributable mainly to the fact that vegetable food and not meat forms the mainstay of their diet. Plant foods are abundant, locally available, and predictable; game animals, in contrast, are scarce and unpredictable. In addition to the mongongo nut, the !Kung have an astonishing inventory of 105 edible plants: 14 fruits and nuts, 15 berries, 18 species of edible gum, 41 edible roots and bulbs, and 17 leafy greens, beans, melons, and other foods. The abundance and variety of plant foods makes it possible for the Ju to feed themselves by an average of about 20 hours of subsistence work per adult per week, a far lower figure than the 40-hour work week we have come to accept in the industrialized countries. In this chapter we explore how this "affluent" way of life is achieved by the Ju in their harsh, semiarid desert environment.

GATHERING AND CARRYING

The tools and techniques of gathering are relatively simple. The knowledge of plant identification, growth, ripeness, and location, however, is extremely complex. The !Kung women are highly skilled at distinguishing useful from nonuseful or dangerous plants and at finding and bringing home sufficient quantities of the best food species available.

Only a single tool, the digging stick, is used in gathering. Carrying, on the other hand, involves the use of several ingenious multipurpose containers and an elaborate body of knowledge.

The versatile digging stick is used to dig out roots and bulbs; it is also used in hunting to dig out burrowing mammals, in water-getting to dig out water-bearing roots, and as a carrying device to transport large roots impaled on it or suspended from it with twine. For the remaining nonroot 75 percent of the vegetable diet—fruits, nuts, gums, melons, and leafy greens—no special gathering tools are used.

Carrying Devices

The kaross Foremost among the carrying devices is the woman's kaross (*chi!kan*), a formidable one-piece combination garment-*cum*-carrying device that also does service as a sleeping blanket (Figure 4–1). The men manufacture these for the women from the hides of the female kudu, gemsbok, wildebeest, or eland. This suede garment is worn draped over the wearer's back. Tied at the waist with a leather thong, the lower half of the kaross conceals the wearer's backside, and the upper half forms a pouch for carrying vegetables, water containers, firewood, and babies. With a center of gravity close to the body, the kaross is ideal for carrying heavy loads. In Ju/'hoan thought, the kaross is so characteristic of women and their work that the knot (*!kebi*) that ties the kaross at a woman's waist is also an affectionate colloquial term for "women" (*!kebisi*).

Leather bags A variety of sturdy leather bags are made from the skins of the steenbok and duiker. Both men and women wear small "handbags" over the shoulder and under the armpit for keeping handy tobacco, fire-making kits, sewing materials,

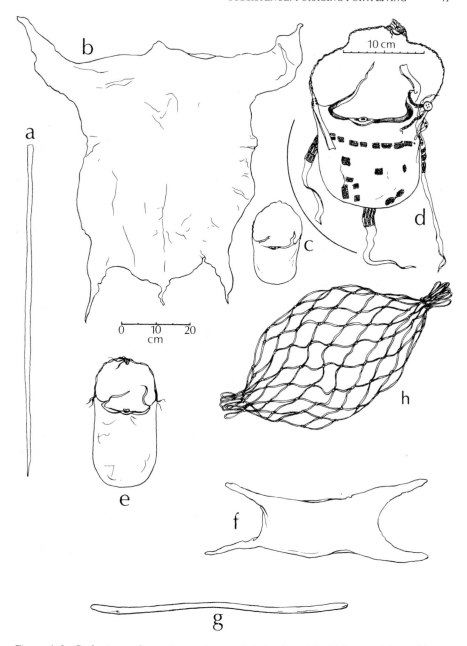

Figure 4–1. Gathering and carrying equipment: (a) digging stick; (b) kaross; (c) small bag; (d) small bag (detailed); (e) man's bag; (f) baby carrier; (g) carrying yoke; (b) man's net.

and other items. The women's bags are brightly decorated with beadwork. For carrying foodstuffs and larger items, large bags called / *tausi* are used, ranging up to the size of a grocery shopping bag.

Baby sling   For carrying a young infant, a mother employs a special leather baby carrier (Figure 4–1), tied around her waist and over her shoulders, that fits inside the

Women carrying loads in their karosses.

kaross on her hip and allows the baby access to the breast. This special baby carrier is lined with soft grasses and other absorbent materials and is frequently cleaned and aired. When an older, toilet-trained child is carried, he or she sits directly in the main pouch of the kaross or is carried on the shoulder by a woman or man.

Carrying net   Men make an ingeniously intricate knotted net, called */wisi,* for use as a carrying device (Figure 4–1). This wide-meshed net, 100 centimeters (3 feet) long and 40 centimeters (16 inches) across, can be lined with long grass and used to carry quantities of such small items as nuts and berries.

Carrying yoke   The carrying yoke *(!garo)* is easily made from a rough wooden branch. Full bags, nets, bundles of meat, and haunches of freshly killed game are slung from either end, and the load is shouldered by a man for the long trips between camps.

Because the essence of the Ju/'hoan adaptation is mobility, and because their daily diet consists mostly of hundreds of small nuts, berries, and roots, San life would not be possible without means of carrying quantities of these small foods back to the camp or home base. Ju/'hoan carrying technology is well developed and well designed. A similar degree of development is reflected in their vocabulary, which has a multitude of terms for different ways of carrying. A partial list is shown in Table 4–1 and illustrated in Figure 4–2. One cannot overstate the importance of carrying and carrying devices for San life and for the life of hunting and gathering

TABLE 4–1   CARRYING VOCABULARY (SEE FIGURE 4-2 FOR ILLUSTRATIONS)

To Carry on the Back		To Carry Otherwise	
1. A child	*maa*	11. On the head	*ku≠tem*
2. A load (males)	*//xam*	12. On the belt	*!uu*
3. A load (females)	*//kei*	13. To drag (not shown)	*!gwe*
4. A *kaross* package	*!guu*	14. To carry firewood in a *kaross*	*!gaba*
To Carry on the Shoulders		**To Carry with a Carrying Yoke**	
5. A child	*chi*	15. To stick a load through (not shown)	*/di*
6. An object	*!kai*		
7. A bag or quiver	*!wana*	16. to hang a load from	*//gau*
8. A carrying yoke	*//wana*	17. To impale a root and carry	*!n//xam*
9. A *kaross*	*//gama*	18. To carry with two carrying yokes	*du tsiu*
10. A spear	*!kei//kun*		*!garo*

peoples in general. The universality of the carrying device and its functional importance among all recent hunter-gatherers has implications for the evolution of human subsistence during the Pleistocene Era, because a device for carrying vegetable foods would seem to be a prerequisite for human economic and social life (see Lee, 1979:489–494).

Major and Minor Foods[2]

Over 100 species of wild plants are classified by the Ju/'hoansi as edible. However, not all plant foods are valued equally. Some are prized and eaten daily; others are despised and rarely eaten. Complex criteria are applied by the Ju to arrange their plant foods into a hierarchy of classes of desirability. Abundance, duration of eating season, ease of collecting, tastiness, absence of side effects, and nutritional value are six of the criteria Ju use to classify their food as / *gau* (strong) or / *ta/tana* (weak) foods. To their own judgments I have added my observations on frequency of eating and quantities eaten and have drawn up a six-class hierarchy of foods:

---

[2]The research on which this discussion is based was carried out from 1963 to 1969. In the 1970s, models of optimal foraging strategy began to be widely applied to gathering and hunting humans (e.g., Winterhalder and Smith, 1981; Bettinger, 1992). The discussion presented here closely anticipates the spirit and underlying assumptions of optimal foraging theory (OFT), although I have several points of disagreement with optimal foraging as currently applied to humans.

OFT assumes that humans, like other species, will make their subsistence choices based on an underlying cost-benefit calculus. They will rank-order foods, giving priority to those that yield the highest returns (in terms of energy and protein) for the least amount of effort. Elaborate models, often accompanied by pages of mathematical formulae, are constructed around this rather simple proposition, usually linked to neo-Darwinian arguments about genetic fitness or differential reproductive success.

While OFT has its adherents, others have been critical of its explicit reductionism. Do people always behave so rationally? Are foraging decisions never affected by outside factors, such as government or missionary policies, or the price of flour at the trading store? I wonder if OFT models, when used single-mindedly, are not enforcing a kind of tunnel vision by focusing on a limited range of behavior (foraging) at the expense of a richer understanding of economic life in its social and historical context.

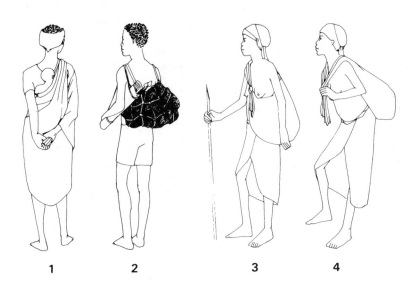

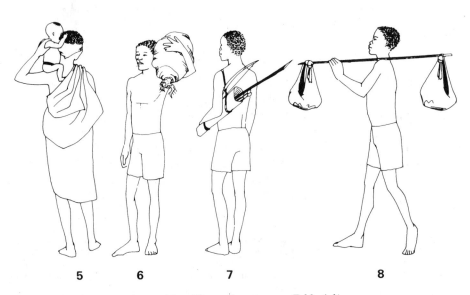

Figure 4–2. !Kung carrying positions (for explanation, see Table 4-1).

Food Classes:		Criteria:
1. Primary	1 species	widely abundant year-round
2. Major	13 species	widely abundant
3. Minor	19 species	locally seasonally abundant
4. Supplementary	30 species	locally seasonally available
5. Rare	19 species	rarely observed to be eaten
6. Problematic	23 species	!Kung classify as edible; not observed to be eaten

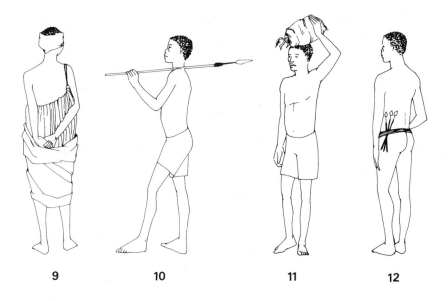

9   10   11   12

14   17

18

16

The mongongo (fruit and nut) is in a class by itself. All the Dobe !Kung agree that it is their most important vegetable food. It is superabundant, found near all water-holes, and available in all months of the year; it is easy to collect, tasty, and highly nutritious. Only meat rivals the mongongo as the most desirable food of the !Kung. I asked one informant to tell me what his idea of an ideal diet would consist of. Without hesitation, he listed four items: meat and mongongo for strength, honey for sweet-ness, and wild orange fruits for refreshment.

Thirteen additional species are considered major foods. These are rated high on most, but not all, the criteria of desirability. Most are seasonal and therefore not available year-round, and most are not universally distributed at all the waterholes. All are abundant, and each may exceed the mongongo in importance at certain waterholes at certain times of the year. Baobab, for example, is tasty and abundant but is mainly concentrated in a few waterholes such as !Kubi and is rare or absent at others. Marula is found at most of the waterholes, but its nutmeat is smaller than that of mongongo, and its shell is harder to crack.

Nineteen of the species are listed as minor foods; these rate high on one or two criteria of desirability. Included are seven species of roots and bulbs that, taken individually, are not important, but that as a group become a major item of the diet during the winter dry season, when the major summer foods are not available. All the species of class III are seasonally limited.

The largest class is supplementary foods, with 30 species. As the name implies, these food supplement the foods in classes I, II, and III or are eaten when the more desirable foods become locally exhausted. The list includes 6 species of fruits and berries, 10 of edible gum, 12 roots and bulbs, a bean, and a leafy green. In general, the foods of class IV are both less abundant and less tasty than the corresponding foods of class III.

The rare foods (19 species) were observed to be eaten on only a few occasions each year. Many were quite scarce; others were plentiful but were downgraded because of poor taste or undesirable side effects.

Finally, there are the 23 species listed as problematic foods. The !Kung said that these were edible, but I did not observe them to be eaten during the study period.

Food Classes and Subsistence Strategy

The way the Ju/'hoansi hierarchically evaluate their plant inventory in order of importance as food suggests a productive analogy to the way they utilize space in the short run in subsistence activities. The Ju typically occupy a campsite for a period of weeks and eat their way out of it. For instance, at a camp in the mongongo forest the members exhaust the nuts within a 1.5-kilometer (one-mile) radius the first week of occupation, within a three-kilometer (two-mile) radius the second week, and within a five-kilometer (three-mile) radius the third week. The longer a group lives at a camp, the farther it must travel each day to get food. This feature of daily subsistence characterizes both summer and winter camps. For example, at the Dobe winter camp in June 1964 the gatherers were making daily round trips of 9 to 14 kilometers to reach the mongongo groves. By August the daily round trips had increased to 19 kilometers.

This progressive increase in walking distance occurs because the Ju are highly selective in their food habits. They do not eat *all* the food in a given area. They start by eating out the most desirable species, and when these are exhausted or depleted they turn to the less desirable species. Because plant food resources are both varied and abundant, in any situation where the desirable foods are scarce, the !Kung have two alternatives in food strategy: (1) they may walk farther in order to obtain the more desirable species, or (2) they may remain closer to camp and exploit the less desirable species. In fact, both alternatives are practiced simultaneously: the younger, more active camp members go

Cooking the fruit of the mongongo.

farther afield to bring back foods of classes I and II, and the older, more sedentary camp members collect class III and IV foods closer to home. Because the day's foods are pooled within families and shared with other families at adjacent fires, the net effect is that every camp member has a variety of food available at the end of the day—and no one goes hungry.

HUNTING

Though vegetable foods provide the bulk of the diet, we should not underestimate the returns from hunting. Meat contributes about 30 percent of the calories to the diet and hunting was the major occupation of the men, up to about 1970. All !Kung, men and women alike, rate meat among their most valued foods. Part of its value comes from its scarcity. Steak is always better than potatoes. But its social value is, I think, paramount. Whenever a large animal is killed it is the occasion for feasting. Great cauldrons of meat are cooked round the clock, and people gather from far and wide to eat. Distribution is done with great care, according to a set of rules, arranging and rearranging the pieces for up to an hour so that each recipient will get the right proportion. Successful distributions are remembered with pleasure for weeks afterwards, while improper meat distributions can be the cause of bitter wrangling among close relatives.

Tools and Techniques

The hunting weaponry consists of major tools and minor ones. The major ones are the bow and arrow, spear, knife, springhare hook, and rope snares (see Figure 4–3). The minor tools include the digging stick and fire-making equipment. In addition, the knife, ropes, and carrying yoke are used in butchery and in carrying the meat back to camp. Guns are almost entirely absent in Dobe !Kung hunting. Though some men had hunted with guns borrowed from the Herero, only one man out of 151 Ju owned a gun and used it for hunting while I was there.[3]

The Ju/'hoansi have four types of hunting techniques. First is the mobile hunt, with bow and poisoned arrows, for plains game such as kudu and gemsbok and wildebeest. This is the kind of hunting most outsiders associate with the !Kung and other hunting peoples (see John Marshall's film, *The Hunters*). It may surprise some that the other hunting techniques produce many more kills than the classic bow-and-arrow hunt.

Hunting with dogs is the second kind of hunt. Warthog, steenbok, duiker, and hares are taken this way. Well-trained hunting dogs bring small game to bay, and the hunter finishes it off with a spear. N!eishi's son ≠Toma had a famous pair of dogs named Swoiya and Foiya, with which he killed warthog at the rate of three per month.

I was surprised to find that the Ju do much of their hunting *underground,* pursuing burrowing animals into their lairs. Ant bear, warthog, and porcupine are taken this way. The latter two are hunted above ground as well. The nocturnal springhare sleeps in narrow burrows during the day. Ju hunters have developed a special tool, a 13-foot-long pole with an iron hook at the end, for probing springhare burrows and impaling the animals underground. The burrow is then excavated with a digging stick to retrieve the kill. This is hot, dusty work, which the Ju were only too glad to turn over to the visiting anthropologist.

The fourth technique is snaring, employed particularly by older hunters whose mobility is limited. A man surveys an area of bush for fresh tracks, then he lays down an unobtrusive line of brush to accustom the animals to cross at certain gaps. The

[3]Even in the late 1980s, firearm ownership was virtually nil among the Dobe area Ju/'hoansi.

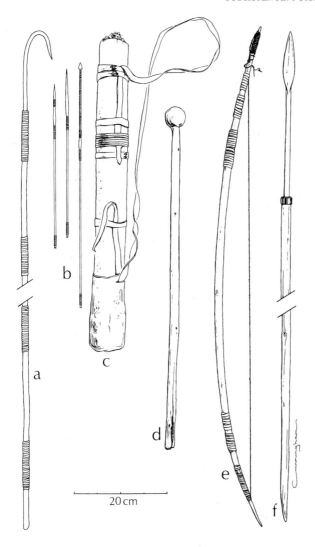

Figure 4–3. !Kung hunting weapons: (a) springhare probe; (b) arrows; (c) quiver; (d) club; (e) bow; (f) spear.

snares are made of rope from local fiber plants with a delicate wooden trigger attached to a bent-over sapling. When the hare, guinea fowl, or small antelope steps in the snare, the noose tightens and the sapling springs up, leaving the quarry dangling. Snaring does not produce a large quantity of meat. In July 1964 at Dobe, 18 animals were killed, 11 of them by snares. These 11, however, provided only 20 percent of the meat of the camp.

The Joys of Tracking

The Ju/'hoansi are such superb trackers and make such accurate deductions from the faintest marks in the sand that at first their skill seems uncanny. For example, both men and women are able to identify an individual person merely by the sight

≠Toma and his father, N!eishi, butchering a warthog.

of his or her footprint in the sand. There is nothing mysterious about this. Their tracking is a skill, cultivated over a lifetime, that builds on literally tens of thousands of observations (see also Liebenberg, 1990). The Ju hunter can deduce many kinds of information about the animal he is tracking: its species and sex, its age, how fast it is traveling, whether it is alone or with other animals, its physical condition (healthy or ill), whether and on what it is feeding, and the time of the day the animal passed this way.

The species, of course, is identified by the shape of the hoofprint and by the dung or scat; this is the simplest information to be deduced, and any 12-year-old boy can accurately reproduce in the sand the prints of a dozen species. The size or age of an animal correlates directly with the size of its print. The depth of the print indicates the weight of the animal. An old or infirm animal may be distinguished by a halting gait or uneven stride length. Evidence of crippling is eagerly sought and is discerned when one hoofprint is deeper than the others.

Knowledge of the animal's habits aids in determining the time of day it passed by. Some of the signs are surprisingly simple. If the tracks zigzag from shade tree to tree, the animal went through during the heat of the day. If the tracks go under the west side of the trees, the animal was catching the morning shade; if under the east side, the afternoon shade; and if under either side, the animal passed at midday. Milling tracks within a small radius out in the open suggest that the animal was there at night and was sleeping. Tracks leading into a dense thicket indicate the animal rested up during midday.

Perhaps the most amazing skill is in the hunter's ability to figure out the number of minutes or hours elapsed since the animal went through. This is crucial information; to obtain it, the Ju have developed their discriminating powers to the highest degree. After a print has been made, it provides a miniature physiographic feature that is acted upon by natural processes. Consider a simple example. When fresh, the print is clean-cut, but after an hour (or less, if the day is windy) a fine covering of wind-blown sand collects in the depression. Later, twigs and grass fall in, and then insect and other animal tracks are superimposed. The moisture content of the soil one, two, three, or four centimeters below the surface and the rate at which soil dries out after being exposed by a footfall are two variables that are exceedingly well studied by the Ju. When an animal is being closely followed, the present position of the shade in relation to the animal's footprint plus these other signs can indicate to within 15 minutes the time the animal passed by.

All these kinds of information and more are interpreted by the hunter in order to decide whether a trail is worth pursuing. Ideally, a hunter looks for an older or infirm animal moving slowly in thick brush. The hunter then can creep up to get within firing range while the quarry is unaware. A final stalk may take up to 40 minutes, with the hunter creeping on his elbows and knees. To have a reasonable chance of placing an arrow, the hunter should be within 100 feet.

Once the animal is hit, the poison must do its work. Well placed, a poisoned arrow can kill a large antelope within 6 to 24 hours. After the hunter examines the tracks for signs of blood, he does a surprising thing: he goes home. There is no point chasing an animal to its death place, which could be miles away. Instead, the hunter heads back to camp for the night. In the morning the hunter, accompanied by a party of carriers, goes out to pick up the wounded animal's trail. They follow the prey to its place of dying, butcher the carcass, and bring it home.

Not all hunts are successful. In fact, on most days of hunting a man will come back empty-handed. And even if an animal is wounded, there is no guarantee that the meat will ever reach camp. As many as half the animals shot by the Ju either recover from their wounds or run so far that they die out of range of the carrying party. An individual hunter is deemed fortunate if he kills as many as two large antelopes per year. Most of the meat consumed by the Ju comes from hundreds of kills of smaller animals.

INSULTING THE MEAT

When a hunter returns from a successful hunt, or when meat is brought into a camp, one would think that this would be met with open glee and the hunter praised for his skill. Quite the contrary: the people often display indifference or negativity at the news of a successful kill, and I was surprised to see the low-key way in which the hunters would break the news of their success. /Xashe, an excellent hunter from /Xai/xai, put it this way:

> When you come home empty-handed, you sleep and you say to yourself, "Oh, what have I done? What's the matter that I haven't killed?" Then the next morning you get up and without a word you go out and hunt again. This time you *do* kill something, and you come home. My *tsu* ("older kinsman") sees me and asks: "Well what did you see today?" "Tsutsu," I reply, "I didn't see anything."

I am sitting there with my head in my hands but my *tsu* comes back to me because he is a Ju/'hoan. "What do you mean you haven't killed anything? Can't you see that I'm dying of hunger?"

"Well, there might be something out there. I just might have scratched its elbow."

Then you say, as he smiles, "Why don't we go out in the morning and have a look." And so we two and others will bring home the meat together the next day.

Men are encouraged to hunt as well as they can, and the people are happy when meat is brought in, but the correct demeanor for the successful hunter is modesty and understatement. A / Xai/ xai man named / Gaugo said:

Say that a man has been hunting. He must not come home and announce like a braggart, "I have killed a big one in the bush!" He must first sit down in silence until I or someone else comes up to his fire and asks, "What did you see today?" He replies quietly, "Ah, I'm no good for hunting. I saw nothing at all . . . maybe just a tiny one." Then I smile to myself because I know he has killed something big.

The theme of modesty is continued when the butchering and carrying party goes to fetch the kill the following day. Arriving at the site, the members of the carrying party loudly express their disappointment to the hunter:

You mean you have dragged us all the way out here to make us cart home your pile of bones? Oh, if I had known it was this thin I wouldn't have come.

People, to think I gave up a nice day in the shade for this. At home we may be hungry, but at least we have nice cool water to drink.

To these insults the hunter must not act offended; he should respond with self-demeaning words:

You're right, this one is not worth the effort; let's just cook the liver for strength and leave the rest for the hyenas. It's not too late to hunt today, and even a duiker or a steenbok would be better than this mess.

The party, of course, has no intentions of abandoning the kill. The heavy joking and derision are directed toward one goal: the leveling of potentially arrogant behavior in a successful hunter. The !Kung recognize the tendency toward arrogance ($\neq$ *twi*) in young men and take definite steps to combat it. As $\neq$ Tomazho, the famous healer from /Xai/xai, put it:

When a young man kills much meat, he comes to think of himself as a chief or a big man, and he thinks of the rest of us as his servants or inferiors. We can't accept this. We refuse one who boasts, for someday his pride will make him kill somebody. So we always speak of his meat as worthless. In this way we cool his heart and make him gentle.

Insulting the meat is one of the central practices of the Ju/'hoansi that serve to maintain egalitarianism. Even though some men are much better hunters than others, their behavior is molded by the group to minimize the tendency toward self-praise and to channel their energies into socially beneficial activities. As a result, the existence of differences in hunting prowess does not lead to a system of Big Men in which a few talented individuals tower over the others in terms of prestige.

I didn't really understand the importance of meat insulting until the Ju/'hoansi tried it on me. Visiting anthropologists, I found, are not immune to the faults of arrogance and self-praise. One Christmas I planned to slaughter an ox as a way of saying thank you to the Ju for their cooperation over the past year. The Ju didn't see it that way and harassed me mercilessly in a way that was both hilarious and painful. The tale is told in a story called "Eating Christmas in the Kalahari," which is reproduced in Appendix A.

Though painful, the experience gave me a deeper insight into their core system of meaning. Insulting the meat is just one of a whole set of rough practices that allow the !Kung to sustain a sharing way of life (see also Chapters 7 and 8).

The theme of egalitarianism is also seen in several other hunting practices. Hunting magic and divination are frequently used to help a hunter who is down on his luck. And the widespread sharing of arrows also helps to reduce the considerable individual differences that exist in hunting ability.

The Ju/'hoan rule for allocating ownership of meat from a kill is "the owner of the arrow is the owner of the meat." Ownership here means primarily the right to distribute the meat. Men circulate arrows widely in the *hxaro* trade network. A man will say to another, "Give me an arrow, and if I kill something with it I will give the meat to you." Weeks or months later, when he kills an antelope, he shares the carcass with his trading partner if the latter happens to be in his camp. If the arrow-giver is elsewhere, the hunter saves a portion of the dried meat for him. This trading of arrows strengthens the bonds between men and is especially used between such kin categories as brothers-in-law. Women may own arrows too, trade them with men, and become owners of meat.

The reason for this high incidence of arrow sharing is not hard to find. A meat distribution brings prestige to the hunter, but it also can be a heavy burden, bringing with it the risk of accusations of stinginess or improper behavior if the distribution is not to everybody's liking. A practice that tends to diffuse the responsibility for meat distribution and spread the glory (and the hostility) around is therefore a blessing in such tense situations. Lorna Marshall makes this apt comment on the practice: "There is much giving and lending of arrows. The society seems to want to extinguish in every way possible the concept of the meat belonging to the hunter" (1976:297).

WORK EFFORT AND CALORIC RETURNS

As my research on the Ju/'hoansi proceeded I was struck by the apparent lack of effort that went into the food quest. In the bush camps half or more of the adults seemed to be resting or sleeping in the camp on any given day. I had seen the abundance of mongongo nuts that the Dobe group had gathered the day after my arrival (see pp. 37–39), but didn't know whether this was a fluke made possible by the presence of my truck. I had learned to mistrust first impressions, and so I decided the only way to settle the issue was to make some systematic observations. How hard or easy was it to make a living? How many hours a day or days per week did the Ju have to devote to subsistence activities? How adequate was their diet in meeting their nutritional needs? In July 1964 I started a daily work diary of the Dobe camp's activities.

The whole camp was checked at sunrise and sunset to determine what each person was doing that day. The comings and goings of Ju/'hoan visitors were also recorded in order to establish a count of the number of mouths being fed each day. And the hunters were checked as they came home each day with or without meat. Women were monitored to see what species of plant foods they had gathered, and samples of their backloads were weighed on a simple scale.

July was neither the best nor the worst time of year for subsistence. The days were sunny and warm; the nights went down to freezing. Mongongo nuts were the major food, with smaller quantities of roots and bulbs. Berries, leafy greens, and other rainy-season foods were scarce or absent.

During the work study, the population of the Dobe camp ranged from 23 to 40. On an average night there were 31 mouths to feed in the camp. I calculated work effort in terms of workweek, not because the Ju think that way (they don't), but because it is a form that is easily understandable to us and makes possible comparison with other societies.[4]

At the end of four weeks I plotted out the figures (see Table 4–2). When the actual number of days of work was plotted, it turned out to be surprisingly low. From week to week the !Kung spent from 1.9 to 3.2 days in finding food. The overall average was 2.4 days of food-getting per person per week. Translated into hours, this worked out to about 20 hours of work per week, about half of the 40-hour workweek that is standard in industrial societies.

Breaking down the figures by age and sex, I found that men worked more days per week than women, about 2.7 days for men compared to 2.1 days for women. Another interesting point was that though women did not hunt, men did gather: about one-fifth of all men's working days were spent in gathering and men's gathering accounted for about 22 percent of all the gathered foods. When I looked at the total contribution of all forms of activity to the diet, I saw that men provided about 45 percent of the food, and women 55 percent, even though men worked harder than women. Overall, vegetable foods provided 70 percent of the diet, and meat the other 30 percent.

How general was the low level of work seen at Dobe in July 1964? In 1969, Pat Draper studied work effort at seven foraging camps in the /Du/ da area, 70 miles south of Dobe. She found that the workweek varied from 1.2 to 3.5 days, with an average of 2.3 days of work per week, very close to the Dobe average of 2.4 days (Draper, personal communication). Thus later studies at other waterholes showed that this leisurely pace of life was not unique to Dobe.

It would be misleading to leave the discussion of work effort here, since subsistence work is not the only kind of work the Ju/'hoansi have to do. In addition, there are the important tasks of manufacturing and maintaining their tool kit and, of course, housework—for the Ju this involves food preparation, butchery, drawing water and gathering firewood, washing utensils, and cleaning the living space. These tasks take many hours a week. (But we should also remember that when Western economists calculate on-the-job work time, they do not include this type of work in their figures.)

---

[4]For a detailed discussion of methods and results, see Lee, 1979:249–280.

TABLE 4–2 RESULTS OF THE DOBE WORK DIARY

Week	Group Size			Total Person-Days of				Meat Consumption	
	Mean	Range	Adult-Days	Child-Days	Consumption	Work	Work-Week	Kg.	lbs.
I (July 6–12)	25.6	23–29	114	65	179	37	2.3	42	92
II (July 13–19)	28.3	23–37	125	73	198	43	2.4	36	79
III (July 20–26)	34.3	29–40	156	84	240	42	1.9	80	176
IV (July 27–Aug. 2)	35.6	32–40	167	82	249	77	3.2	57.5	127
Total	30.9		562	304	866	199	2.4	215.5	474

TABLE 4–3   ESTIMATE OF OVERALL WORK EFFORT IN HOURS PER WEEK
FOR MEN AND WOMEN

	Subsistence Work	Tool Making and Fixing	Housework	Total Workweek (hours)
Men	21.6	7.5	15.4	44.5
Women	12.6	5.1	22.4	40.1
Average both sexes	17.1	6.3	18.9	42.3

The traditional Ju/'hoansi make use of some 28 different tools and devices for gathering, hunting, cooking, and fetching water. In addition, their wardrobe consists of leather garments that have to be manufactured from the hides of game animals. They have to construct their houses, and their living and sleeping sites have to be cleared and maintained. These kinds of tasks add about an hour's work per day for men, and 45 minutes for women.[5] Finally, the tasks of housework, including an hour of nut-cracking per person per day, plus all the other tasks, add another 2 to 3 hours per day to the total work effort.

The overall estimate of hours per week shown in Table 4–3 is about 44.5 hours for men and 40.1 hours for women, with an overall average of 42.3 hours of work per person. This figure is still far below that level of work expected of people in our society. Studies have shown that North American wage-earners, those with many children especially, will spend up to 40 hours per week *over and above their wage-paid* job doing housework, shopping, washing, etc. This amount of work is not necessarily decreased by "labor-saving" washing machines and other appliances (Meissner et al., 1975).

The Quality and Quantity of the Diet

During the 28 days of the study the hunters brought in 18 animals yielding 454 pounds of meat, and gifts of meat from outside made up another 36 pounds of meat, for a total of 490 pounds. This works out to a daily consumption of 9.1 ounces of meat for every man, woman, and child. None of the kills were made with bow and poisoned arrows. ≠Toma, with his excellent hunting dogs, killed four warthogs, and these alone provided two-thirds of all the meat. Snaring and clubbing provided the remaining third of the meat.

Hunting success rates were not high. In all, seven men spent 78 man-days hunting. Since only 18 kills were made, it works out to only about 1 kill for every 4 man-days of hunting. Nevertheless, over a whole year, the average Ju will consume between 175 and 200 pounds of meat, a very good level of nutrition by world standards, comparable to the level of meat consumption in the developed countries.

Although meat consumption was high, how adequately did the !Kung level of work effort meet their *overall* caloric needs? And did their diet provide them with the

---

[5]The calculation of these figures is discussed in detail in Lee, 1979:272–280.

TABLE 4–4   CALORIES AND PROTEINS IN THE !KUNG DIET

| Class of Food | Percent contribution to Diet by Weight | Per Capita Consumption | | Calories/Person/Day |
		Weight (g)	Protein (g)	
Meat	31	230	34.5	690
Mongongo nuts	28	210	58.8	1365
Other vegetables	41	300	3.0	300
Total	100	740	96.3	2355

range of nutrients and minerals needed to maintain a healthy population? By weighing the food and calculating the nutrient composition, I was able to come up with a rough estimate of the calories and proteins available in the daily diet. The figures are shown in Table 4–4.

Meat and mongongo nuts comprised the major part of the diet, contributing 31 and 28 percent of the weight respectively. About 20 species of roots, melons, gums, bulbs, and dried fruits, including some mongongo fruit, made up the remaining 41 percent of the diet. In all, the work of the Ju/'hoansi made available a daily ration of 2355 calories of food energy and 96.3 grams of protein to each person. The diet was well-balanced in terms of vitamins and minerals, and if it was lacking anything it was an abundance of refined carbohydrates: there was no equivalent in the Ju/'hoan diet to the white bread, rice, pasta, and sugar-rich food that form so large a portion of our Western diet (and which may be responsible for our rapid growth rates). The caloric levels were more than adequate to support the Dobe population and to allow the people to live vigorous, active lives without losing weight.

The July work diary showed a good level of nutrition at one time of the year, a time of relative plenty. It was important to know how well people did at times of the year when food was scarcer. I did not collect work diary information at other times of year, but in a subsequent study Nancy Howell and I weighed people at various times of the year (Lee, 1979:281–308). We reasoned as follows: though individual weights might vary, if overall weights remained fairly stable, that was a clear sign that nutrition was adequate. Conversely, if overall weights dipped sharply at one time of year, it would indicate a hungry season when the !Kung adaptation was put to the test.

In July 1968, Howell and I toured the Dobe area, stopping at all waterholes to weigh as many people as we could find. We repeated this weighing in October and again in January of 1969. In all, we were able to weigh 201 people in all three weight campaigns. The results showed that adult weights remained essentially stable from July to October, but dipped slightly from October to January, with a weight loss of 0.7 percent at Dobe and Mahopa and of 2.3 percent at /Xai/ xai (Lee, 1979:303). This loss of weight was statistically significant (it was not due to chance) but it was very small by the standards of other African societies, where seasonal weight losses of 6 or more percent were not uncommon.[6]

---

[6]This point has been disputed by Wilmsen (1978b, 1989:303–312). For a discussion, see Lee (1979): 281–308; 440–441.

JU/'HOANSI SUBSISTENCE: AFFLUENCE OR ANXIETY?

The evidence from the study of seasonal weights therefore supported the evidence from the work and caloric studies. Ju/'hoansi appeared to have the happy combination of an adequate diet and a short workweek. Over the course of a year, the picture of steady work, steady leisure, and adequate diet was maintained.

In summary, we have learned from the study of Ju/'hoan subsistence that despite the popular stereotypes, the Ju do not have to work very hard to make a living. In assuming that their life must be a constant struggle for existence, we succumb to the ethnocentric notions that place our own Western adaptation at the pinnacle of success and make all others second or third best. Judged by these standards, the Ju are bound to fail. But judged on their own terms, they do pretty well for themselves.

If I had to point to one single feature that makes this way of life possible, I would focus on *sharing*. Each Ju is not an island unto himself or herself; each is part of a collective. It is a small, rudimentary collective, and at times a fragile one, but it is a collective nonetheless. The living group pools the resources that are brought into camp so that everyone receives an equitable share. The !Kung and people like them don't do this out of nobility of soul or because they are made of better stuff than we are. In fact, they often gripe about sharing. They do it because it works for them and it enhances their survival. Without this core of sharing, life for the Ju/'hoansi would be harder and infinitely less pleasant (see Chapter 13).

5/Kinship and Social Organization

One day in March 1964, I was visiting a !Xabe village, when Hwan//a, a woman about my age who was married to one of the Tswana Headman Isak's three sons, playfully began to call to me, "Uncle, uncle, /Tontah, come see me."

Puzzled, I drew closer; until that time the Ju had referred to me simply as the White Man (/ Ton) or the bearded one, *Tsikoie* (*Mandavo,* in Herero). Hwan//a smiled and said, "You are all alone here and I have no children, so I will name you /Tontah after my *tsu* /Tontah who is dead, and, as I have named you, you shall call me mother."

Pleased, I asked Hwan//a to tell me how she decided on the name /Tontah. She explained that I was a European, a "/ *ton,*" and the traditional Ju name /Tontah sounds like it. Since her late *tsu* had no namesake, she decided to name me /Tontah to do honor to him and to my exotic status.[1]

It was hard for me to think of the young and attractive Hwan//a, not yet 30, as my mother, but I was happy to have a name other than White Man.

This was the famous name relationship—the Ju/'hoan custom of naming everyone after an older person according to a repertoire of personal names. I had read about it in the writings of Lorna Marshall (1957) and I was excited to be named in this way.

The name stuck. Soon people all over the Dobe area were calling me /Tontah, and I began to sense some of the possibilities of the name relationship when a very beautiful woman, on whom I had a terrible crush, playfully said, "Your old name called me *tsiu* [wife], so I will call you *mi!kwah,* my husband."

But there was more to come. A few weeks later, back at the Dobe camp, I was sitting in the shade working on some notes when N!eishi; his son ≠Toma, the hunter; and N!eishi's ex-wife, the redoubtable //Gumi; approached me with some ceremony and sat down.

"*Mba,*" N!eishi began, calling me by the term "father," a not uncommon form of greeting, "*Mba,* we see that you are all alone here; your family is far away, and we too are all alone. We have no family. No one pays attention to us. So from now on I am your father, and //Gumi here is your mother, and ≠Toma is your older brother. From now on call me '*mba.*'"

---

[1]Often elders have several people named after them. Years later I was to meet another namesake of the late / Tontah, a prominent member of the /Gausha group that was studied by the Marshall family and featured in many of their films. This was / Tontah, the husband of N!ai of *N!ai: The Story of a !Kung Woman.* This younger / Tontah, a man in his fifties, took our name relation seriously, befriended me, and taught me much about conditions on the Namibian side of the border (see Chapter 12).

//Gumi broke in. "And you call me *aiye.*" She used the vocative form for mother, the first word every Ju infant learns, like *mama* in English.

"And call me *!ko!ko,*" added ≠Toma, using the vocative form for older brother.

With my limited language, I signified my pleasure with the turn of events. Here was a whole family to be a part of, one with genealogical links throughout the Dobe area. It did not seem to bother anyone that I was named from one family and adopted into another. And with great cordiality people in the distant villages began to instruct me in what I was to call them.

But soon things got very complicated. My knowledge of the kinship terminology was minimal. A few people were calling me by kin terms that flowed from their genealogical connection to my own "parents," N!eishi and //Gumi. And a few others were using kin terms because they were related to other /Tontahs through the name relationship. But many others were using kin terms that made absolutely no sense to me, either as genealogical kin or namesake kin. It was clear that I had a lot to learn about the kinship system and social organization in general.

The process of discovery is the subject of this chapter. After describing the group structure of the Ju, we will enter the fascinating world of Ju/'hoan kinship and its principal genius stroke: the name relationship.

The Ju/'hoansi commonly live in camps that number from 10 to 30 individuals, but the composition of these camps changes from month to month and from day to day. In essence, a Ju/'hoan camp consists of relatives, friends, and in-laws who have found that they can live and work well together. Under this flexible principle, brothers may be united or divided; fathers and sons may live together or apart. Further, during his or her lifetime a Ju/'hoan may live at many waterholes with many different groups. Given their flexible lifestyle, and lacking a system of state organization as we know it, what principles *do* the Ju rely on to give their life stability and coherence?

As in all other prestate societies, the central organizing principle of Ju/'hoan life is kinship. Kin terms are applied to everyone, related or not, and kin ties extend to the very borders of the known world. Kinship provides the structure of everyday life and enables the society to reproduce itself socially from generation to generation. But the multifold principles of kinship do not constitute an invariant code of laws written in stone, but instead a whole series of codes, consistent enough to provide structure but open enough to be flexible. I found the best way to look at !Kung kinship is as a game, full of ambiguity and nuance. The game of kinship has a serious side to it, but it is also fun, providing lifelong opportunities for deep play.

JU/'HOANSI LIVING GROUPS

In recent years the Ju/'hoansi have had two kinds of living groups. The first kind has a coherent internal structure, is usually fairly large (10 to 30 members), and is economically self-sufficient; most are based on hunting and gathering. The second kind is attached to Black cattle posts. These groups are usually units of one or two families whose menfolk work on the cattle; sometimes they are larger, composed of 30 or more individuals, and sometimes smaller—as small as a single Ju woman married to a Herero man. I call the first kind of grouping a *camp,* a close translation of the Ju term *chu/ o* (literally, "the face of the huts"), and the second I call a *client group,* reflecting its dependent status in relation to the Blacks.

In 1968 there were 18 camps ranging in size from 4 to 34 people, and 16 client groups with a range of 1 to 44 people. The mean size of camps was 17.8; client groups were about half as large, with a mean size 8.6. In 1968 about 70 percent of the Ju lived in camps and 30 percent in client groups. Camps were usually based on hunting and gathering, although several owned cattle and/or practiced agriculture. Client groups, by contrast, were always dependent on cattle herders for milk, meat, and grains.

The basic traditional Ju/'hoan living group is the camp, a noncorporate, bilaterally organized group of people who live in a single settlement and who move together for at least part of the year. The camp is a flexible but not a random assortment of individuals. At the center of each camp is a core of related older people—usually siblings or cousins—who are generally acknowledged the owners—*k"ausi*—of the waterhole. Around each waterhole is a bloc of land—the *n!ore*—which contains food resources and other waterpoints and which is the basic subsistence area for the resident group. The *k"ausi* are generally recognized as the "hosts" whom one approaches for permission when visiting at a waterhole. The *k"ausi* are simply the people who have lived at the waterhole longer than any others. They include both male and female kin and their spouses. The name of one member of the core group through time becomes associated with the camp as a whole, and the camp becomes known by that person's name. An example is *≠Toma//gwe chu/ to* (*≠*Toma//gwe's camp) at Dobe.[2]

The *k"ausi* provide continuity with the past through an association with a waterhole that may extend over 50 years or more. Rarely, however, does this association go back as far as the grandparent generation of the oldest *k"ausi*. To put it another way, the half-life of a core group's tenure at a waterhole can be estimated at 30 to 50 years (Lee, 1972:129). A second integrative role for the *k"ausi* is the genealogical focus they provide. A camp is built up gradually through time by the addition of in-marrying spouses of the core siblings. These spouses in turn may bring in *their* siblings and their spouses, so that the basic genealogical structure of the camp assumes the form of a chain of spouses and siblings radiating from the core, as shown in Figure 5–1. At a given time the camp is composed largely of persons related by primary ties: almost every member has a parent, a child, a sibling, or a spouse to link him or her to the core.

Let us examine the process of group structure by looking at the evolution of a single camp, the Dobe camp (Figure 5–2). The core siblings, //Koka and her younger brother N!eishi, moved into Dobe around 1930. After the former owners died or moved away, they became the *k"ausi*. They brought in their spouses (3, 4, 5), and the children of these marriages (6, 7, 8, 9) later brought in their spouses (10, 11) to live at Dobe (segments 1 and 2). After N/ahka (11) had been married to /Xashe (6) for several years, her entire family joined her at Dobe, including her six brothers and sisters (13, 14, 15, 16, 17, 18), her parents (19, 20), her maternal grandfather (21), and her mother's brother (22). Later, when two of her siblings (17, 18) married, their spouses also came to Dobe (23, 24) (segment 3).

[2]This leader is *not* in any sense a headman. Lorna Marshall (1960:344ff) originally argued that ownership of each waterhole resided in the person of a band headman, who was always male and who inherited his position patrilineally. My research indicated that no headman existed either among the Dobe or the Nyae Nyae !Kung, and subsequently Marshall revised her view accordingly and retracted the headman concept (1976:191–195). (See also Chapter 8.) In the 1970s, the Botswana state formalized the office of village headman as an elected position.

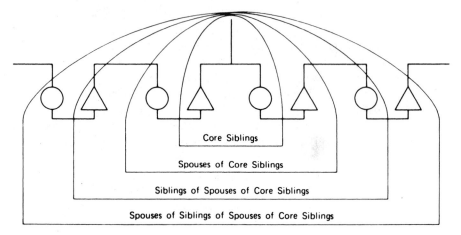

Figure 5–1. Groups are formed through chains of siblings and their spouses, and their siblings and their spouses.

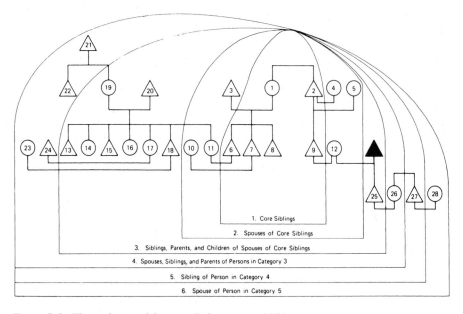

Figure 5–2. The evolution of the main Dobe camp to 1964.

On the other side, in 1955, ≠Toma (9) married a 45-year-old widow, Tin!kai (12), who brought her adolescent son (25) to Dobe. Around 1960, the son married a woman (26) who, in turn, brought her younger brother (27) along. Finally, in 1964, the last link was established when 27 married and brought his wife (28) to Dobe.

Of the 28 persons in the Dobe diagram, 6 are cores and another 6 are spouses of cores; 9 more members are the siblings, parents, and children of the in-marrying spouses; and 7 are more distantly related. All camp members, however, can trace their relation to the core through the primary ties of sibling, parents, offspring, or spouse.

Do core groups tend to be dominated by males or females? An older theory of band organization, traceable to Radcliffe-Brown (1930), put male siblings at the center of groups. In the Dobe case, however, the core group is composed of siblings of *both* sexes, and this is typical of the core groups in the Dobe area as a whole. An analysis of 12 camps in 1964 showed that a brother and sister formed the core in 4 cases, two sisters and one brother in 2 cases, and two brothers and one sister in 1 case. In addition, 4 camps had cores composed of two sisters, and 1 had a core composed of two brothers. These combinations are to be expected in a strongly bilateral society such as the Ju/'hoansi, and the results serve to emphasize the futility of trying to establish whether the Ju have matrilocal or patrilocal residence arrangements.

What makes camps change in numbers and composition? Short-term processes of three kinds set people in motion: exhaustion of local food resources, visiting and receiving visitors, and conflict within the group. In actual practice, it is often difficult to distinguish between each of these causes. When an argument breaks out in a camp, suddenly the food resources of another area become more attractive. Ju love to go visiting, and the practice acts as a safety valve when tempers get frayed. In fact, Ju usually move, not when their food is exhausted, but rather when only their patience is exhausted (see also Chapter 8).

In the longer run, processes that affect group composition include residential shifts at marriage, the adjustment of sex and dependency ratios, and the adjustment of overall numbers. In the first instance, the marriage of a boy to a girl usually results in the boy taking up residence in his in-laws' village. This practice, known as brideservice, is discussed in Chapter 6. But frequently the boy's brother or sister and their spouses may also join him for weeks or months, and occasionally his parents as well. Thus entire families may come together at the time of a marriage, and not just the bride and groom.

When a group's dependency ratio—the proportion of dependents per 100 ablebodied producers—gets too high or too low, steps may be taken to bring this ratio back into line. For example, if a camp has many young children to feed, this creates a burden on the working adults. One or more of the young families may be encouraged to hive off and join other camps where the dependency ratios are more favorable. Similarly, a group with few or no young children may see its future in jeopardy and take steps to recruit a related family with young children to take up the *n!ore*. By these means the reproduction of the groups is perpetuated and the burden of work effort is evenly allocated throughout the area.

In spite of these mechanisms, however, groups don't survive indefinitely. Each decade some disband and their members distribute themselves among their kin in other camps. For example, of the 16 Dobe-area camps in 1964, 10 were intact in 1973, while 6 had disbanded, and 6 new camps had come into being.[3]

All this visiting, shifting, and adjusting of numbers will make sense to us when we realize that the Ju camp is a unit of sharing. The food brought into a camp each day is distributed widely so that each member receives an equitable share. Thus, it is crucial that the people in the camp get along well together. If arguments break out,

---

[3]I'm sure that a certain amount of group disbanding occurred in every decade, but I now believe that the groups were more stable in the past than they were in 1963–1973, a period leading up to major socioeconomic changes (see Chapters 10, 11, and 12).

then sharing breaks down, and when that happens the basis for camp life is lost. Only when one or both of the feuding parties leave or when they settle their differences can the sharing be restored.

The dynamic of Ju/'hoan camp life is thus composed of work and leisure, harmony and conflict, and group solidarity interspersed with periods of group fission.

THE KINSHIP SYSTEM

We have said that kinship is the central organizing principle of societies like the Ju/'hoansi. The purpose of this section is to spell out the particular features of the Ju/'hoan kinship system and to get you inside the system so that you can see the world around you as the Ju see it.

In order to do this we have to build up our kinship picture in three phases. We start with the kinship terminology as we usually think of it, a genealogical diagram with *ego* at the center and the terms she or he applies to all kin. We'll call this the normal kinship, or Kinship I. Next we will introduce Ju personal names and the name relationship and show the rather different set of kin terms generated by this method, which we'll call Kinship II. As we look further into the name relationship a problem emerges between the rules of Kinship I and Kinship II: the latter seems to destroy the sense of the former. Just when you are beginning to despair, we introduce the key that resolves the contradiction and unlocks the secret of Ju/'hoan kinship. This key is the principle of *wi,* which I call Kinship III. As you grasp the inner meaning of the *wi* principle, a new sense of the beauty and coherence of Ju/'hoan kinship begins to emerge. Armed with that sense you will, I hope, be able to see the !Kung world as they themselves see it.[4]

Kinship I

Let us begin by introducing the kin terms for the immediate family. We will present the English-language equivalent first, then the anthropological short form, and then the Ju/'hoan kin term.[5]

	Short Form	*Kin Term*
Father	F	*ba*
Mother	M	*tai*
Son	S	*!ha*
Daughter	D	*≠hai*
Older Brother	OB	*!ko*
Older Sister	OZ	*!kwi*
Younger Brother	YB	*tsin*
Younger Sister	YZ	*tsin*

---

[4]This presentation draws upon my own data and also the analyses of Marshall (1976) and Fabian (1965). An expanded version of this discussion is found in Biesele ed. 1986.

[5]We will be using English kinship terms, not because they always fit Ju concepts (they don't) but as an aid to students' understanding.

Women and girls participating in a joking relationship.

So far the kin terms follow our system, in that there are separate terms for F, M, S, and D, that is, F≠FB, M≠MZ, S≠BS, and so on. The Ju differ from English usage in the kin terms for siblings. There are separate terms of OB (*!ko*), OZ (*!kwi*), and younger siblings of both sexes are lumped under the term *tsin*. Furthermore, sibling terms are different, as we shall see, from cousin terms.

Let us consider next the terms used to apply to grandparents and grandchildren.

Father's father	FF	*!kun!a*
Mother's father	MF	
Father's mother	FM	*tun, mama*
Mother's mother	MM	
Son's son	SS	*!kuma*
Daughter's son	DS	
Son's daughter	SD	*tuma*
Daughter's daughter	DD	

The term *!kun!a* means literally "old name" and refers to the fact that male children are preferentially named after their grandfathers. The term *!kuma* means "small name" and is a reciprocal of *!kun!a*. The term *tun* for "grandmother" also has a reciprocal form, *tuma*, that is, granddaughter. These pairs highlight an important principle of Ju/'hoan kin terms: almost all of them have an older–younger reference depending on the relative age of the speaker. In a society like the Ju/'hoansi, with few social statuses, relative age is one of the few status distinctions that can be made. Older–younger reciprocals are found in several other kin term pairs: *tsu–tsuma, //ga–// gama, tun!ga–tun!gama.*[6]

Next we consider the terms for the relationships we call in English aunt, uncle, cousin, niece, and nephew. I will give you these terms now, but remember that these will have to be modified later when we introduce Kinship II, the name relationship.

Father's brother	FB	*tsu*
Mother's brother	MB	
Father's sister	FZ	*//ga*
Mother's sister	MZ	
Father's brother's son	FBS	*!kun!a or !kuma*
Mother's brother's son	MBS	
Father's sister's son	FZS	
Mother's sister's son	MZS	
Father's brother's daughter	FBD	*tun or tuma*
Mother's brother's daughter	MBD	
Father's sister's daughter	FZD	
Mother's sister's daughter	MZD	
Brother's son	BS	*tsuma*
Sister's son	ZS	
Brother's daughter	BD	*tsuma* (man speaking)
Sister's daughter	ZD	*//gama* (woman speaking)

Careful study of these tables will reveal one important principle of !Kung kinship: the principle of alternating generations. For ego's *own* generation and for the *second* up *and* down, ego will generally use the *!kun!a–tun* pair of terms. But for the *first* generation up and down, ego will use the *tsu–//ga* pair of terms. To put it another way,

ego's own generation	
ego's grandparent's generation	are *!kun!a, tun*
ego's grandchildren's generation	
ego's parental generation	
ego's children's generation	are *tsu, //ga*

Following this principle, which pair of terms would ego use for great-grandparents and great-grandchildren? If you answered *tsu-// ga,* you are correct.

The principle of alternating generations relates to another principle of kinship: joking and avoidance. All Ju kin relations are either joking (*k″ãi,* "to joke" or "to

---

[6]The Ju have a universalistic kinship system in that every single person in the society can be linked to every other by use of a kin term (see Alan Barnard, 1976, 1978, 1992a: ch. 15). The only exception to this rule, and the only nonkin term of address, is *≠dara,* meaning "equal." It is used for people of the same sex who are so close in age that an older–younger pair of terms can't be used. *≠dara* also means "friend."

Kumsan!a and his small name, Kumsama; they are in the !kun!a–!kuma *relationship.*

play") or avoidance (*kwa,* "to fear" or "respect"). And all of ego's kin fall into one or another of the two categories.

For a woman, here is how the kin universe is divided:

Joking Kin	Refers to	Avoidance Kin	Refers to
!kwi	OZ	*ba*	F
tsin (female)	YZ	*tai*	M
!kun!a	FF, MF	*!hai*	S
tun	FM, MM	*≠hai*	D
!kuma	SS, DS	*!ko*	OB
tuma	DS, DD	*tsin* (male)	YB
		tsu	FB, MB
		//ga	FZ, MZ

And for a man, the universe of kin divides as follows:

Joking Kin	Refers to	Avoidance Kin	Refers to
!ko	OB	*ba*	F
tsin (male)	YB	*tai*	M
!kun!a	FF, MF	*!ha*	S
tun	FM, MM	*≠hai*	D
!kuma	SS, DS	*!kwi*	OZ
tuma	SD, DD	*tsin* (female)	YZ
		tsu	FB, MB
		//ga	FZ, MZ

A person's behavior is very different toward joking kin compared with avoidance kin. With a joking relative one acts in a relaxed fashion and speaks on familiar terms. The fact that *!kun!a* and *tun* fall into this category highlights the affectionate relationship that exists between grandparents and grandchildren, a quality that is found in many cultures, including our own. But unlike our own, the Ju/'hoansi take the kin terms for immediate relatives and extend them widely. The terms *!kun!a* and *tun* will be applied to dozens of people, and the feelings of affection are also widely extended. People in the *!kun!a–tun* category who are unrelated are not only treated with affection but, if they are of appropriate age, they may be prime candidates for marriage.

Toward an avoidance relative one must show respect and reserve, and one will often use the second person plural as a form of address (The Ju/'hoansi make the same distinctions between familiar and formal that in French are represented by *tu* and *vous*). The fact that one's parents (and children) and one's parents' siblings fall into the avoidance category is indicative of the authority that parents exercise over their children. People in the avoidance relation may *not* marry, even if they are unrelated. In extreme cases, such as mother-in-law/son-in-law avoidance (see below), the two parties in theory may not even speak directly but must use a third party as intermediary. Many of these relationships, however, can be warm and friendly as long as proper reserve is shown in public.

Among joking relatives, too, there is a considerable range of behavior. Toward your own grandparent you can be affectionate, but you may not engage in overt sexual joking. With an unrelated *!kun!a* or *tun* of the opposite sex you can engage in bawdy joking of the most overt kind, called *za* (see Chapter 8).

Finally, it is worth noting that the principle of alternate generations implies that if you avoid person "A" you will generally joke with his or her parents and children, and if you joke with person "A" chances are you will avoid his or her parents and children. All of a person's kin will fall into one or the other category. There are no neutrals.

These same principles apply to "affines," relations through marriage, which we now consider. The affinal terms are as follows:

AFFINAL TERMS:

	Short Form	Kin Term	Joking or Avoidance
Woman Speaking:			
Husband	H	*!kwa*	J
Husband's father	HF	*≠tum*	A
Husband's mother	HM	*/ otsu*	A
Husband's brother	HB	*tun!ga*	J
Husband's sister	HZ	*/ otsu*	A
Brother's wife	BW	*/ otsu*	A
Sister's husband	ZH	*tun!ga*	J
Man Speaking:			
Wife	W	*tsiu*	J
Wife's father	WF	*≠tum*	A
Wife's mother	WM	*/ otsu*	A
Wife's brother	WB	*tun!ga*	A
Wife's sister	WZ	*tun*	J
Brother's wife	BW	*tun*	J
Sister's husband	ZH	*tun!ga*	A

AFFINAL TERMS: *(Continued)*

Man or Woman Speaking:

Son's wife's father	SWF ⎱	*n!unba*	J
Daughter's husband's father	DHF ⎰		
Son's wife's mother	SWM ⎱	*n!untai*	J
Daughter's husband's mother	DHM ⎰		

Note that the !Kung joke with spouses and with spouses' siblings of the same sex as their spouse. This is because a man's wife's sister (or brother's wife) is herself a potential wife, and therefore a joking relation is allowed. The same holds true for a woman and her husband's brother or her sister's husband.[7] Relations between men and brothers-in-law and women and sisters-in-law, however, are tinged with respect. (An important variation is discussed in Chapter 10; see *Swara* and the *Sarwa*.)

The most heavily weighted avoidance relations occur between a man and his mother-in-law and between a woman and her father-in-law. Here even direct speech communication is not supposed to occur. (In practice it frequently does, however.)

Summing up the presentation of Ju/'hoan kinship, so far one can see that it makes a logical, internally consistent whole. Kinship analysts classify the Ju/'hoan system as an "Eskimo" type of kinship, in that it has terms that separate the nuclear family from collateral relatives. Fathers are distinguished from father's brothers, mothers from mother's sisters, siblings from cousins, own children from nephews and nieces, and so on. If this system has a familiar ring, it's not surprising. North American English kin terminology (and that of most European languages) is also of the Eskimo type. The Ju/'hoansi make many of the same distinctions that we do.

But unlike American kinship, the Ju/'hoan kinship system makes extensive use of personal names in structuring kinship, and it is to names and naming that we now turn.

Kinship II: Names and the Name Relationship

Among the Ju/'hoansi there are a very limited number of personal names in use. Only 35 men's names and 32 women's names were in use in the Dobe area in 1964. Names are inherited from ancestors according to a fairly strict set of rules. Every child must be named for somebody. A first-born son is supposed to be named after his father's father, and the first-born daughter after her father's mother. Second-born children are supposed to be named after the mother's father and mother's mother, and additional children are to be named after father's brothers and sisters and mother's brothers and sisters, in that order. More distantly related kin, and affines, may also provide names to a family. Parents may *never* name a child after themselves.

All Ju/'hoan names are sex-linked. A man and a woman may never have the same name. Further, the Ju have no surnames. The result of this naming is that each man's name may be inherited and shared by up to 25 other men, and each woman's name by up to 26 women. Table 5–1 lists the 35 men's names in use in the Dobe area in

---

[7]If a man dies his brother may inherit his wife; this practice is called the *levirate*. Similarly, if a woman dies her sister may inherit her husband, a practice called the *sororate*.

TABLE 5–1   MEN'S NAMES LISTED IN ORDER OF FREQUENCY

Most Popular Names	*Number of Men with That Name*
1. ≠Toma	25
2. K"au	24
3. Kashe	15
4. /Ti!kay	15
5. /Twi	14
6. /Gau	14
7. /Tashe	12
8. Bo	11
9. /Kan//a	11
10. Dam	9
11. !Xam	9
	159

Percentage of all men with 11 most popular names = 74%

Other Men's Names

— /Tishe	6
— N//au, N!eishi, ≠Gau	5 each
— Debe, Tsaa, Tsau, //Kau	3 each
— Hxome, N//u, /N!au, /Tontah (!), ≠Daun, !Xoma, //Koshe	2 each
— Ko/tun, Kum/to, N!ani, Tsama, /Tan!au, /Tuka, /Tushe, ≠N//au, !Kaha	1 each
	56

Percentage of men bearing 24 less popular names = 26%
n = 35

1964, and Table 5–2 lists the 32 women's names. It is interesting to note that almost 75 percent of all the men have one or another of the 11 most popular men's names, while 73 percent of all women have one of the 12 most popular women's names.

Since the Ju/'hoansi have no surnames, there is a real problem in sorting out one ≠Toma from another. The Ju get around this by using nicknames extensively, usually highlighting, or spoofing, some characteristic or quirk of their owners: ≠Toma short, Bo tall, Debe big belly, N!ai short face (of John Marshall's film *N!ai*) are some examples. The leader of Dobe camp is ≠Toma//gwe—≠Toma sourplum, referring to his liking for the fruit but also nicely capturing his acidic personality. East of Dobe, many men and women have nicknames given to them by Herero and Tswana, nicknames such as Kasupe, Kashitambo, Kopela Maswe, and others.

What is the relation between people bearing the same name? If your name is ≠Toma, for example, you are likely to find about 24 other ≠Tomas in the population, all of whom claim descent from the same original ≠Toma and claim to be related to you. All ≠Tomas older than yourself you address as *!kun!a* (old name) and all ≠Tomas younger than yourselves you address as *!kuma* (young name), regardless of what your genealogical connection is and even if you have no discernible genealogical connection at all.

In reckoning kinship, the possession of a common name thus leapfrogs over the genealogical ties and creates close kinship even with distant relatives. Similarly,

TABLE 5–2   WOMEN'S NAMES LISTED IN ORDER OF FREQUENCY

Most Popular Names	Number of Woman with That Name
1. N!uhka	26
2. Chu!ko	23
3. N≠tisa	19
4. /Twa	16
5. //Kushe	15
6. N/ahka	14
7. Di//kau	13
8. N!ai	13
9. Hwan//a	11
10. Karu	10
11. /Tasa	9
12. //Koka	8
	177

Percentage of all women with 12 most popular names = 73%

Other Women's Names	
— Bau, Sa//gai, Tin!kay,//N	7 each
— Chwa,/Toishe	6 each
— Kun//a	5
— Kwoba	4
— //Gau	3
— Be, Kxore, N//au, ≠Tabo	2 each
— !Ku, Kxamshe,/Tam,/Xia, //Kau!kobe,//Gumi,//Nsa	1 each
	67

Percentage of all women bearing 20 less popular names = 27%

n = 32

anyone with your father's name you call "father," anyone with your wife's name you may call "wife," anyone with your son's name you may call "son," and so on. And you will be called various kin terms by others according to what your name means to them.

The name relationship has an important bearing on marriage arrangements. A woman may not marry a man with her father's or brother's name, and a man may not marry a woman with his mother's or sister's name. Thus, for a man, if your mother has a common name and you have several sisters with common names, up to 50 percent of all the potential spouses may be off limits to you. For example, a man named ≠Toma will be ineligible as a spouse for the approximately 50 women with fathers or brothers named ≠Toma. And if his mother is a N!uhka and he has sisters named Chu!ko and N≠tisa, another 68 women will be barred from marrying him.

The principle of the name relationship has a certain logic to it, and it is obviously of great benefit in tying society together by making close kin out of distant strangers. But it should be clear that it is a great *destroyer* of the logic of the standard kinship system we outlined on pages 64–69. In fact, the two systems are often completely at odds.

To illustrate, let us take the not infrequent case of a man who is named after his father's or mother's brother and not for his father's or mother's father.[8] His FB becomes his *!kun!a,* a joking term, and his FF becomes a *tsu,* an avoidance term. Now what about his FBS, who ordinarily would be a *!kuma?* He now must become a *tsuma* if the principle of alternating generations is to hold. In short, in up to half the cases ego will find himself out of step with Kinship I and out of step with his brothers and sisters, who will joke with those he avoids and who must avoid those he jokes with.

But the problem doesn't stop there. The name relationship also introduces complications into the marriage market. For instance, consider the case of a young man named ≠Toma who finds an attractive young woman named Chu/o. She happens to have the same name as his *tun;* this makes Chu/o not only a joking partner but also highly eligible as a spouse for ≠Toma. But wait! The attractive woman's father's name happens to be ≠Toma as well, and this makes our young ≠Toma strictly off limits *to her.* His name system makes her an eligible spouse; her name system makes him *verboten.* Whose view is to prevail? When such an impasse occurs, the Ju say *sa ge a // kemi*—"they are in the middle"—that is, they are halfway between the joking and the avoidance categories. In such cases avoidance takes priority over joking and a marriage is unlikely to occur.

Because so many Ju/'hoansi share the same names, this sort of problem crops up again and again. Given these contradictions between the "normal" kinship of system I and system II generated by the name relationship, how can we go about finding out which system takes primacy, or at least how the two systems interlock?

Kinship III: The Principle of *Wi*

The method I first used to tackle this problem in the field was to interview many people and ask them to give me the kin terms they applied to each of up to 30 relatives. This task proved extremely time consuming and frustrating. At first everything went smoothly with each informant: father was called *ba,* mother *tai,* older brother *!ko,* and so on, as they should be in Kinship I. Other kin were called *!kun!a* or *tun* if they had ego's grandfather's or grandmother's name, or *!ko* if they had ego's brother's name, as they should in Kinship II. But every informant had many kin whose terms of address *did not make sense either in terms of Kinship I or Kinship II!* Each older Ju/'hoan could rattle off terms for all his or her kin without hesitation, but when I asked why they used a particular term the answer made little sense to me.

I resolved that there must be some additional principle or principles that were escaping me. After months of muddle, the clue came when I asked the following question of !Xam, a 70-year-old /Xai/ xai man: "When two people are working out what kin term to employ, how do you decide whose choice is to prevail?"

"In our way," !Xam replied, "it is always the older person who '*wis*' the younger person. Since I am older than you, I decide what we should call each other."

I had heard this argument before but hadn't grasped its full significance. The Ju/'hoan concept of *wi* is an interesting one. I had understood it to mean "to help" or "to assist"; now I learned that it also had the sense of exercising authority. !Xam explained that relative age was very important in Ju/'hoan kinship. In a society with no

---

[8]Lorna Marshall's data show that only 51 percent of the Ju/'hoansi are named for grandparents (Marshall, 1976:244).

chiefs or headmen or ranked statuses, relative age was one of the few bases for status distinctions. It was crucial in determining who should choose the kin terms to be used.

As I explored the concept of *wi* further, its full meaning began to dawn on me. In fact, its use constituted a third principle of Ju/'hoan kinship, on a par with Kinships I and II. The principle that elders chose kin terms for juniors, when combined with the name relationship, make kinship appear quirky and unpredictable. Yet these choices made perfect sense when you grasped *wi*'s inner meaning. Finally, after months of plodding along, I finally felt that I had cracked the code; this is what I wrote in my fieldnotes in March 1969:

> *Wi* is the great rattler and destroyer of systems. Because for the first half of your life you have to take all your elders' various *wis* according to *their* lights, not yours.
>
> But then turning around [in midlife] you take these well-established *wis* and impose them on your juniors of various names in ways that have little meaning to them *just as your wis originally had little meaning to you!*
>
> Thus *wis* seemingly devoid of logic keep getting passed on and such neat rules as alternating generations from either Kinship I or Kinship II can never get going.
>
> Against this trend toward nonlogical *wis* there is the continuing refreshing of kinship with terms drawn from real parents, real siblings, real *!kun!as* and later, real spouses and real in-laws. These give the individual's personal *wi* system a semblance of order, especially with his or her juniors (Fieldnotes 21/3/69).

Moments like this in fieldwork are wonderful; with this new insight, I found that the seeming confusion surrounding Ju/'hoan kinship was replaced by clarity. As the smoke cleared, I was able to further unravel the system.

First, learning the system is a lifelong affair. Your kin universe evolves as you grow. As you pass through marriage, the birth of your children, and later their marriages, you add new names and new twists to the application of kinship terms.[9] Take the simple fact of growing older. Since elders determine the kin term juniors apply to them when you are young, everyone is older than you, and you play an essentially passive role in the game of kinship.

For instance, if your name is / Gau and an older woman named N!uhka marries a / Gau, she will call you *mi !kwa*—husband—or *mi !kuma*—small name—and this term will stick even if you have no N!uhka's in your kindred, or if you do have a N!uhka to whom you would apply a different name.

Now let's say that this N!uhka becomes a grandmother and a baby N!uhka is named after her. You will now apply the term *tsiuma*—small wife—or *!kuma*—small name—to the baby N!uhka! The kin tie that originally had no logical basis gets perpetuated and, more importantly, *begins to develop a logic of its own.*

As you get older, more and more people are born after you, and for these juniors you are in the driver's seat; you may establish the appropriate term in light of your situation. The older you get, the more "control" you have over your kinship, until at the end of life you will have *wi*ed everybody in the kin universe. In fact, when I asked a very old man how old he was, he replied, "All the people who *wi*ed

---

[9]The kinship system is such a wonderfully complex affair that certain older people, usually women, become specialists in keeping track of how everyone is related to everyone else. I used to sit in amazement as Sa//gain!a rattled off names, terms, and rationales for dozens of kin pairs.

me are *kwara* (dead), and all who live I have *wi*ed [that is, I am the oldest person around]."

A second aspect of kinship and the life cycle is the changes that take place at marriage. When a man marries, new vistas of kinship immediately open up. If I marry a N≠*isa,* then:

1)   all women named N≠isa could call me husband (*!kwa*);
2)   all husbands of N≠isas could call me brother or co-husband (*!gwaba*);
3)   all fathers and mothers of N≠isas could call me son-in-law (≠um);
4)   all siblings of N≠isas could call me brother-in-law; and so on.

Whether any of these terms are actually used depends on what the older person wants to do, but kin terms flowing out of marriage names, because they are reciprocal, are among the most popular of the name-relation kin terms.

/ TONTAH MEETS / TONTAH

Armed with my new knowledge, my new name, and my new kinship network, I plunged with enthusiasm into the world of Ju/'hoan kinship. Every day, new relationships were unfolded as people from distant waterholes explained their ties to me. Women named Hwan//a called me son, men named N!eishi did the same. Sa//gais and ≠Tomas called me brother. Because I was a new person and genealogically a child, young and old alike *wi*ed me. Soon I was engulfed in a dense network of kin ties and obligations. In only one respect was I lacking kin ties. My name, / Tontah, was a rare one, being shared with only two of the 250 men in the greater Dobe population (see Table 5–1). Thus encounters with my actual *!kun!as* were few and far between.

It wasn't until my second field trip that I really came to understand what having a namesake meant. I was visiting a group to the south of Dobe, and I was told that farther on there was a very large camp of San led by a man named /Tontah. He had heard about me, his namesake, from visitors from the north, and he was anxious to meet me. Would I come down and visit him? When we arrived at his camp at /Du/ da, my *!kun!a* was standing by the road waiting to meet me. / Tontah was a tall (by Ju/'hoansi standards), good-looking man in his forties with an open face framed by a short goatee. I liked him immediately. He greeted me with some ceremony and said, "Come, let us go to the camp to meet *our* people," placing a particular emphasis on the word *our.* He was living with his wife's family, so most of the people were his in-laws. In fact, they turned out to be *our* in-laws.

"And here is *our* father-in-law and mother-in-law," he said, introducing me to an elderly smiling couple. "And here is our brother-in-law," pointing out a handsome young man whittling a spear. "And here is *our* wife, Hwan//a," said my *!kun!a,* presenting me to an absolutely stunning woman in her late thirties with almond eyes and a disconcertingly direct gaze. I noted that her name, "Hwan//a," was the same as that of my "mother." This put us into an ambiguous situation, intimate yet respectful at the same time.

"And here are our children," /Tontah continued, pointing out first a fourteen-year-old girl as striking as her mother, then an eight-year-old girl and a five-year-old boy.

Wanting to play my role as namesake to the hilt, I sat down to talk and said to the eight-year-old, "Daughter, I am thirsty, give me water to drink." In a twinkling an

Hwan//a, the wife of /Tontah.

ostrich egg canteen was produced and a cup of passable water poured. Refreshed, I spent the afternoon talking with /Tontah about the other members of his large camp—actually three semicontiguous camps of over 100 people—and how *we* were related to them. At the end of our talk my *!kun!a* made a comment on Ju/'hoan kinship that has stuck in my mind:

"If your name is /Tontah," he said, "all /Tontahs are your *!kun!as*. All who /Tontahs birthed are your children. All who birthed /Tontahs are your parents, and all who married /Tontahs are your wives."

Which is more important to the Ju/'hoansi, I wondered, the genealogical tie or the name relationship? It is difficult to answer this question, but one line of evidence may be useful. I was both given a name relationship and adopted into a Ju/'hoan family. Most of the other anthropologists, scientists, and filmmakers who have worked with the Ju—now over two dozen in number—have only been given namesakes, and that alone, the Ju feel, is more than sufficient to plunge them into the kinship network. The strength of the name relationship and of the principle of kinship in general is illustrated by the experience of a British film crew from the BBC. Within an hour of arrival at Dobe in July 1980, the entire party had been given Ju/'hoan names and had been "adopted" by their namesakes, who proceeded to call them by their Ju/'hoan names for the rest of their stay and who never even bothered to find out what their English names were.

6/Marriage and Sexuality

Hwan//a, a handsome young woman of 18, had just given birth to a beautiful baby after an affair with a young Herero man. The man would not marry Hwan//a, nor did Hwan//a's parents want him to. They wanted her to marry a Ju/'hoan, but who would take her now that she was a mother of another man's child? In 1964 the problem of "illegitimate" children was still relatively rare, since most girls were married before or soon after menarche (first menses).

Several years before, a Ju/'hoan named Bo had approached Hwan//a's parents for her hand in marriage, but her father refused, having another suitor in mind. But when Hwan//a's affair with the Herero boy started, these other negotiations were dropped.

Three days after the baby was born, Bo's mother, Karu, and her husband !Xam, came from a village 12 miles away to visit Hwan//a's parents with an interesting proposition.

"We want to ask you for Hwan//a for our son Bo," said Karu.

Hwan//a's father refused, saying, "My daughter was spoiled by the Herero. If you take her, you will get into arguments with her about the child. And I fear that you will not take care of the child properly because it is born Herero, not Ju/'hoan."

"We are not worried about that," Karu replied. "We want to take both the mother *and* the child, and we will take care of them just as well as you would yourself."

After further discussion and exchange of gifts, Hwan//a's parents agreed, and Hwan//a herself agreed, and she and her new baby accompanied Karu and !Xam back to their village. A new marriage was consummated and a new alliance forged between the two villages.

The marriage of Hwan//a and Bo illustrates several themes of Ju/'hoan marriage: the arrangements between the parents, the giving of gifts, and the generally flexible and humane attitude towards sexual "indiscretion." The "unwed" mother Hwan//a was not stigmatized or cast out but instead welcomed with her child into the boy's family, even though he was not the father.

However, in other respects the case above is not typical of the way Ju do things. The purpose of this chapter is to discuss the changing patterns of Ju/'hoan marriage and sexuality, and to show the central role each plays in Ju/'hoan politics and culture.

THE ARRANGEMENT OF MARRIAGES

Traditionally, the search for a marriage partner for a girl or boy usually begins soon after a child is born. All first marriages are arranged by the parents and may involve a decade or more of gift exchange before the children are actually wed. Typically, a boy's mother would approach a girl's mother and propose a marriage. If the girl's side was agreeable, the betrothal would be sealed with the giving of *kamasi*—a kind of gift specifically exchanged between parents of prospective brides and grooms.

Girls or boys are strictly constrained in who they may or may not marry. In seeking a suitable spouse parents must pay particular attention to the kinship and name relationships of the prospects. There are both primary and secondary prohibitions. In addition to obvious incest taboos against marrying a father, brother, son, uncle, or nephew, a girl may not marry a first or second cousin.[1] Additionally, she may not marry a boy with her father's name or her brother's name, and a boy in turn may not marry someone with his mother's or sister's name. Secondary prohibitions refer to anyone standing in an avoidance kinship relation to ego, including the kin terms, *tsu, tsuma, // ga, // gama, !ko, tsin,* and so on (see Chapter 5).

The result is that when a boy's and a girl's prohibitions are all put together, up to three-quarters of all potential spouses may be excluded by reason of real kin ties or name relations. In practice, parents of girls tend to be very picky about who their daughters marry, and if a young man is unsuitable for any reason, a kin or name prohibition can always be found to justify it.

A case in point is Tin!ay, a beautiful pubescent girl who was still unbetrothed in 1969 at the ripe old age of 15. When I presented her mother /Tasa with a list of eligible young men of suitable age, she cordially but firmly vetoed each one in turn.

"What about Kau?" I asked.

"No, he's her *tsu;* he has the same name as her father."

"What about Bo?"

"No, he is my *// gama*'s child! We are too closely related."

"What about Kashe?"

"No, he has the same name as Tin!ay's brother. I won't have my 'child' as an in-law."

"What about Dam?"

"No, my own sister N!uhka birthed him."

"What about / Gau?"

"Isn't he betrothed to //Kushe?"

"What about Tsaa?" (He was married to Tin!ay's older sister N!uhka.)

"No, I refuse *!gwa* [plural marriage]. N!uhka must be the only one!"

In / Tasa's eyes no one would do for Tin!ay, and several years passed before she was finally married to one Samk″au, a man whose name relation to Tin!ay was one of the joking variety.

In the Ju/'hoan mother's view of things, an ideal son-in-law is an unrelated or distantly related man whose name relation to the girl is *!kun!a* (old name), the most cordial of joking relations. Whenever possible the husband is drawn from this pool of fictive kin, though other joking kin are also eligible.

Besides the proper kinship-name connection, the parents of a girl look for several other qualities in a son-in-law. He should be a good hunter, he should *not* have a reputation as a fighter, and he should come from a congenial family of people who like to do *hxaro,* the Ju/'hoan form of traditional exchange. The last criterion is tested before the marriage as the parents of the prospective bride and groom exchange a series

---

[1]The prohibition of cousins as spouses is a highly unusual aspect of !Kung marriages. Foraging peoples throughout the world actually *prefer* or *prescribe* a cousin as a spouse.

A young woman nearing the
age of puberty and marriage.

of *kamasi* gifts to reinforce their relationship. If either side does not keep up the gift exchange, the deal may be called off and a new betrothal sought.

The first two criteria can only be satisfied by close observation of the young man for an extended period. Thus the preferred form of postmarital residence is uxorilocal— the groom comes to live with the bride's family for a period of years and to hunt for them. Only after several children are born can he take his wife and family back to his own people. Frequently, after 8 to 10 years of bride service, the couple elects to stay with the wife's people. Hwan//a, in the case study at the start of the chapter, made the unusual move of going directly to her husband's family.

Traditionally, girls were married at ages 12 to 16, boys at 18 to 25. In certain regions such as southern Nyae Nyae, according to informants, the girls' age at marriage was even younger: 10, 9, or even 8 years of age! When combined with the practice of long nursing and late weaning, one might see the amazing situation, in the words of one informant, of "a girl going from her mother's breast to her husband's bed in one day." However sexual consummation of the marriage would be delayed for a number of years after the actual ceremony.

The marked age difference between spouses was another important reason given for bride service: a girl of 12 or 14 was simply too young to leave her parents, therefore the husband had to "move in" with his in-laws.

By the 1960s and 1970s, the age of marriage had increased somewhat. Marriage of the very young had ceased altogether—the youngest age of marriage we recorded for girls was 14—and the girls tended to marry between the ages of 15 and 18. Boys were further delayed in finding spouses, and their marriage age had increased to 22–30. The greater delay in marriage for boys compared to girls had an important social consequence. Because the husband was 7 to 15 years older at marriage than his wife, this had the effect of giving him a disproportionate influence over the marriage partnership. The wives, however, as we shall see, had ways of evening up the score.

THE MARRIAGE-BY-CAPTURE CEREMONY

The Ju/'hoansi marriage ceremony involves the mock forcible carrying of the girl from her parents' hut to a specially built marriage hut, and the anointing of bride and groom with special oils and aromatic powders. Unlike our Western fairy tales in which the couple live happily ever after, !Kung marriages start on a stormy note and continue in that vein for weeks or months after. In fact, the "normal" Ju marriage has many aspects of marriage-by-capture, an ancient and controversial form of marriage in which a groom steals a bride. Today, elements of this ancient custom appear in the marriage rituals of many societies.[2] In the case of the Ju/'hoansi, the elements of marriage-by-capture present are not entirely ritual in nature. They express real conflict between husband and wife and between parents and children.

These themes are illustrated in this account of a marriage at / Xai/ xai between //Kushe, a girl of 16, and a young man named ≠Toma, who was living in the east. The informant is / Twa, the mother of //Kushe.[3]

When ≠Toma comes from the east we will hold the [marriage] ceremony. First we will build a house for them to live in. Then ≠Toma will go and sit in the hut, while we "mothers" and "grandmothers" (tunsi) will go and bring //Kushe to him. She will be crying and crying and refusing and she will be kicking and screaming against us. With some girls it is necessary to carry them bodily to the hut on the back of one of the women. But all the while we are talking to her and saying, "This is the man we have given you to; he is not a stranger; he is our man and a good man; he won't hurt you, and we, your tunsi, will be right here with you in the village." When we get her calmed down we will put her inside the hut and all sit around the fire talking. Then as everyone gets sleepy we leave her there with an older girl who will sleep beside her so that //Kushe will be in the middle with her girl friend on one side and her husband on the other.

The next morning we will wash and paint them. First we will wash them with a mixture of mongongo oil and the seeds of tsama melons. Then we will take both husband and wife and paint them head to toe with red ointment.

When I married my husband Tsau [/ Twa continued] I didn't fight too hard, but I cried a lot when I was taken to sleep in his hut. When the elders went away I listened carefully for their sleeping. Then, when my husband fell asleep and I heard his breathing, I very, very quietly sat up and eased my blanket away from his and stole away and slept by myself out in the bush.

[2]Marriage-by-capture was a favorite subject of nineteenth-century anthropologists, who traced its occurrence throughout Europe and the world.

[3]Similar accounts of conflict at marriage are found in L. Marshall (1976), Shostak (1981, 1983), J. Marshall (1980), and Volkman (1983).

In the morning the people came to Tsau's hut and asked, "Where is your wife?" He looked around and said, "I don't know where my wife has gone off to." Then they picked up my tracks and tracked me to where I was sitting out in the bush. They brought me back to my husband. They told me that this was the man they had given to me and that he wouldn't hurt me.

After that we just lived together all right. At first when we slept under the same blanket our bodies did not touch, but then after a while I slept at his front.

Other girls don't like their husbands and keep struggling away until the husbands give up on them and their parents take them back.

This apparent struggle at the time of marriage is partly customary, but another part of it reveals a genuine underlying conflict. All first marriages are arranged by parents, and the girls have little say in the matter. If the choice is unpopular, the girls will show their displeasure by kicking and screaming, a way of asserting their independent voice in decision making against the alliance of parents and potential husband. If they protest long and hard enough, the marriage will be called off. The fact that close to half of all first marriages fail among the Ju/'hoansi is eloquent testimony to the independence of Ju women from both parents and husbands. In some cases girls have been known to attempt suicide rather than allow a marriage to be consummated. (We know of no successful suicide attempts, and in all cases the marriage was called off.) But even if the protests subside and the marriage takes root, the struggles of the bride during the ceremony serve notice that she is a force to be reckoned with within the marriage and within the family. Another function of the marriage-by-capture motif may have something to do with the relationship of violence and sexual arousal. A prize that is won after a struggle is always more appealing than one that is handed over on a platter. The arousal effect may work equally on both partners. The notion that only males are sexually aggressive may be a projection of our own Western biases on our concept of human nature in general, as will be discussed later.

However, this level of conflict is not sustained indefinitely. After the initial stormy period Ju/'hoan couples usually settle down in a stable long-term relationship that may last 20 or 30 years or more, terminating in the death of one or another spouse. There is ample evidence that Ju men and women develop deep bonds of affection, though it is not the custom of the Ju/'hoansi to openly display it. Successful marriages are marked by joking and ease of interaction between the partners. Only about 10 percent of marriages that last five years or longer end in divorce. When divorce does occur, the initiative comes from the wife far more frequently than from the husband (L. Marshall, 1976:286). Divorces are characterized by a high degree of cordiality, at least compared with Western norms. Whatever the cause of their split, ex-husband and wife may continue to joke and may even live in adjacent huts with their new spouses. (My "mother"// *Gumi* and my "father" *N!eishi* lived this way.) Since there is no legal bond or bride price, divorce is a simple matter subject to mutual consent. The same, for that matter, is true of marriage. The Ju/'hoansi have no system of legal checks and balances apart from their own goodwill and desire to live in harmony. Thus we have seen marriages, especially of older people, occurring without any ceremony at all. A couple simply takes up residence together, and the community acknowledges that they are married.

//Gumi, holding forth on the subject of marriage negotiations.

PLURAL MARRIAGE AND REMARRIAGE

In a sample of 131 married men in 1968, 122 (93 percent) were living monogamously, 7 (5 percent) were living polygamously (6 with 2 wives, 1 with 3), and 2 men (2 percent) were living in a polyandrous union, sharing 1 woman. These figures illustrate the point that the overwhelming majority of Ju marriages are monogamous. Although polygamy is allowed and men desire it, it is the wives who in general oppose this form of union. Polyandry is even less common and is considered an irregular union. When it occurs it is usually among older people past childbearing age.

Polygyny (marriage of 1 man to 2 or more women) is uncommon. Of the 7 cases in our sample, only 4 were producing children. In 3 others the co-wife was an older woman in a secondary marriage. ≠Toma// gwe of Dobe had a long-standing marriage with //Koka that had produced three grown sons. When //Koka's younger sister N!ai was widowed at age 60, she became a co-wife, with //Koka, of ≠Toma// gwe. An example of a younger plural marriage is N// uwe, the San constable attached to Headman Isak's tribal court. N// uwe married two sisters. The older woman has borne him five children; the younger sister is infertile. But the three-way marriage has lasted over 35 years. Three of the 7 cases were sororal polygyny, while in 4, the co-wives were unrelated.

When looking at the reasons why some men marry two women and most do not, an interesting correlation emerges. All 7 polygynous men are healers (see Chapter 9), and 5 of the 7 have reputations as being among the strongest and most effective healers in the Dobe area. The ability to heal is shared by about 45 percent

≠Toma// gwe and his wives N!ai (left) and //Koka (right).

of all Ju men. Therefore, if the ability to heal is a sign of power among the Ju/'hoansi, then taking two wives may be one of the very few status symbols associated with it. The wives of the strong healers express pride in their husbands' ability, and they are also among the strongest singers at the all-night healing dances.

Against the express desire of men to take a second wife stands the overwhelming opposition of their first wives. Many married men have started negotiations with prospective parents-in-law only to have their wives threaten to leave them if a second wife enters the union. Sexual jealousy, pure and simple, is the reason given for the wives' objections, and in most cases the husband's plans are dropped. This underlines again the point that women are a force to be reckoned with in Ju/'hoan society.

Given women's objections to the idea of co-wives, it may come as a surprise that those women who *are* in this type of marriage get along with each other very well! The co-wives, whether sisters or not, strive to maintain harmonious relations, cooperating in food gathering and child care. The three marriage partners sleep under the same blankets, and sexuality is carried on discreetly with each wife in turn.

The Ju/'hoan term for polygamy of either the two-wives *or* two-husbands variety is *!gwah,* and the kin term for co-wife is *!gwah di-* (literally, co-woman). This term is also used widely among unrelated but friendly women as a term of cordiality. For example, women whose husbands have the same name may call each other *!gwah di-,* as do women who were formerly married or betrothed to the same man. The term for co-husband is *!gwah ba* (literally, co-father) and a similar rule of cordiality prevails among men married to women of the same name. For example, when my then-wife Nancy Howell was adopted into the name system as N!uhka, her namesake's husband /Twi immediately began calling me his *!gwah ba* (co-husband), as did other men married to N!ukhas.

Despite this cordiality, sexual jealousy appears to be strong among the Ju/'hoansi. Women apparently love to joke about co-wifery with other women as long as they don't have to become actual co-wives.

Given the realities of divorce and life expectancies, many Ju/'hoansi, male and female, find themselves without partners in middle or old age. Although some remain unattached—out of choice or necessity—many do remarry, and for those who do, these second (or third) marriages often prove to be happy and fulfilling. One interesting aspect of marriage in later life is the number of older women who marry younger men—men who are 10, 15, or more years younger than their wives. At /Xai/ xai in the mid-1960s a remarkable 27 percent of all married couples (8 out of 29) had the wife older than the husband. One reason these marriages work so well is that, freed from the tasks of childrearing, middle age tends to be a carefree time of life for Ju/'hoansi women, a topic discussed in Lee (1992c).

//N, a vigorous older woman, was about 55 when she married /Tontah, who was about 30, the same age as her son ≠Toma from a previous marriage. In an interesting twist, the son ≠Toma then married Tin!kay, his stepfather's older sister, who was five years older than ≠Toma. Neither marriage produced children, and no one at /Xai/ xai regarded these arrangements as too out of the ordinary. Since such linked marriages occur in many cultures, I wonder if readers are aware of similar marriages in their own or friends' families?

Of course the age difference between spouses can go in the other direction—with a husband much older than his wife. In 1985, Kumsa, a widower in his sixties, gave his teenage daughter in marriage to another widower about his age. It proved to be a good marriage and when children were born, Kumsa was encouraged to remarry himself, this time to a very young woman in her mid-teens. Nearly everyone regarded this marriage as an excellent one for both partners, except the bride herself, who ended the union after several months.

In most cultures remarriages tend to occur with couples who are closer in age than these examples, but here other problems emerge; for example, the principle of sibling solidarity may come into conflict with the desire to remarry. As we have emphasized, sibling relations are crucial in structuring Ju/'hoansi living groups (pp. 60–63). Adult or elderly siblings constitute the core of most living groups. So the main alternative to remarriage for widows and widowers is to take up residence with an adult sibling or siblings.

For some it is possible to have the best of *both* worlds and live with both a sibling and a spouse. N≠isa, a twice-divorced 60-year-old at /Xai/ xai, was living happily with her older brother Segai and his wife, until an old friend, ≠Tomazho, a dashing 70-year-old widower, came into her life. When ≠Tomazho—a famous healer—married N≠isa she was faced with a dilemma of leaving her brother's village where she was very comfortable. All ended happily when ≠Tomazho agreed to leave his married daughter's village and move in with his wife and her brother. The photo above shows N≠isa, flanked by her brother Segai on her right, and her husband ≠Tomazho on her left, all of them smiling and in excellent spirits.

N≠isa flanked by her brother Segai (left) and her husband ≠ Tomazho.

INTERGROUP ALLIANCE AND CONFLICT

In a society like the Ju/'hoansi, with so little property to argue about, sexuality and marriage choices are two of the main foci both of social solidarity and of social conflict. When homicide occurs it is likely to have been triggered by an argument between men over a woman. Because of this, the negotiations over marriage have an undercurrent of danger to them. If a promise is broken, or two men feel they have a legitimate claim to the same woman, a fight may break out, sometimes with fatal results (see Chapter 8).

It is the threat of violence that may account for the fact mentioned earlier that some Ju/'hoan girls were married *very* young, at age 10, 9, or even younger. A clue is given when we note that the area where the girls were married youngest—Nyae Nyae—was also an area that had a high incidence of blood feuds (see Lee, 1979:387). Informants argued that the young age at marriage at Nyae Nyae was due to the desire of parents to have their daughters safely married *before* rivals could stake their claims, or before the girl was old enough to have an affair with one man after her parents had betrothed her to another. If a girl was married before she became sexually active, peace could be assured in the community.

Though conflict might erupt over a betrothal, it would be a mistake to exaggerate its importance. After the early stormy period, the great majority of Ju marriages are established without stress, and the couples live in peace and harmony. In fact, marriage is one of the major forms of intergroup alliance among the Ju/'hoansi. The marriage of a young couple creates an important bond between the two families and their camps. The kin terms *n!unba* and *n!untai* refer to child's spouse's father and child's spouse's mother respectively. (There are no equivalent terms in English, although there are in many other languages.) The in-laws collectively are known as *n!un k"ausi* (or /twisi). The n!un relationship between affines is very strong among the Ju/'hoansi. If the two families live far apart they will likely exchange visits of a month's duration each year. The n!un k"ausi are usually strong partners in the hxaro network, exchanging gifts through their children over a period of years or decades. In some cases the entire family of the groom may take up co-residence with the family of the bride. An example of this was the family of N/ ahka, who married / Xashe, ≠Toma// gwe's eldest son at Dobe. After finishing his bride service, / Xashe brought his wife back to Dobe to live. In 1963–1965 a large party of her kin came to live with her and her in-laws at Dobe, including her father, her mother, her married sister with her husband and two children, a married brother and his wife, four more unmarried siblings, her mother's brother, and her maternal grandfather—a total of 14 people (Chapter 5, Figure 5–2).

To understand the true nature of marriage in societies like the Ju/'hoansi, you have to see that marriage alliances form an important part of the system of social security. If one has good relations with in-laws at different waterholes, one will never go hungry. If wild food resources give out in your home territory, you can always go visit your in-laws. *This* is the secret of why Ju/'hoansi marriages are so important to individual and group survival.

THE "MARRIAGE" OF /TONTAH

In the winter of my first year of fieldwork I was staying in the bush with / Xashe and N/ ahka, and with her parents, Kasupe and / Tasa. One evening as we sat around the campfire telling hunting stories, / Xashe turned to me and asked,

"/Tontah, back in your n!ore, your parents, are they living or dead?"

"Living," I replied. "Why do you ask?"

"And your wife and children," he responded, sidestepping my question, "where are they?"

"I have no wife and no children. I'm still too young to marry."

The people laughed at my response. With my beard and my obvious wealth, I certainly appeared to them as part of the marriageable age group.

"Well," / Xashe continued, "who have your parents betrothed you to?"

"No one! The girls have all refused me." Another stock answer, and good for a laugh. "But I do have a girl friend. And one of these days we might marry." This was true. My good friend Marie Kingston had lived in the Kalahari for several months, and they had met her.

Turning serious, / Xashe said, "/Tontah, a man like you, owning many things, can afford many wives, and even if you have a wife in your n!ore you should have a wife from this n!ore. I, /Xashe, as I am sitting here today, take my daughter //Toka and give her to you."

The people at the fire loudly indicated their approval of this move, while the object of this discussion, a perky four-year-old, averted her glance and cuddled in the arms of her mother.

I had heard about the practice of early betrothal among the !Kung, but this was ridiculous!

"But, but," I stammered, "by the time she is old enough to marry me she will have an old man for a husband."

"Not so," replied /Xashe. "She is young now, but it won't be long before she can marry you. Two, three rainy seasons at the most," he gestured, holding up his fingers, "and you will be together."

"And think of what it will be like," said N/ ahka, the mother of the "bride" and my potential mother-in-law. "In the morning you are sleeping by your fire and your young wife is up and around drawing water, roasting nuts, and cooking food." All this N/ ahka pantomimed with gusto. "Then you wake up and stretch, you have a nice cool drink of water and a wash-up, and then your breakfast is ready." The people nodded and murmured approvingly.

Now N/ ahka was really warming to her subject. "Refreshed and well fed, you are now ready to hunt. You test your arrows and choose the ones to take; you shoulder your quiver and you are off. All day long you criss-cross the country. Then you spy an animal, stalk carefully, and let fly. The animal is hit; you give chase; it's up, it's down; you finish it off with your spear and it's yours. You shoulder the load of meat and stagger home, hot and dusty. Your *tsiu* has a nice cold egg of water waiting for you. You drink and wash up, and then *sha,* and // *gxa,* and leafy greens are cooked and ready to eat. You drink, you eat, you butcher and cook the meat, and drink and eat again. Around the fire your wife spreads your blankets, and you lay down to a good night's sleep."

The group was chuckling and clucking in appreciation of our domestic bliss-to-be. But N/ ahka pressed on. "*Mi≠tum,*" she said, using the kin term for son-in-law, "that is how it will be. But first we must teach you how sons-in-law behave. Some men hunt for their in-laws, but as you have no quiver there are other ways. You can give us things: clothes, blankets, shoes, beads, food, sugar, tea. All this will show us that you are a serious suitor."

The group was particularly pleased with this last bit. They knew that *kamasi,* the gifts that flow between prospective in-laws, circulate widely in the recipients' village, and so all stood to benefit from having me as a son-in-law.

It was my turn to speak. "*Mi≠tum,*" I said to / Xashe, "and *mi/ totsu,*" addressing N/ ahka, "your words make my heart feel glad. I like you and I would like to be your ≠*um.* But I don't know what my family would say. I will write them and find out. In the meantime, let us do *kamasi.*"

This answer seemed to satisfy people. N/ ahka, beaming, turned to her daughter and said, "//Koka, greet your husband."

While her age-mates giggled, //Koka stared sullenly and stuck her tongue out at me.

SEXUALITY

The learning of sexual behavior begins for Ju children at an early age. Parents and young children sleep under the same blanket, and parental sex is carried on discreetly while the children sleep. Older children run naked through the village until age seven or eight, and it is only when they reach their early teens that they are finally expected to cover up the genitals.

There is a natural and unselfconscious attitude toward sex on the part of the Ju/'hoansi, and this attitude is imparted to the children. Sexual play is considered a normal part of childhood. N≠tisa, a 50-year-old !Kung woman from !Kangwa, was interviewed in depth by Marjorie Shostak about her life experiences. Here N≠tisa speaks about her first experiences of sex:

> When a child sleeps beside his mother, in front, and his father sleeps behind and makes love to her, the child watches. Perhaps this is the way the child learns. Because as his father lies with his mother, the child watches. The child is still senseless, is without intelligence, and he just watches.
>
> Then, when he and the other children are playing, if he is a little boy, he takes his younger sister and pretends to have sex with her. And as he grows, he lives in the bush and continues to play, now with other children, and they have sex with each other and play and play and play. They take food from the village and go back to the bush and continue their games. That's the way they grow up.. . .
>
> Some days I refused and remained in the village and just stayed with mother. Some days I went with them. Sometimes I refused to play, other times I agreed. The little boys entered the play huts where we were playing and then they lay down with us. My boyfriend came to see me and we lived like that and played. We would lie down and they would have sex with us.
>
> /Ti!kay taught it to me, and because of that I liked him. I really liked him! When we played, the other children said I should play with someone else, but I refused. I wanted /Ti!kay only. I said, "Me, I won't take a horrible man."
>
> They teased /Ti!kay. "Hey . . ./Ti!kay . . .you are the only one N≠isa likes. She refuses everyone else."
>
> He taught me about men. We played and played, and he grabbed me, and we played and played. Some days we built little huts, and he took me. We played every day. I used to think, "What is this thing that is so good? How come it is so good and I used to refuse it? The other children knew about it, and I had no sense. Now I know when you are a child, this is something you do. You teach it to yourself. (Shostak, 1976:262–263).

From this account it will be clear that the concept of virginity can have no real meaning in the !Kung context. Most boys and girls will have had some experience of sexual intercourse by age 15. It is curious, therefore, that girls express so much fear and resistance toward their husbands at the time of marriage. As we noted on pages 80–81, Ju girls struggle to avoid sexual intercourse with their husbands for weeks or months after the marriage. N≠tisa, too, resisted strenuously the advances of her husband, / Xashe, even tying a branch between her legs with leather to prevent her husband's penetration (Shostak, 1976:272–73). Finally, after many further struggles, N≠tisa's attitude began to change:

> We lived and lived and soon I started to like him. After that I was a grown person and said to myself, "Yes, without a doubt a man sleeps with you. I thought maybe he didn't."
>
> We lived on, and then I loved him and he loved me, and I kept on loving him. When he wanted me I didn't refuse, and he slept with me. I thought, "Why have I been so concerned about my genitals? They are after all not so important. So why was I refusing them?"
>
> I thought that and gave myself to him and gave and gave. I no longer refused. We lay with one another, and my breasts had grown very large. I had become a woman. (Shostak, 1976:274–275)

Marital sex after the excitement of the children's play groups is of necessity rather restrained. The presence of young children and the lack of privacy further inhibit sexual expression. The preferred position for intercourse is man-behind, woman-in-front, with the two lying on their sides as they face the sleeping fire.

Younger couples may vary this by going out gathering together and making love in daylight out in the *t'si*. Except for young infants, children are left behind on these expeditions. Interviews with informants suggested that the Ju/'hoansi use a variety of sexual positions, including male superior, female superior, front and rear entry. The goal of sex for both partners is orgasm, and it is clear from informants that Ju/'hoansi have a clear conception of female orgasm. Several women said they regularly experienced *tain,* the Ju word for orgasm, the same word used to describe the indescribably delicious taste of wild honey.

A number of forms of sexual behavior that are common in our society are rare or absent among the Ju/'hoansi: oral and anal sex, coitus interruptus, bondage, and sadomasochistic practices do not appear to be part of the Ju/'hoan repertoire. Similarly, rape seemed to be extremely uncommon among the Ju/'hoansi (L. Marshall, 1976:279). However, with the rise of alcohol consumption in the 1990s, sexual assault was become more common.

Homosexuality is not common, but both gay and lesbian forms do occur. N≠tisa described a number of same-sex sexual experiences with childhood playmates (Shostak, 1983:120). A few adult men and women have experimented with same-sex sexual partners, with male homosexuality being the more common. Of the two women and six men reported to have had homosexual experiences, all were married, indicating that all were bisexual. Ju/'hoan nonparticipants in these activities expressed attitudes of curiosity and bemusement toward them rather than embarrassment or hostility.

The question of marital fidelity and extramarital affairs is one that has fascinated several observers, but the data are contradictory. In many Ju marriages the partners are strictly faithful to one another, while in a large minority there is evidence of extramarital affairs. For example, at one waterhole with about 50 married couples between the ages of 20 and 50, we recorded 16 couples in which one or another was having an affair. Both husbands and wives take lovers; there is no double standard among the Ju/'hoansi. In confiding to Marjorie Shostak (1981, 1983), Ju women spoke warmly of their lovers and the rare and precious moments they spent with them. Both partners, however, had to be discreet. If an outraged husband or wife discovered the liaison, a major fight could break out. Women, if anything, expressed more sexual jealousy than men, and if they caught wind of an affair, they have been known to attack their rivals or their husbands, or both.

MALE AND FEMALE AMONG THE JU/'HOANSI

We have looked at marriage and sexuality and have found that they are sources of strength and cohesion in Ju/'hoan society, as well as sources of conflict, disharmony, and stress. On balance, though, the cohesive side predominates: male–female relations are not riven with stress and dissension, and most Ju/'hoansi would be considered (by our standards at least) to be blessed with happy marriages and good sex lives. Now we have to ask the question, is this blessing achieved at the expense of women, who are subordinated to their husbands' interests? Or, conversely, is it the men who are subordinate to the interests of women? Let us review the evidence.

Arranged marriages do put a young woman at a disadvantage as her parents and her husband make arrangements about her future. But the young woman can make her needs known by vetoing the marriage, an option not offered women in many tribal and peasant societies. During marriage both men and women work around the "home," with the men doing more subsistence work and tool-making and women doing more housework and child care. No evidence of exploitation here.

The marriage ceremony does act out a ritual of marriage-by-capture and, as we noted, it conceals a real source of generational and gender conflict beneath the surface. However, the many forms of sexual oppression that women experience in other societies, such as rape, wife battering, purdah, enforced chastity, and sexual double standards are rare or absent in Ju/'hoan society. In their sexual life both men and women appear to enjoy sex and to seek and expect to achieve orgasm, and both may seek lovers outside a primary relationship. And both men and women experience sexual jealousy and may act out their anger on spouses or rivals. The evidence on balance supports neither of the two alternatives mentioned above. Rather, we see a picture of relative equality between the sexes, with no one having the upper hand. There is no support in the Ju/'hoansi data for a view of women in "the state of nature" as oppressed or dominated by men or as subject to sexual exploitation at the hands of males.

7/Complaint Discourse: Aging and Caregiving Among the Ju/'hoansi[1]

BY HARRIET G. ROSENBERG

INTRODUCTION

The study of Ju/'hoan kinship and marriage (Chapters 5 and 6) increased my understand-ing of some of the deeper aspects of their life, but other important areas remained a mys-tery to me. I had come to the Kalahari to learn about their hunting and gathering way of life, but I hadn't been prepared for the Ju/'hoansi's raucous sense of humor or the sharp-tongued wit that characterized their daily conversations. But most puzzling of all had been the litany of complaints and put-downs that passed their lips every day, a level of rude ban-ter that would be hard to tolerate in North American society, yet which they seemed to take in stride.

The level of complaint was especially high among older Ju/'hoansi. As 80-year-old //Kokan!a told us: "Old people have long complained: it is an old thing. Even if the child did everything for them, they would complain."

My wife, Harriet Rosenberg, is a medical anthropologist who teaches at York University in Toronto. In 1986 and 1987 Harriet and I and our daughter Miriam trav-eled to the Dobe area to study aging and caregiving. Her insights illuminated that sub-ject but yielded an important bonus: It was through the study of aging, in fact, that we were able to make sense of one of the most fundamental truths of Ju/'hoan life. Complaining is not just a chance occurrence, but an integral part of the Ju/'hoan way of life. It provides a key to understanding the quality of interpersonal relations, of Ju core values, the discourse that has enabled them to live up to the demands of sharing and egalitarianism. RBL

How do Ju/'hoansi care for elders, and what is the language through which care is negotiated? Do the Ju follow patterns of caregiving familiar in North American society

[1]This chapter is adapted from a paper that originally appeared in two editions of *The Cultural Context of Aging*, edited by Jay Sokolovsky (1990; 1997). The "we" used here refers to a team of investigators, in-cluding Richard B. Lee, Meg Luxton, and Harriet Rosenberg; research assistants Nandi Ngcongco, Dorothy Molokome, Leonard Ramotakwane, and Makgolo Makgolo; and translators Gakekgoshe Isaaka and Gai !Koma. In addition, we thank Megan Biesele for the careful translation/transcriptions she made of interviews she conducted in Ju/'hoansi in Namibia.

The investigators wish to thank the Social Science and Humanities Research Council of Canada for pro-viding funding for this project, "Aging, Caregiving and Social Change in an African Population." In addi-tion, Rosenberg would like to thank Patricia Draper, Christine Gailey, Mathias Guenther, Richard Katz, Robin Oakley, and Polly Wiessner for their gracious assistance with this version.

The "Young-Old": A Woman in her fifties holds the group's attention.

or does their management of these difficult relationships differ significantly? This chapter explores the social basis of caregiving discourse among the Ju/'hoansi. Despite the changes in economic and social life that the Ju/'hoansi have experienced in the last 30 years, caring discourse appears to be autonomous in the Dobe area, in the sense that it is constructed within the culture itself, with very little influence from state agencies (legal, health, educational, military, social services) or non-Ju/'hoansi religious philosophies.

To review some relevant points of background, in the late 1980s the 700 Ju/'hoansi of the Dobe area shared their eight waterholes with about 325 pastoralists, mainly of the Herero ethnic group. Until the 1960s and 1970s the majority of Ju/'hoansi had lived in small camps of about 15 to 30 people, often centered around a core of siblings, their spouses, and children. The groups relied on wild food products for the bulk of their subsistence needs and moved three to six times a year in search of food and water. These camps were characterized by egalitarian social relations and the widespread sharing of foodstuffs—the typical features of a small-scale communal social formation. The language and kinship system were intact and fully functioning.

After 1968, conditions began to change rapidly, with the opening of a store in 1968 followed by a school in 1973 and a health clinic and airstrip in 1978. During this period the Ju/'hoansi began to shift over to small-scale livestock and crop production and settle into semipermanent villages. Cash became a common medium of exchange that coexisted with the traditional regional gift exchange system

The monthly mobile clinic from !Kangwa making its rounds and treating patients at Dobe.

called *hxaro*. Migrant labor, livestock sales, and craft production became sources of cash income.

By the mid-1980s, in their dress and economy, the Dobe Ju/'hoansi's lifestyle came to resemble that of many impoverished southern African peasants. They received drought relief in the 1980s and 1990s, and empty bags and containers from overseas countries littered their villages. Their children went to school, but most dropped out in the early grades. A few went on to high school and have become literate in English and in other African languages. People now seek health care at local clinics or from mobile health units, and they often spend their modest incomes on transistor radios, European-style clothing, tea, sugar, tobacco, and beer.

Their transition to an agricultural way of life has had only mixed success. In the mid-1980s, over half the families lacked livestock, and even the most "affluent" herders numbered their stock in the range of 10 to 20 head of cattle. Foraging declined in the mid-1980s with the introduction of drought relief but bow and arrow hunting once again increased in Botswana, encouraged by the Game Department (Lee and Rosenberg, 1994). The knowledge of Dobe area elders about their environment and seasonal variations, and their technical advice about hunting and gathering became highly prized as younger community members intensified foraging activities (Lee and Biesele, 1994; in press).

On a deeper level the Dobe Ju/'hoansi are struggling—not without success—to adhere to the values and beliefs of their ancestral culture. This cultural context has continued to generate the motifs, themes, and rationales about aging and caregiving that we explore in this chapter.

AGING AND SOCIAL CHANGE IN JU/'HOAN SOCIETY

Like most foraging peoples, the Ju/'hoansi were not interested in and did not keep track of chronological age. Birthdays and anniversaries were not social markers and age segregation has been noticeably absent. Major life transition hallmarks existed at the younger end of the age spectrum, distinguishing among infants, children, adolescents, and adults. No ceremonies, such as retirement events or anniversary celebrations, marked the onset of old age or menopause, but all elders (including those without children) carry the honorific *n!a* in their names. *N!a* is an interesting word which combines the meanings of "old," "big," and "great." No ritual occasion marks the moment when one becomes *n!a,* usually in one's mid to late forties; certainly, everyone 50 or over is called *n!a.*

Old age is divided into three broad categories. All elders are *n!a,* those who are very old are called "old/dead" *m≠da !ki,* a term that designates extreme old age and one that is also a joking term. A sick or decrepit elder may be referred to as "old to the point of helplessness" *m≠da kum kum.* The terms *≠da !ki* and *≠da kum kum* do not denote a sharp decline in social status; the frail elderly are neither a particular butt of ridicule nor a source of fear and anxiety.

It should be noted that growing old and the changes that accompany it are a constant topic of conversation and a source of humor. Linking sexuality and aging seem to make the best jokes and much of campfire discussion features endless stories about decline in sexual prowess, especially among men. Post-menopausal women also delight in engaging in broad sexual joking (Lee, 1992c).

Although the Ju/'hoansi do link old age with degeneration, elders are also associated with generative and life-giving activities, as Biesele and Howell (1981) have pointed out in their analysis of a beautiful folktale of a grandmother/granddaughter relationship. Similarly, elders are felt to have special powers that permit them to eat certain foods (e.g., ostrich eggs) considered too dangerous for younger people to consume. Even elders with physical infirmities have taken strong leadership roles, as for example in the case of four blind seniors whose decision-making advice and curing roles were very influential in the political and social life of one waterhole in the 1960s. Also, it is worth noting that death is not exclusively connected with old age. Historically, the Ju/'hoansi have had a high infant mortality rate, and now tuberculosis is prevalent in the Dobe area. Thus, death can and does occur at any age.

In the realm of sociopolitical power, Ju/'hoansi elders have had limited prerogatives. Traditionally, they commanded control over defining kinship relationships (see Chapter 5). A senior person, male or female, has the right to decide who fits where in the kinship system and to determine an avoidance or a joking framework for social interactions. This system of seniority gives elders power within the social universe, but it does not constitute a gerontocracy (rule by the elderly). Before settling down, the Ju/'hoansi were for the most part without property and could not wield the threat of disinheritance to encourage compliance. When an adult daughter of an elder with cows was recently asked how cattle ownership affects the quality of care, she responded by saying, "It hasn't changed things. We took care of our elders then and we still take care of them" (Lee, fieldnotes, May 1995). However, this mother of six children also indicated that at her passing, her eldest child (female) would inherit her cattle and that she

≠da !ki but still spry. Kaincha, the well-known healer and his wife Be.

alone among her siblings anticipated receiving her mother's property, because she saw herself as the principal caregiver. But when her eldest daughter was asked to confirm this she allowed that she might decide to share her inheritance with her siblings (Lee, fieldnotes, May 1995).

How property and inheritance will, in the long run, influence personal relationships including eldercare, is still very much in the process of being worked out. Sedentary life has brought changed patterns in subsistence and marriage customs that may also create significant changes in the lives of Ju/'hoansi elders. In the past, old people, by dint of their personal authority, attempted to construct marriage alliances that seemed sensible to them, but young people often refused such arrangements, thwarting the intentions of their seniors. Nowadays, an emerging pattern of bride wealth in lieu of bride service[2] and an increase in informal liaisons of local girls with Black boyfriends has made marriage a contentious issue in the Dobe area. As some young women find themselves locked into restrictive arrangements (especially problematic is the new pattern of *paternal* child custody at divorce within bride wealth systems), many women have chosen to avoid marriage altogether (Lee and Rosenberg, 1994; see also Draper and Keith, 1992).

[2]*Bride wealth* is a common part of marriage arrangements among pastoral peoples in Africa. The bride's family is given cattle and/or other property to mark the marriage. Customarily, bride wealth is related to the bride's residence with the groom's family (virilocal residence). Should the betrothal or the marriage fail, the cattle are returned. Furthermore, if the union produces children, custody would normally reside with the father and his family.

By contrast, *bride service* is associated with the groom's responsibility to move to the bride's family (uxorilocal residence) and to provide subsistence for his in-laws for a specific period of time, often several years. If a divorce should occur, any children would normally remain with the mother and her family.

Despite the changes in social practices, the elders we interviewed argued that they saw no real change in their own lives as a result of the displacement of bride service by bride wealth, and that receiving a cow at the marriage of a daughter seems to be equivalent to having a son-in-law's hunting skill at their disposal. Lee's 1995 interviews indicate that elders are promoting cattle exchange at marriage *in combination with* bride service (not instead of it) and that they are resisting paternal child custody at divorce. In response to a question about child custody, he was told by one senior woman that "that is very tough. If there is divorce, we would not permit the children to go [to the ex-son-in-law's family] regardless of the cow." Thus current Ju/'hoansi marriage arrangements are in a state of flux and the implications for elders are unclear.

Another arena of personal authority for elders has been their role as healers. Richard Katz, who did fieldwork among healers in the Dobe area in the 1960s and late 1980s, notes that the social status of certain elderly healers is very high (personal communication, 1995; see also Katz, Biesele, and St. Dennis, 1997). These old men are "the healers' healers" and it is their experience and their strength in not being overpowered by the supernatural forces with which they work that command respect. In a culture where boasting of any kind is frowned upon, these senior healers are permitted to talk about their skill and achievements. Not all old people develop the power to heal—to sing, dance, go into a trance, and "pull sickness" out of others. Those who do can often go on until they are quite old, teaching other healers and participating in healing the community at large. Katz (1982) has described the charismatic energy of some elderly healers and their aura of exceptional strength and spirituality.

FIELD RESEARCH ON AGING: THE 1986–1987 PROJECT

The following discussion is based on participant observation, formal questionnaires, and open-ended, unstructured interviews with the Ju/'hoansi in 1986 and 1987 (updated by Lee in 1995) and on the accumulated work of anthropologists who have been working with them since 1963. We were, thus, able to compare our informants' retrospective accounts with field descriptions of observed behavior over a period of three decades, an ability that provided in one instance (see text) a key insight.

In 1964, 9 percent of the population was over age 60.[3] By 1973, that proportion had risen to 10.5 percent, and in 1986 the figure was 12.5 percent, with 7.5 percent over age 65. In addition, the birth rate has risen. As of 1986, almost 40 percent of the population was under 15 years of age. Thus, at the time of our field research, 48 percent of the population was between 15 and 49 and supported both the young and the elderly.

Our discussion of the social experience of aging among the Ju/'hoansi focuses on four topics:

1. Complaint discourse
2. Narratives of neglect and abandonment
3. Entitlement
4. The social organization of care

---

[3]The Ju/'hoansi themselves do not mark chronological age. The ages used in this essay represent estimates made by the demographer Nancy Howell during fieldwork in 1968 (see Howell, 1979; 2000) and revisions made according to census updates by Lee during field trips in 1973, 1983, and 1986–1987.

Older women's power: the women's trance dance and healing.

COMPLAINT DISCOURSE

The Ju/'hoansi are known to their neighbors and anthropologists alike as extremely talkative people and much of their talk verges on argument, often for its own sake (Lee, 1979:372). Thus Chu!ko's stream of complaints is not viewed within the culture as unusual or as a particular attribute of old age. Campfire conversation often swirls around accusations of improper meat distribution, improper gift exchange, stinginess, and the shortcomings of others, but usually delivered in a kind of good-natured joking manner.

Complaining thus serves as an important leveling device but also may be a medium for the expression of a variety of other, more complex feelings. In describing the circumstances around the deaths of three elders, Wiessner (1983) noted vociferous complaints about the adequacy of care in all cases, even in a family where adult children and more distant kin were doing everything they possibly could, including purchasing and slaughtering goats and holding healing ceremonies. "These accusations," according to Wiessner, are part of "the rhetoric of reciprocity which pervades San life" (1983:1). Complaining is a public exhortation to keep goods and services circulating: It warns against hoarding.

Complaining rhetoric may also have been part of Chu!ko's individual efforts to keep herself visible. Just as Jewish elders in Barbara Myerhoff's classic study of a Los Angeles senior's drop-in center used "competitive complaining" (1978:146) as a performance strategy to mark their continued presence in the world, so Chu!ko's constant hum of words may well be her way of saying, "I'm still here."

We wondered if the move to a cash economy would mean a decline in sharing. Yet even with these changes, sharing remains strong. There is no language yet to express a world of personal needs that would take precedence over obligations to others, and there is very little leniency shown to those who struggle with conflicting obligations. Individuals who have attempted to become more self-sufficient and to limit the circle of reciprocity when they switched from foraging to farming and herding have found it difficult to explain why they were not sharing their crops or killing their goats and cattle to feed their kinspeople. Some suffered ostracism (Lee, 1979:412-414).

An incident reveals the deeper cultural meaning of complaint discourse. One woman in her early sixties who owns several head of cattle has been observed to be among the loudest of complainers, denouncing all and sundry for their failure to share. One day, while following an anthropologist back and forth while he was packing up camp, she delivered a blistering tirade against his hard-heartedness. Back and forth from tent to truck they trudged, the anthropologist silent, carrying bundles of goods, Nuh!ka on his heels, yelling at him. Suddenly, she stopped and like a scene in a Brecht play, stepped out of character, altered the tone of her voice, and in a whisper announced, "We have to talk this way. It's our custom." Then she stepped back into character and resumed her attack.

The Ju/'hoansi have a name for this type of discourse: It is called *horehore* or *obaoba* and can be translated as "yakity-yak." In the case above, Nuh!ka stepped out of character to break the tension of the verbal assault she had mounted. In other cases, the tension can be broken by a joke that leaves ". . . the participants rolling on the ground helpless with laughter" (Lee, 1979:372). Complaint discourse is, thus, not peculiar to elders but may be invoked by anyone at any time to decry real or potential stinginess.

NARRATIVES OF NEGLECT AND ABANDONMENT

To the observer, Ju/'hoansi elders appear to be hale and hearty[4] and well integrated into the social life of their community. Frail[5] elders are embedded in caregiving networks of several on-site carers, who provide for their needs. Yet the discourse used by elders to describe their situation is often one of unrelenting complaint and blaming. In general, the most common response to the question, "Who looks after old people?" is "Their children." But when we stepped outside the normative system and asked elders, "Who looks after you?" the response was very frequently, "No one. Can't you see that I am starving and dressed in rags?"

Elders frequently complained about the neglected state they were in and told lengthy tales about the deficiencies of those who *should* be caring for them but were not. Although neglect discourse took on a variety of forms, two common styles will be examined here—the nagging style and broad melodrama.

Chu!ko's Story

The first style is typified by Chu!ko, age 72. At the time of the interview (the mid-1980s), Chu!ko lived with her husband, her daughter, and her son-in-law, all of whom shared in the caregiving. Yet Chu!ko described herself as neglected because her three half-brothers and their children who lived nearby did not provide for her.

I asked Chu!ko if she could give me an example from her "own memory" of how an old person was looked after until she or he died. "Do you know of any old person who was abandoned?" Chu!ko was not interested in the past just then:

> I have no story, but the only example that I can give you is my own. I have younger siblings with children. And I am old. I have no niece or nephew that brings food from my siblings. And I just see that they are not looking after me.

The care that she received from her daughter, son-in-law, and husband was scarcely acknowledged. Chu!ko asserted that caregiving had deteriorated in the present. She maintained that in the past, children were collectively responsible for all elders.

---

[4]In 1967–1968, Truswell and Hansen (1976) conducted a health survey of the region. They found Ju/'hoansi elders to be remarkably fit and not suffering from high blood pressure or other stress-related illnesses. More recent research indicates that changed diet has produced elevated blood pressures in the population (Kent and Lee, 1992; Hansen, Dunn, Lee, Becker, and Jenkins, 1994).

[5]We divided the elderly into five categories of functionality: category one was the most fit, and five represented those who were completely dependent. "Frail" refers to those in categories four and five, a total of 12 people.

Chu!ko n!a, wife, mother, and older sister, in a more cheerful moment.

When I say the past was better I mean this: before, the child listened to his/her[6] parents. When children went out to play and an adult who saw an elder ailing came upon them, s/he scolded them for letting the elder die of thirst and ordered them to attend to [the elder]. Today an adult will merely look and say or think: "Let his/her children take care of him/her." And even the children themselves are not caring by nature.

She then reiterated her complaints against her half-siblings.

Two of her brothers agreed to be interviewed, and they defined themselves as being caregivers to their sister and pointed out that they sent food and water to her via their children and grandchildren. Nevertheless, Chu!ko maintained a persistent litany of complaint. Far from not wishing to seem a burden or a dependent, she went out of her way to publicly blame her brothers and their families as being delinquent caregivers. Her form of expression was often a quiet oration to no one in particular.

Chu!ko's complaint discourse can be interpreted in a variety of ways. She may have been detecting changes in the distribution of social obligations that have accompanied settlement, and may indeed have picked up a drift away from sibling care

---

[6]The third person singular is not gendered in the Ju/'hoansi language. Thus, we use the English terms "his/her" or "she/he" in the text to translate the speaker's usage. While "he/she" may seem awkward to some English speakers it is consistent with the Ju/'hoansi language, which does not distinguish between male and female in the third person singular, just as English does not in the third person plural "they" but French does in the forms "ils/elles."

towards a more nuclear pattern. Her family and her brothers had lived together in the past in a traditional sibling core unit, but at the time of the interview, the brothers lived a half-mile away, on the other side of Dobe. Two of these brothers have many children, grandchildren, and other elders to care for and may well have been preoccupied with their immediate situations. The third sibling is often dismissed as a person with no sense who cannot be relied on. Thus, Chu!ko may be complaining about a new experience of social distance that has fractured horizontal bonds and is delimiting caregiving responsibilities within the nuclear family.

Kasupe's Story

The second style of complaint discourse, broad melodrama, came home to us in a striking account by a Ju/'hoan elder with a flair for the dramatic. Kasupe, age 74, a skilled storyteller, surrounded by family, responded to our interview question of who looked after him by denouncing his entire family. First, he attacked his children:

> My own children do not look after me. See the clothes I am wearing—these rags I'm wearing—I get them from my own work, my own sweat. None of them have done anything for me. Because they do not look after me, I, their parent say they are "without sense."

He went on to discuss his future prospects:

> I do not know who will take care of me when I am old and frail. Right now I can manage; I still have some strength. But as I grow old, I cannot point out a child—a person—about whom I can say, "This one will take care of me." Perhaps I will perish.

Warming up to his tale of woe, Kasupe also denounced his brothers and sisters, ultimately dismissing all of his relatives as being uncaring. To illustrate the depths of their neglect, he launched into the following story:

> Here is proof of the uncaring nature of my children. I will tell you a story. [Years ago] I'd gone hunting with some Herero and we had split up, agreeing to meet later at a certain point. Those Herero warned me that they had set a steel trap in the direction I was headed. I went on but because it was dark, I could not see and was caught in the trap. It grabbed my ankle. I stayed there and my wife and children were following me. None of them came to see how I was. I was only helped by you Gakegkoshe [the translator] and /Tontah [anthropologist Richard Lee]. You helped me heal and saw to it that I got better. None [of my family] came to see how I was doing. It was only you. Even my brothers and sisters in Namibia did not come to see how I was doing.

The story had a familiar ring. Richard Lee had recorded the incident in detail in the first edition of the present volume (Lee, 1984), and the details he recorded were completely at odds with Kasupe's version of the story. After the interview we fetched a copy of the first edition and returned to Kasupe. There on page 111 was a photo of Kasupe on the day of the crisis lying on the ground surrounded by family and Ju/'hoan healers (see p. 127, this edition). The text also included a lengthy account from Lee's field notes describing Kasupe's wife and children sobbing and wailing as community members worked on curing him. Lee administered some penicillin. The next day Kasupe began to improve, and within three months he was hunting again (Lee, 1984:104–106).

Feeling some glee in having caught Kasupe in a contradiction, we laid the story out before him. Far from neglecting him, here was the evidence, with photograph, of his family and community making heroic efforts to save his life. Kasupe's only response was to break out into a loud, long, thigh-slapping laugh which was immediately echoed by the Ju/'hoansi audience and the anthropologists.

Kasupe was completely unabashed and expressed no regret at having "accused" his relatives of neglect, abandonment, and death-hastening behavior. Whether there was any "truth" to his narrative was quite irrelevant. His version of events made a good story. It was gripping and dramatic; he was impressive as he told it. The listener was captivated by "the utterance" (Eagleton, 1983:115).

But like Chu!ko's less melodramatic narrative, Kasupe's performance also had another side to it. Kasupe had expressed what "might" happen if caregivers were not to do their duty. He had described aloud what the world would be like should the caring system not be reproduced. His narrative allowed his audience to imagine the dire scene of family neglect. By negative example, he restated the social contract of caregiving obligations. His laughter, and the audience's laughter, did not mean that the complaint lacked seriousness, only perhaps that he had been topped by a better story this time. But the complaint was important: the Ju/'hoansi system of mutual responsibility and caregiving requires constant lubrication, and complaining greases the wheels.

In a more serious vein, !Xoma, a respected elder, who was not given to extravagant rhetoric, pointed out that there were indeed cases of real abandonment in the past. He explained the circumstances of abandonment in a previous generation:

> They'd leave him/her and go off, because they didn't know what to do with him/her. Naturally, they had no truck, no donkey, nothing. And they were also carrying her/his things on their bodies. Sometimes they'd try to carry the person where they were going. Someone else would carry the person's things, if there were many people. But if the people were few, or if there was only one man, they didn't know what to do with the old person. They would admit defeat, leave him/her, and go.

It is likely that there have been cases of death-hastening among the Ju/'hoansi in the past, although we do not have any sustained ethnographic account of such behavior. The Ju/'hoansi, themselves, use the equivocal term *n/a a tsi* (to leave in the bush), which implies abandonment. As !Xoma's dispassionate analysis implies, the term "burden of care" was not a metaphor, but a concrete description of physically carrying a frail elder on one's back. When this was the only means of transportation, there were likely to have been times when the coping skills of the caregivers were stretched to the breaking point, and the elder was abandoned in the bush.

Settled life has made a difference in elder care. In the mid-1980s, we found incapacitated elders being scrupulously cared for by kin and community. The conditions of a settled lifestyle, the availability of soft foods, and access to vehicles in cases of medical emergency all make it easier to care for frail elders today in comparison to 30 or more years ago. Furthermore, settlement has meant that Ju/'hoansi practices are now more closely scrutinized by the state than they were in the past. The presence of a police post in the Dobe area has likely influenced community thinking on abandonment of elders.

The irrepressible Kasupe enjoying the joke.

The discourse of neglect is thus quite complicated. It is used to describe cases in which "real" abandonment may have occurred. It is used as a social regulatory mechanism to reinforce sharing and caregiving. It is used as a vehicle to tell a good story. What is most apparent about this discourse is that words and words alone have up until very recently been the main social regulators of behavior. The Ju/'hoansi themselves have no legal/police system with which to coerce behavior or punish offenders.

ENTITLEMENT

"I would not want to live with my family. They are nice people, very generous, but it would not be fair to them."

82-year-old North American woman

Ju/'hoansi elders do not see themselves as burdens. They are not apologetic if they are no longer able to produce enough to feed themselves. They expect others to care for them when they can no longer do so. Entitlement to care is naturalized within the culture: Elders do not have to negotiate care as if it were a favor, rather, it is perceived of as an unquestioned right.

The needs of elders are not defined as being markedly different from the needs of anyone else. The material aspects of caring for elders was uniformly defined by our

//Gumi n!a (right), who "still knows how to talk properly," and her daughter Sa//gai at Mahopa village.

informants as providing *da, !gu, msi* (firewood, water, and food). These are the basics of life which are procured and shared among all members of the community. Obtaining these necessities in the past has not been especially onerous, requiring on average 20 hours of work per week in food gathering from the active population, but today those with herd animals work longer hours. Thus elders have not been experienced as a particular economic burden or a category of people with "special needs." In fact, in terms of health care, elders are both givers and receivers of care. Even with the arrival of government health workers in the district, healing dances continue to flourish, giving elders a prominent role in community life.

One rarely hears an old person express appreciation for the care that he or she receives, and one never hears elders express the desire to live alone so as to not burden the family with caregiving obligations. The desire to live alone is classified as a form of mental illness. "Only a crazy person would live alone," said one young informant. For some, entitlement to care flows directly from the parent–child relationship. /Tasa, age 65, described this process of socialization:

> When a child is born you teach that child to care for her/his parents throughout the time the child is growing up, so that when the child is older s/he will willingly care for his/her parents. But if that child has a crippled heart, is a person with no sense, that will come from inside her/him and s/he will neglect the parents.

THE SOCIAL ORGANIZATION OF CARE

Caregiving is normatively described as being the responsibility of all adult children. No elder thought the responsibility was linked to gender or that daughters should do more than sons. According to N/ahka, a woman with many children and grandchildren, feminization of caregiving is not a social norm.

> In my household, both my sons and daughters help me. The care they give balances so that I see no difference. I don't think girls are more caring than boys. [Is this the same for others at Dobe?] Yes. I give the example of N!ai who has no daughters but the care that her sons give her is of the same quality as that which I get from my children.

Most caregivers subscribed to this version, but a few women felt they were doing more than men. //Gumi's daughter, Sa//gai, was particularly angry with her brother, ≠Toma, and fought with him about his lack of attention to their mother. On the other hand ≠Toma felt that his sister had not been sufficiently attentive when their father was ill and dying.

For our informants it was not gender that divided the population between active caregivers and delinquents, but rather a personal quality or quirk. One elder noted, "If you have a child and that child has a good heart, regardless of whether s/he is male or female, s/he will look after their parent."

Nothing can be done to force a child to be a good caregiver. If a child fails to do his or her duty then others are expected to pitch in, especially if the old person has no children. The situation of Chwa is illustrative.

Chwa was in her late eighties at the time of the interview, had poor eyesight, though good hearing, and could still walk. She had no children and lived with her co-wife Bau and their husband, both of whom were in their early eighties. Throughout our discussion, neighbors dropped by with food and water. Chwa entered a conversation that compared past caregiving of the elderly to the current situation. One of her neighbors commented that she had never heard of elders being left in the bush in the past. Chwa stated that she had "heard of people carrying those who were sick on their backs from village to village," but today, she continued "people do not look after the old sufficiently." Two of her neighbors immediately disagreed and took turns affirming that the young do *n!abe n!abe* (care for) the old.

Chwa, however was adamant. She pointed out that her nephew Tsau, was derelict in his duty. (Tsau was her brother's son, a man of about 60, married and living at another village.) "He wants to," she went on, "but his wife won't let him. But those who do take care of me are this N≠isa here [an elderly neighbor] and that woman there, my co-wife [Bau], while our husband tends the cattle."

She then proceeded to recount this positive description of care, one of the very few that I had ever heard from an elder.

> Once, when I was very sick, I was burning with fever, she [N≠isa] poured water on me, and then she held me in her arms. These women, N≠isa, Tan//kae [an elderly neighbor], and my co-wife cared for me. I slept in their arms. This happened this past summer, when the wild onions came out of the ground and the Grewia berries were already on the bushes [February–March]. My heart craved bush food and these women collected it for me.

One of the caregivers explained further:

> We collected the Grewia berries; we gave her some and sold the rest to the school people [parents who had children at /Xai/ xai school and could not easily go gathering]. And then we bought sugar and tobacco for this old one.

I asked, "What made you think of doing that?" And Bau, Chwa's co-wife, using her hands for emphasis, responded, "What is there to think about? You see an old person. She is your person. She can't walk. She can't do it for herself, so you do it."

Thus, although Chwa has no children of her own, she was firmly anchored in a responsive caregiving network. She also felt it her right to demand caregiving from her nephew, even though he had other obligations elsewhere. She dismissed this situation of competing caregiving responsibilities by claiming that it was the nephew's wife who prevented him from doing his duty. From her perspective, he still had a duty to her. He, on the other hand asserted that she was being looked after by "her people" or *ju*.

As stated previously, although the caregiving role for someone who is "your person" is naturalized, it is not feminized. Caregiving is explained as a quality of human, not female, nature. We have observed male and female carers providing food, firewood, and water, although the foods may represent a gendered division of labor, with men hunting and women gathering. Government drought relief food will be carried to elders who cannot manage to go to the relief trucks themselves by any of "their people." Both men and women also care in other ways. Massage is an important service rendered by carers. Both men and women will gather the plants and nuts used to prepare the ointments used during massage. Women are more likely to provide other, smaller services for female elders, such as grooming hair, but both men and women spend time visiting, talking, and drinking tea with elders. However, in the delicate area of toileting old people, there did seem to be a gender link. Male caregivers would take responsibility for guiding male elders in and out of the bush and female caregivers would look after the needs of women elders.

Children, regardless of sex, were enlisted in caregiving as well. Sometimes the special relationship of grandparent–grandchild was used to mobilize care. This relationship is quite expandable into an inclusive kinship mode, which draws in distant kin. Elders, for example, may invoke the "name" relationship so that children with the same name as the old person will be regarded as grandchildren and available to perform such services as fetching water, if they are willing. The web of caregiving thus moves well beyond the limited confines of the nuclear family.

Elders are independent and autonomous (as are all members of the community) in the sense that can do what they wish when they wish. Able-bodied elders forage, fetch water, visit, trade gifts, make crafts, dance, sleep, and eat whenever they choose. They do not face fears of pauperization with old age or the struggles of living on a "fixed income." Their old age is not filled with anxieties about personal security: They have no fears about interpersonal violence, robbery or abuse. They do not lock themselves in their houses at night. Their conversation is not filled with talk of loneliness, or the difficult decisions about whether to sell their homes and lose a whole way of life in order to seek a diminished but more secure living environment (Draper and Keith, 1992).[7]

Frail Ju/'hoansi elders are enmeshed in a network of caregiving. The eight frail elders we interviewed had between 4 and 8 people looking after them for a total of 44 people undertaking frontline elder care responsibilities.

---

[7]Draper and Keith (1992) elaborate on the contrast drawn here between the feelings of personal security among Ju/'hoansi elders and the fears and painful choices of elders within a North American community.

Even those who were extremely weak were not segregated from the social land-scape. We observed a situation in which ≠Dau, a very sick elder, who slept almost all the time, was placed in the center of social life. Around him gathered family and neighbors who chatted, smoked, and cooked together. Nearby his son hacked up the carcass of a kudu, and the old man's wife, //Koka, stirred the cooking pot, children played, and an infant nursed. As the meat cooked, his wife lifted his head every few minutes and fed him a morsel of food. He chewed silently, his eyes shut. When he was done, he rested his head on the blanket. In the meantime, his wife chatted with those at the fire. Both the old man and his caregivers were rooted in a social matrix which undoubtedly eased the burden of care and perhaps enhanced the quality of this very frail person's last days.

CONCLUSION: THE PARADOX OF SHARING AND COMPLAINING

By North American standards the material situation of the Dobe Ju/'hoansi is poor, but the social circumstances of elders is quite positive (see also Draper and Harpending, 1994; Draper and Keith, 1992). They have personal autonomy and re-spect, and live in a culture that strongly values caregiving and support. Old people participate in social, political, economic, and spiritual life. They may regret growing old and ask someone to pull out the first few grey hairs, but they are also equipped with rich cultural resources for articulating their concerns, fears, and anxieties and for ensuring support.

Yet the Ju/'hoansi complain all the time. They are cranky, funny, and loud. They live in a moral universe of high caregiving standards, in which the ideal seems to be that every person is directly obligated to meet the needs of every other person all the time. But since such a perfect world is impossible to obtain, they find ample justifi-cation for their complaints of inadequate caregiving. Furthermore, personal prefer-ences, personality conflicts, and old unresolved grievances enter into the caregiving equation, making it a far from ideal universe. There is always someone who is not do-ing enough. And there is always someone ready to denounce that person in terms nei-ther pleasant nor polite.

The cultural forms that reproduce respect and care for elders through complaint discourse reflect deep patterns in Ju/'hoansi culture. Boasting, self-aggrandizement, or displays of pride are strongly discouraged as behaviors that impede sharing and that may lead to violence. Thus, it is not polite etiquette, but ". . . rough humor, back-handed compliments, put-downs and damning with faint praise" (Lee, 1979:458)—the rhetoric of complaint—which is in constant use to constrain potentially danger-ous behaviors. Complaining is the only social arena in which the Ju/'hoansi are competitive and it is hardly surprising that elders are so good at it. They have been practicing their whole lives.

FUTURE PROSPECTS: HOW WILL "DEVELOPMENT" AFFECT CAREGIVING?

These discourses and practices have not abruptly unraveled with changes in ma-terial culture such as the appearance of transistor radios, cassette tape players, and bicycles. In other words, cultural formations are resilient, and contrary to the highly romanticized myth presented in the film *The Gods Must Be Crazy*, the world is not turned upside down by the introduction of a minor artifact of Western society. The Ju/'hoansi of Botswana drink soda pop and still conduct trance dances, still complain about those who do not share, and still care for their elders.

Of more far-reaching significance for the Dobe area in general and elder care in particular are the major infrastructural transformations in subsistence patterns; integration into state educational, legal and medical systems; the role that tuberculosis and alcohol consumption play; and the transformations in southern Africa as a whole with the end of the war in Namibia and the fall of apartheid in South Africa. These new elements in the Ju/'hoansi world create unpredictable challenges. For the time being they are meeting these challenges with a powerful cultural pattern of sharing/complaining—one that can still produce the following discourse, The speaker is N≠isa, a 60-year-old woman in /Gausha, Namibia, recorded by Megan Biesele in 1987:

> Here are words about caring for an old person. Words like if a person is old, you take care of her. You put your heart into it, and scold others, saying, "Don't you see this person is old? Take care of her today, you take care of her today. Do you say she has strength? She has no strength. Now you put your heart into her." That's what you say to another person. You're telling him/her to put his/her heart into an old person. That's what you say. . . . Now I'm finished.

8/Conflict, Politics, and Exchange

Before their incorporation into the Botswana polity, the Ju/'hoansi were a people without a state; they had no overriding authority to settle disputes, maintain order, and keep people in line. Whatever order there was had to come from the hearts and good-will of the people themselves. This was no small task. The Ju/'hoansi, like all of us, are subject to the emotions that afflict people who live in social groups: anger, jealousy, rage, greed, and envy, to mention a few.

Yet the Ju/'hoansi managed to live in relative harmony with a few overt disruptions. How the Ju/'hoansi and people like them could live as peacefully as they did has puzzled and mystified observers for decades. Understanding their methods of handling conflicts is the purpose of this chapter.

First let us look at the Ju/'hoan system of ownership and leadership; then we will go on to look at conflict and violence, and, finally, at the mechanisms the Ju/'hoansi have evolved to maintain peace.

OWNERSHIP AND LEADERSHIP

Groups of people, not individuals, own the land among the Ju/'hoansi. Each waterhole is surrounded by an area of land with food and other resources that a group depends on. This territory, or *n!ore*, is owned by a group of related people who collectively are called the *k"ausi* (owners). It is these people to whom you must go for permission if you want to camp there. Under most circumstances this permission is rarely refused.

The Ju/'hoansi regard the *n!ore* as their storehouse or larder, and if food runs out in one *n!ore* all people have a claim on the resources of several other *n!ores*. The principle of reciprocity specifies that if you pay a visit to my *n!ore* in one season, then I will pay you a visit in another. In this way, guest and host relations balance out in the long run. As a result, there is rarely any cause for conflict over land among the Ju/'hoansi.

I was fascinated by the smooth way these permissions were granted, and I kept asking the Ju to explain how the system worked. /Xashe, a 40-year-old /Xai/ xai man and a superb hunter, explained it this way:

> /Xashe: When I want to hunt at ≠Toma/ twe's *n!ore* I say, "My *!kun!a,* I would like to hunt on your ground." ≠Toma would reply, "My *!kuma,* I'm hungry too, tomorrow you hunt and we will eat together."

RBL: How would you split up the kill?

/Xashe: I would take a portion and give the rest of the animal to the *n!ore* owner. In my own *n!ore,* //Gum// geni, all others have to ask my siblings and me for permission. I have refused some people. For example, I once refused / Twi from Due. We lived together but we didn't get along. He was selfish to me. When he distributed the meat he would get mad and not give me any; so I refused him.

RBL: Are *n!ores* ever owned by one person?

/Xashe: Never, even if you are the oldest you always say this *n!ore* is your siblings'.

RBL: Is it only siblings who own it?

/Xashe: No, other family members can also own the *n!ore.* They don't ask us permission. They just tell us, "We are going to the *n!ore."*

Every Ju/'hoan has rights to at least two *n!ores,* the father's and the mother's. Wherever a person is living will be the strongly held *n!ore,* and the other will be weakly held. With marriage a claim is also established to the spouse's *n!ore,* and in the course of visiting and of siblings' and children's marriages, other *n!ores* become part of your universe.

The Problem of the Headman

We have seen that mechanisms exist for owning and using the land, but how are the major decisions arrived at? How is order and harmony maintained without formal political institutions? Some early observers of the Ju/'hoansi reported the existence of chiefs or headmen, who held political power among the !Kung as a first among equals (Schapera, 1930; Fourie, 1928). Lorna Marshall in her earlier writings (1960) spoke of a !Kung headman in whom resided the ownership of the group's resources and who inherited his position patrilineally.

If a headman existed, I resolved to find him, and in 1964 I set out to do just that.

After reading Marshall's 1960 article and the earlier writings of others, I made widespread inquiries in the Dobe area to find out who was the headman or chief (// kaiha) at each waterhole. The answers people gave were almost entirely negative. The younger people did not know who, if anyone, was the headman, and the older people were obviously puzzled by the question. Some people offered a variety of names, but most answered that the only headman they knew of was Isak, the Black headman sent out by the Tswana chief. Finally I discussed the question with K"au, a senior /Xai/ xai man originally from /Gam. "Before the Tswana came here," I asked, "did the San have chiefs?"

"No," he replied. "We had no one set apart like a chief; we all lived on the land."

"What about /Gaun!a? Was he a chief of /Xai/ xai?" I asked citing the name of a man the Herero had mentioned as a former San headman.

"That is not true," K"au responded. "They are mistaken. Because among the Blacks the chief's village is fixed; you come to him, speak, and go away. Others come, speak, and go. But with us San, we are here today, tomorrow over there, and the next day still elsewhere. How can we have a chief leading a life like that?"

"If the San have no chiefs," I asked, "then how did /Gaun!a come to be labeled as the chief here?"

"I can tell you that. /Gaun!a was living at /Twihaba Caves east of /Xai/ xai when the Blacks came. They saw evidence of his many old campsites and so they called him '// *kaiha.*' But they named him something that no Ju/'hoan person recognizes.

"But even that is lies," the old man continued, "because /Gaun!a was not even the real owner of /Twihaba! His proper *n!ore* is N!umtsa, east of /Gam. /Twihaba properly belongs to the people of a ≠Toma whose descendants now live mostly in the east."

Other Ju informants corroborated K″au's statements about the absence of a headman among themselves, but the most striking confirmation of the point came from a conversation with another K″au, a short, lively Dobe resident nicknamed Kasupe who had originally come from the Nyae Nyae area. In her detailed discussion of the headman, Lorna Marshall (1960:344–352) had used the /Gausha waterhole as a prime example. The headman of /Gausha, according to Marshall, was one Gao who "chose to renounce his headmanship and to live with his wife's people in [Dobe]. . . . However, should Gao change his plan and return to Band 1, the headmanship would automatically fall on him again, as he is the eldest son" (1960:350).

Marshall's Gao turned out to be none other than our K″au (Kasupe), living at Dobe. When I asked him how it felt to be the absent headman of /Gausha, he expressed surprise, shock, disbelief, and then laughter. With a keen sense of the irony of the situation, Kasupe insisted that he was in no way the headman of /Gausha; the Ju/'hoansi did not even have headmen. If they did, he, Kasupe, would be the headman of //Karu, not /Gausha, because the former was his father's true *n!ore.* Finally, asked Kasupe, if he was such a headman, how did it happen that he, the boss, was living in rags at Dobe, while underlings like his brother and sisters were living in luxury at the South African settlement of Tjum!kui?

Kasupe's genuine surprise at being named the headman of /Gausha, along with the abundant corroborating evidence from other informants, convinced me that indeed the Ju/'hoansi have no headmen. Years later, speaking with /Twi!gum, one of the owners of !Kangwa, I casually asked him whether the Ju/'hoansi have headmen.

"Of course we have headmen!" he replied, to my surprise. "In fact, we are all headmen," he continued slyly. "Each one of us is headman over himself!"

It is clear that, as K″au suggests, the headman concept probably came into existence as a result of contact with the Blacks, who wanted to incorporate the Ju/'hoansi into their hierarchical system, and *not* as a result of indigenous Ju/'hoan politics.

The Ju living groups do have leaders who may develop considerable influence in group decisions. These leaders work in subtle ways; they are modest in demeanor and may never command, but only suggest, a course of action. There is no hereditary basis to their role, and as often as not they are outsiders—men who have married into a group of *n!ore* *k″ausi* (landowners). This absence of hereditary leadership works for the !Kung, but it is a mixed blessing. When fights do break out there is no one within Ju society with the force of law behind him or her to separate the parties and reach a settlement. Both the strengths and shortcomings of the egalitarian society are illustrated in the following account.

A FIGHT ABOUT ADULTERY

N≠isa was a beautiful married woman in her early twenties with a reputation for jealousy. Following the birth of her daughter in late 1967, she became subject to bouts of depression. For weeks she was brooding and sullen, and finally, on a very cold, clear night in late June 1968, as the Dobe people huddled around their fires, her anger boiled over. She started declaiming to the village at large that her husband had shamed her. She said dirty women with long black labia (a grave insult) were screwing him. She knew who they were and was going to name names. The camp was in an uproar. She began shouting insults at several of the other young mothers in the village, accusing them in the most vulgar language of having relations with her husband. Amid heated denials from the other women and the group in general, N≠isa then shouted that she was so ashamed that she was going to throw herself into the fire. She stood up and dove into the flames, only to be caught by three other women, who leaped up to restrain her. Finally Kwoba, one of the accused women, could take it no longer. She rose from the other side of the fire and came over to N≠isa and slapped her hard on the face. N≠isa jumped up and started grappling with her as other women intervened to lift the now-screaming infants off the women's backs. In a few minutes the fighters were pulled part, but the shouting and recriminations continued. N≠isa's husband Kashe angrily denied the accusations, while the other men urged that Kashe give N≠isa a good thrashing for causing so much ruckus. The accused, Kwoba, repeated over and over, *"Au zhi! Au zhi!"* ("She lies, she lies"), and others said, "This girl is the jealous type. This isn't the first time this has happened."

The cooler-headed observers agreed that N≠isa's suspicions were unfounded. Kashe was a serious-minded husband and father and, unlike some of his peers, was *not* running after other women.

By midnight the Kalahari subfreezing night had brought the conversation to a halt. The next morning, N≠isa and Kashe left Dobe with their infant daughter for a three-day visit to another waterhole. In later weeks the couple continued to live in harmony without further incidents, and N≠isa tried to mend fences with the women she insulted, who in turn were quick to forgive her.

LAUGHTER AND DANGER

The fight between N≠isa and Kwoba was typical of the dozens of minor and major fights we witnessed or recorded in interviews.[1] Far from being harmless, the Ju/'hoansi can be scrappy and violent, and the violence sometimes leads to fatal results. My research on the period 1920–1955 turned up 22 cases of homicide, and although homicide ceased between the mid-1950s and the mid-1970s, and in the 1990s, it flared up alarmingly in the late 1970s (see Chapter 12).

Given the lack of property and the widespread practice of sharing, what is there for the Ju/'hoansi to fight about? And given the lack of governmental structures, when fights do break out, what prevents them from escalating out of control? We will try to answer these questions in the remainder of this chapter.

Four years before my arrival at Dobe, Elizabeth Marshall Thomas (1959) published *The Harmless People,* a book on the !Kung that portrayed them as likable and inoffensive people who posed no threat to their neighbors. The phrase "harmless people," which has since become famous, is Thomas's free translation of their term for themselves, *zhu/ twasi,* meaning "true or genuine people" or "just folks."

---

[1]Eighty-one disputes were recorded in all, including 10 major arguments without blows, 34 involving fights without weapons, and 37 with weapons.

I was attracted by the characterization of harmlessness and was disposed to believe it. It seemed to correspond to Rousseau's eighteenth-century characterization of the "noble savage," a view of "primitives" with which I was in sympathy at the time. But my early fieldwork interviews turned up pesky and oblique references to a Ju/'hoan past that was decidedly not "noble" and that was out of kilter with the harmless image. Informants would preface remarks about some past event with statements like, "It was the year of the big fight at /Xai/ xai," or "the year I married was the year that / Gau killed Kashe," or "My child was born the year after the Nyae Nyae people killed So-and-so."

After first ignoring these signals as evidence at odds with my prior position, I soon reversed my field and decided to make a systematic study of conflict and violence. My reasoning was as follows: because a body of evidence contradicts my *a priori* belief is *precisely* the reason to investigate it. (This advice, given by Charles Darwin in the introduction to *The Origin of the Species* [1859], is good advice for all scholars to follow.) I systematically began inquiring about homicides and gradually, reluctantly, people began mentioning cases. In all, 22 cases of homicide came to light, and 15 other cases of nonfatal fights, most of which had happened 20 to 40 years before, but some as recently as 8 years before my arrival. But I also found that the Ju/'hoansi had many mechanisms for controlling aggression and preventing serious fights from breaking out.

The Ju/'hoansi distinguish three levels of conflict: talking, fighting, and deadly fighting. A *talk* is an argument that may involve threats and verbal abuse but no blows. A *fight* is an exchange of blows without the use of weapons. And a *deadly fight* is one in which the deadly weapons—poisoned arrows, spears, and clubs—come out. At each stage attempts are made to dampen the conflict and prevent it from escalating to the next level. It will be useful to look at each level in turn.

Ju/'hoansi are great talkers. They may be among the most talkative people in the world. Much of this talk verges on argument, often for its own sake. Improper meat distribution, improper *hxaro* gift exchange, and laziness or stinginess are the most frequent topics of dispute (see Chapter 7). The Ju call these *horehore* or *obaoba,* meaning "yakity-yak": heated but good-natured conversations often punctuated by laughter. However, there is more to them than meets the eye. Simply because these arguments happen to be funny doesn't mean that they lack seriousness. In fact, they proceed along the knife-edge between laughter and danger.

When real anger replaces joking, a "talk" (*n≠wa*) ensues—an outpouring of angry words delivered in a stylized staccato form. John Marshall's film *An Argument About a Marriage* is a good example of the *n≠wa* form. (See Film Guide.)

The *n≠wa* may escalate further to become a very grave form of argument, involving sexual abuse or *za.* The *za* form occupies the ambiguous position of being both the highest form of affectionate joking in the "joking relationship" (Chapter 5) and the deadliest affront, leading directly to fighting. Male examples include the insult, "May death pull back your foreskin," and female forms include, "May death kill your vagina," and "long black labia." Hurling a *za* insult arouses intense feelings of anger or shame and may lead directly to a fight.

Ju/'hoan fights involve men and women in hand-to-hand combat while third parties attempt to break them up (or in some cases, egg them on). In 34 fights recorded, 11 involved men only, 8 were between women, and 15 were between men and women.

Two men fighting. The fight was broken up before the deadly weapons came out.

Fights are of short duration, usually two to five minutes long, and involve wrestling and hitting at close quarters rather than fisticuffs. Fighters are quickly separated and forcibly held apart; this is followed by an eruption of excited talking and sometimes more blows. Serious as they appear at the time, anger quickly turns to laughter in Ju/'hoan fights. We have seen partisans joking with each other when only a few minutes before they were grappling. The joking bursts the bubble of tension and allows tempers to cool off and the healing process to begin. Frequently the parties to a dispute will separate and go away for a few days or weeks to sort out their feelings. Fission is an excellent form of conflict resolution, and people like the Ju/'hoansi, with little investment in fixed property, find it easier to split up temporarily than stay locked together in a difficult argument. ≠Toma//gwe and his brother-in-law N!eishi have been coalescing and splitting for years. After an argument they might make separate camps for a few months, only to recombine in a single village the following season.

DEADLY COMBAT: JU/'HOAN STYLE

Despite the resort to laughter and fission as means of defusing conflict, not all fights are easily resolved. In all fights efforts are made to keep men between the ages of 20 and 50 apart. These are the people who possess the deadly poisoned arrows and other weapons, and are likely to use them. The pronouncement "We are all men here and we can fight. Get me my arrows." crops up in several accounts of fights. If this level is reached, the situation is out of control and the point of real danger to life and limb has been reached.

The period of my fieldwork, 1963–1969, was a time of relative peace. However, before 1955, poisoned arrow fights occurred somewhere in the Dobe or Nyae Nyae regions on the average of once every two years. My persistent questions succeeded in turning up 22 cases of homicide and 15 woundings during the period 1920–1955 (Table 8–1).

Fights usually broke out between men over a woman and, once started, might degenerate into a general brawl, as in this case (K1), which took place in the 1930s. Two men, Debe and Bo, were fighting for the hand of a woman, Tisa. This is a composite account given by two participants, Debe and Kashe, men now in their seventies. Debe reported:

> We were all living together at N≠wama. Bo started it by refusing me a wife. I wanted to marry Tisa, and her mother and father gave me permission, but Bo had already married Tisa's older sister and he wanted to take her as a second wife, so he refused me.
>
> There was a big argument, and fighting broke out. Bo yelled at my younger sister, "What is your brother doing marrying my wife? I'm going to kill you!" He shot an arrow at her and missed. Then Bo came up to me to kill me, but my father came to my aid. Then Samkau came to Bo's aid. Samkau shot at me but missed; my father speared Samkau in the chest under the armpit. Samkau's father, Gau, seeing his own son speared, came to his aid and fired a poisoned arrow into my father's thigh. I was shooting at Bo but missed him.

The narrative continues with the account of Kashe, the brother of Tisa:

> Then Debe's father, Hxome, stabbed at Gau with his spear. Gau put up his hand to protect himself and the spear went right through it. Samkau rushed at Hxome with his spear and tried to spear him in the ribs. At first the spear jammed, but then it went through.
>
> In the meantime several side fights were going on. My older brother dodged several arrows and then shot Debe's sister in the shoulder blade (she lived). I dodged arrows by two men and then hit one of them in the foot with a poisoned arrow.
>
> After being hit with a poisoned arrow in the thigh and speared in the ribs, Hxome fell down, mortally wounded. Half-sitting, half-lying down, he called for allies. "I'm finished, my arms are stilled. At least shoot one of them for me."
>
> But no more shooting happened that day. We went away and came back the next morning to see Hxome writhing in his death throes. He had been given cuts to draw off the poison, but the poison was in too deep, and he died. We left N≠wama and all came back to /Xai/ xai.

This case illustrates some general features of Ju arrow fights. First, the protagonists are members of closely related living groups. A second point concerns the rapid escalation and drawing in of more participants and the unpredictable outcome. None

TABLE 8–1   !KUNG HOMICIDE CASES 1920–1955

Code No.	Situation
K1*	In a general brawl over a martial dispute, three men wound and kill another east of /Xai/xai (1930s)
K2*	By general agreement, the senior of the three killers in K1 is himself killed in retaliation (1930s)
K3	The notorious /Twi kills a man in a spear fight (/Du/ da area, 1940).
K4	The notorious /Twi kills a second man, an event that later leads to the killing /Twi himself (/Du/ da area, 1940s).
K5	In the course of being fatally attacked, /Twi manages to kill a third man and wound a woman (/Du/ da area, 1940s).
K6	The killer /Twi is ambushed and wounded and then killed by the collective action of a large number of people (/Du/ da area, 1940s).
K7	In a sneak attack one man kills another over the latter's wife. Wife first runs away with the killer, but becomes frightened and returns alone (≠To//gana, 1940s)
K8	A young man kills his father's brother in a spear fight, the closest killer–victim kin connection in the sample (/Du/ da area, 1930s).
K9	A man accuses another of adultery. In the ensuing fight, the accused adulterer is wounded, but succeeds in killing the husband (Bate, 1930s).
K10	In anger over her adultery, a man stabs and kills his wife with a poisoned arrow and flees the area (/Xai/ xai, 1920s).
K11	≠Gau from Tjum!kui kills a /Gausha man with a spear to initiate a long sequence of feuding (Nyae Nyae area, 1930s).
K12	≠Gau's enemies attack him in retaliation, but ≠Gau kills a second man in the attempt (Nyae Nyae area, 1930s).
K13	A relative of ≠Gau's is killed in an earlier fight that is related to K11 and K12 (Nyae Nyae area, 1920s).
K14	≠Gau's enemies attack him a second time at a place called Zou/ toma, and ≠Gau kills a third man; two others are killed the same day; K15, K16. (Nyae Nyae area, 1930s).
K15	The attackers kill a woman bystander of ≠Gau's group in the arrow fight at Zou/ toma (1930s).
K16	The attackers fail to kill ≠Gau himself at Zou/ toma, but they do kill another man of his group (1930s).
K17	A young man not of the /Gausha groups kills ≠Gau in a sneak attack, finally eliminating an unpopular man (1940s).
K18	The younger brother of ≠Gau is attacked by another man in an argument, but in the ensuing fight, the man's wife is killed. ≠Gau's brother goes to jail in South-West Africa for this crime (1950s).
K19	Returning home from jail, ≠Gau's younger brother is met on the road and killed by relatives of the victim in K18 (near South-West African farms, 1950s).
K20	A Black settler was having an affair with a !Kung man's wife. Catching them *in flagrante,* the husband shoots and kills the man. The killer is later jailed in Maun, Botswana (!Kubi, 1946).
K21	A young man kills an older man with a club in a general brawl. The killer is later jailed in Maun (1952).
K22	In a general brawl a young man and his father kill a /Xai/ xai man. Later both are taken to jail in Maun (1955; the last case of !Kung homicide in the Dobe area until the 1970s.

*This case is discussed in detail in the text.

of the four wounded were even principals in the original argument between Bo and Debe over the woman Tisa. Another general feature is that deadly fighting is almost exclusively a male occupation. All 25 of the killers in the 22 cases were male, as well as 19 of the 22 victims. Of the three female victims, only one was a principal in a conflict; the other two were unfortunate bystanders. This contrasts sharply with the high level (25 to 50 percent) of female homicide victims in most Western societies. It may reflect women's high status in Ju/'hoan society (see Chapter 6).

The main weapons used are poisoned arrows, employing the same lethal poison used to kill game. Since a 200-kilogram buck will die within 12 to 24 hours, one can imagine the effects on the body of a human weighing 50 kilograms. Even with prompt treatment, a person shot with a poisoned arrow has only a 50/50 chance of survival.

The popularity of the poisoned arrows puzzled me. Why, I wondered, didn't the men fight with unpoisoned arrows and thus reduce the risk of death? To this question, one informant offered an instructive response: "We shoot poisoned arrows," he said, "because our hearts are hot and we really want to kill somebody with them."

Because of the very nature of homicide, when one killing takes place it is hard not to follow it with another, in retaliation. Feuds, in fact, accounted for 15 of the 22 killings. In only 7 cases was a homicide not followed by another—and another. In one dramatic series 9 people were killed in Nyae Nyae in a series of related feuds over a 20-year period (Lee, 1979:390–391), and other feuds involved another 6 victims. The prevalence of feuds brings us back to our original question: Once the Pandora's box of violence is opened, how is it possible for people to close it down again in the absence of the state or an overriding outside political authority?

The Ju/'hoansi do have one method of last resort, a trump card, for bringing a string of homicides to an end. I listened with amazement to my informant Debe as he unfolded an incredible tale of passion and revenge. This is a continuation of the case discussed above.

> After my father's murder, Debe, a man who was my *!kun!a* [older namesake] complained, "Now my namesake Debe has no father, but Samkau still has a father. Why is this?"
>
> I said, "You are right. I am going to kill Bo, who started it all."
>
> "No," Debe said, "Bo is just a youngster, but Gau is a senior man, a *n!ore* owner, and he is the one who has killed another *n!ore* owner, Hxome. I am going to kill *him* so that *n!ore* owners will be dead on both sides."
>
> One evening Debe walked right into Gau's camp and without saying a word shot three arrows into Gau, one in the left shoulder, one in the forehead, and a third in the chest. Gau's people made no move to protect him. After the three arrows were shot, Gau still sat facing the attacker. Then Debe raised his spear as if to stab him. But Gau said, "You have hit me three times. Isn't that enough to kill me, that you want to stab me too?"
>
> When Gau tried to dodge away from the spear, Gau's people came forward to disarm Debe of his spear. Having been so badly wounded, Gau died quickly, but made no further move to harm Debe. However, fearing more trouble, some of our people brought in the Tswana man Isak to mediate the dispute.

The only word to describe the events above is an execution. There is no other explanation for the fact that Gau's people made no move to aid him as Debe walked into camp and killed him. This was not an isolated case: a similar outcome ended the careers of three other men, all of whom had killed before.

In the most dramatic case on record, a man named /Twi had killed three other people, when the community, in a rare move of unanimity, ambushed and fatally wounded him in full daylight. As he lay dying, all the men fired at him with poisoned arrows until, in the words of one informant, "he looked like a porcupine." Then, after he was dead, all the women as well as the men approached his body and stabbed him with spears, symbolically sharing the responsibility for his death.

I find this image striking. It is as if for one brief moment, this egalitarian society constituted itself a state and took upon itself the powers of life and death. It is this collective will in embryo that later grew to become the form of society that we know today as the state.

THE END OF THE FIGHTING

In recent years the presence of outsiders—Tswana and Herero—has had an important modifying effect on the way the Ju/'hoansi handle conflict. Since the appointment of Isak Utugile as headman at !Kangwa in 1948, Ju have preferred to bring serious conflicts to him for adjudication rather than allow them to cross the threshold of violence. The *kgotla* "court" has proved extremely popular with the Ju/'hoansi, and Tswana and Herero at other waterholes frequently act as informal mediators in Ju/'hoan disputes. Many speak of the bringing of the *molao* "law" to the district as a positive contribution for the Batswana. A number of the Ju men have become knowledgeable in some of the finer points of Tswana customary law.

The reason for the court's popularity is not hard to find: it offers the Ju a legal umbrella and relieves them of the heavy responsibility of resolving serious internal conflicts under the threat of retaliation. The court has also provided the Ju/'hoansi some protection against unfair treatment and land grabs at the hands of the Black settlers (see Chapter 10). On the other hand, the impact of outside law should not be overestimated. Two homicides occurred in the Dobe area after the headman's appointment, and in Nyae Nyae one offender was killed *after* he had been jailed by the South African authorities. Recently the Ju/'hoan homicide rate has flared up again at the South African–run settlement in Namibia (see Chapter 12, p. 176), and violence continued into the 1990s after Namibia's independence.

HXARO EXCHANGE

Despite their occasional flare-ups of violence, the Ju/'hoansi do manage to live in relative harmony. We have already touched upon some of the ways the Ju limit violence: the use of talking and joking to avert a fight or limit its seriousness, and the use of group fission to separate parties in conflict. But the major means of maintaining and fostering amicable relations between groups is through gift-giving (see L. Marshall, 1976). The Ju/'hoan system of gift exchange, called *hxaro,* is a far-reaching and ingenious mechanism for circulating goods, lubricating social relations, and maintaining ecological balance. Polly Wiessner, who has studied *hxaro* in detail, aptly calls it a mechanism for reducing risk.

Hxaro in its essentials is a delayed form of nonequivalent gift exchange: I give you something today, and you give me something in return six months or a year from now. What you return does not have to be of precisely equivalent value as long as things balance out in the long run. The Ju/'hoansi make a sharp distinction between barter and *hxaro*. A barter exchange requires an immediate return of equivalent value. *Hxaro* requires neither. The key to understanding *hxaro* is that, unlike our system of economic value, which is primarily about the exchange of goods and services for money, the Ju/'hoan system is primarily about *social relations* and the goods themselves are of secondary importance.

The clue to this came to me when I was discussing *hxaro* with !Xoma, a wise and dynamic man then in his forties, a leader of one of the Bate camps.

"*Hxaro*," said !Xoma, "is when I take a thing of value and give it to you. Later, much later, when you find some good thing, you give it back to me. When I find something good I will give it to you, and so we will pass the years together."

"How close or similar should my return thing be to the one you gave?" I asked !Xoma.

"We can be living close together or far apart," said !Xoma, apparently misunderstanding my question.

Rephrasing, I asked again, "If you gave me a big thing and I gave you a small thing, would that be all right?"

"Yes, it would be all right," replied !Xoma patiently.

"And if you gave me a small thing and I have you a big thing?"

"That would be very good, if it is your heart," replied !Xoma.

I seemed to be getting nowhere. I tried another tack. "Let's say you gave me a spear and I gave you three strings of ostrich-shell beads, would that be all right?"

"Yes it would," replied !Xoma.

"What if I gave you two strings of beads?"

"Yes, that would be all right."

"One string?"

"Yes."

"What about four or five strings?" I was getting desperate.

!Xoma broke into a broad smile. "I see what your problem is! /Tontah, you don't understand our way. One string, five strings, any return would be all right. You see, we don't trade with things, we trade with people!"

Any two people, regardless of age or sex, may do *hxaro* together, but the most frequent partnerships radiate from the husband–wife relation. A typical pathway goes from mother to daughter, from daughter to husband, from husband to his father or mother, and beyond. In effect, the parents of a couple reinforce their relation by putting goods into circulation through their children. The gifts before marriage, called *kamasi* (see Chapter 6) set this pathway in motion, and the goods, of course, move in both directions. People also do *hxaro* with siblings and their spouses, with parents' siblings, and with more distant relatives.

Every item of Ju/'hoan material culture theoretically may be put into *hxaro: karosses,* dogs, pots, digging sticks, pipes, jewelry, and so on; but the most frequent *hxaro* items are ostrich-eggshell bead necklaces and other beadwork, made by women and traded by both men and women, and arrows, spears, and knives, made by men and traded by both sexes. A particularly popular class of *hxaro* goods has been items of European origin, especially clothing: hats, shirts, pants, dresses, scarves, and shoes; and iron cooking pots, enamelware, and other utensils. Glass beads of European origin (mostly Czech) are highly prized. Using beads of different colors, the women weave and sew intricately patterned headbands, which are a primary medium

/Xai/ xai woman making ostrich eggshell bead necklaces for hxaro.

of *hxaro* exchange. The designs are named and are original to the Ju/'hoansi; they constitute an indigenous !Kung art form. It is likely that European goods reached the Dobe area through long-distance *hxaro* networks long before the Europeans themselves arrived on the scene. The same was probably true for an even earlier period of goods of Bantu origin, such as pottery and iron knives, spears, axes, and arrowheads. Fragments of iron and pottery are found in small numbers on archeological sites in the Dobe area, indicating the presence of trade in prehistoric times. (See Appendix B for more on prehistoric trade.)

Two classes of things were not *hxaro*. Food was never *hxaro*ed, although it could be exchanged in other ways; and people were not objects of *hxaro*, not even in a joking or a metaphorical way. Such institutions as spouse exchange and marital exchanges existed and were thought of as forms of reciprocity, but they were part of a different symbolic system (see Chapters 5 and 6).

Hxaro goods could travel for very long distances. In fact, the Ju would draw diagrams in the sand of what they called *n≠amasi,* the roads or pathways along which goods traveled. A valued item might travel 200 kilometers over the space of two years, and change hands five times; or it could take three years to travel 100 kilometers and change hands only twice. These kinds of data are of great interest to archeologists (see Wiessner, 1977, 1982, 1986).

The Ju/'hoansi love to go visiting, and when they do, *hxaro* exchanges always play a part. In fact, it is not clear if the visit is the excuse for the *hxaro* or the *hxaro* is the pretext for the visit. When a family arrives in a distant camp, first they greet and eat,

A !Kubi woman lavishly adorned with hxaro *beadwork.*

then the next morning they do *hxaro*. Bags of goods are brought out and, one by one, handed over to individual partners with a phrase like "I take out this small thing to give you," or "I couldn't find a really good thing, I just brought you this." Care is usually taken to play down the value of the gift, even if it happens to be a nice one. Then, either at once or a day later, the return gifts are made. When I first saw items being exchanged, I assumed that the *hxaro* was a form of barter, but the Ju/'hoansi were quick to point out that I was mistaken. I was witnessing the halves of *two different transactions*. The first giving was the return gift of the *last* exchange, and the second was the opening gift of the *next* exchange.

The delayed aspect of the exchange was crucial to the !Kung. As one man told me, "If you give me something and I give you something back, we are even, we are finished. In *hxaro* you are never finished. One or the other is always waiting to see what comes back."

Occasionally the Ju/'hoansi had major gatherings, usually in winter, when up to 200 people from eight or more camps would get together for a few weeks. Here the *hxaro* trading would be intense, as people who hadn't seen each other in years would complete transactions and initiate new ones. Old people described the excitement of these events, when dances involving 100 participants would go on for two nights and a day.

Hxaro did not always go smoothly. If a gift did not come up to expectation, it could mean a *hxaro* partner was losing interest in maintaining the relationship and was allowing it to lapse. This was a major source of argument, but fights about *hxaro* were usually a symptom of an underlying conflict rather than a cause in themselves.

Hxaro partnerships could also lapse by mutual agreement. And this was common in later life. People from 30 to 60 were the most active in *hxaro*. As people grew older, they traveled less, and their *hxaro* networks shrank.

Ju/'hoansi bringing a dispute to the Tswana headman's court for adjudication.

Apart from age differences, not all Ju/'hoansi were equally active in *hxaro*. Some men and women had dozens of partners and were constantly on the go. Others maintained only a few close relations with whom they did *hxaro* regularly. I wondered whether the active *hxaro* partners were wealthier than the inactive ones. The Ju/'hoansi do have a word for wealth, "*// kai*," and a term "*// kaiha*," which can be translated either as "rich man" or as "chief." Hanging inside the huts of some of the active *hxaro* people was a bag or bags full of beadwork, ironware, and other valuables. These the people called *//kai*—wealth.

I asked !Xoma, "What makes a man a *//kaiha*—if he has many bags of *//kai* in his hut?"

"Holding *//kai* does not make you a *//kaiha*," replied !Xoma. "It is when someone makes many goods travel around that we might call him *//kaiha*."

What !Xoma seemed to be saying was that it wasn't the number of your goods that constituted your wealth, it was the number of your friends. The wealthy person was measured by the frequency of his or her transactions and not by the inventory of goods on hand.

In fact, according to the logic of the !Kung system, display of wealth would simply result in people asking you to give them the visible items. In Ju/'hoan custom it is very difficult to say no to such requests.[2] Therefore, any accumulation of wealth would be quickly dissipated.

Leveling of wealth differences, therefore, is one of the key functions that *hxaro* serves in Ju/'hoan life. Another function has also been mentioned: the obtaining of exotic goods that are not available locally through long-distance *hxaro*.

---

[2]The only way to say no to such requests is to say that you have already promised the item to another. The listeners will be observant that you keep your promise and will be quick to point it out if you don't.

Several other functions should also be mentioned. *Hxaro* relations give people an entrée into a number of different groups. Thus, in the event of local group conflict the parties may cool off by visiting other groups for the purpose of *hxaro*. This set of options is particularly important ecologically. As I pointed out in Chapter 4, the Kalahari has marked regional and annual variations in the density of plants and animals. A prized food may be rich in one area and completely absent in another. Or a local wild food crop might be abundant one year and scarce or absent the next. Given these conditions, it is essential that groups be able to adjust their numbers by moving to adjacent areas when things get rough. Kin ties maintained and reinforced by *hxaro* are the means by which the Ju/'hoansi are able to move when necessary to preserve ecological balance. In Polly Wiessner's words, *hxaro* is a mechanism for reducing risk by spreading it widely in the population (Wiessner, 1977, 1982).

In all societies, conflict and fighting are always a possibility between groups. We have seen how the Ju/'hoansi manage conflicts and, when they fail to manage, how conflicts escalate to dangerous and even fatal levels. *Hxaro* represents the other side of the coin: the long-term institutions for maintaining ties between the people, circulating useful goods, and spreading the risk of ecological disaster so that everyone may live with an adequate, if not luxurious, food supply.

9/Coping with Life: Religion, World View, and Healing

In previous chapters we have seen how the Ju/'hoansi manage to make a living from their semidesert environment, and how they organize their groups, arrange marriages, and deal with conflict. But like all people, the Ju/'hoansi live in a world of uncertainty, inhabited by forces beyond their control. Like all people they must face illness, misfortune, and the ultimate loss—death. Like others, the Ju/'hoansi seek to counteract these forces and gain what control they can over their lives. Death is inevitable. But the meaning people attach to death, its causes and aftermath, is culturally given. Without meaning, without culture making sense of things, life would be impossible.

The system developed by the Ju/'hoansi to make sense of their world involves forces beyond the natural order. Their universe is inhabited by a high god, a lesser god, and a host of minor animal spirits that bring luck and misfortune, success and failure. But the main actors in this world are the //gangwasi, the ghosts of recently deceased Ju/'hoansi. The //gangwasi, not long before the beloved parents, kin, and friends of the living, hover near the Ju villages, and when serious illness or misfortune strikes, it is almost always the //gangwasi who cause it.

The Ju/'hoansi are far from defenseless in the face of these malevolent spirits. They have many spells, herbs, magic formulas, and practices for restoring health or good fortune. And if these fail, the Ju have the powerful tool of *n/um,* the spiritual medicine or energy given by gods to men and women. Armed with *n/um,* specially trained healers are able to enter trances and heal the sick. They go to the //gangwasi and cajole, plead, argue, and, if necessary, do battle with them to make them give up their grip and leave the living in peace.

The healing trances take place at all-night dances, the major ritual focus of the Ju/'hoansi in the 1960s, 1970s, and 1980s. There are both men's and women's dances, and new manifestations of *n/um* with new rituals are constantly appearing as young healers experience revelations during dreams, trances, or illness.

Though deeply immersed in their own world view, the !Kung are pragmatic about other belief systems, or as they put it, about other forms of *n/um.* They are interested in and fearful of the witchcraft practices of their African neighbors. And they take a similar view of the disease theories and treatments brought by the Europeans. They may seek out both kinds of medicine when circumstances warrant it.

In this chapter we will begin by sketching out their world view and their theory of misfortune. We will then go on to look at two medicine dances in detail: the Men's Giraffe Dance and the Women's Drum Dance. Finally, we will look at the way

Ju/'hoan beliefs are attempting to accommodate the ideas and practices of the Blacks and the Whites.[1]

THE WORLD OF THE *//GANGWASI*

My introduction to the *//gangwasi* came in the winter of 1964. In early July I returned to Dobe after a month's absence to find that misfortune had befallen the people. Entering the village, I found Kasupe, the popular Dobe man whose relatives had figured prominently in the Marshall studies, lying in front of his hut surrounded by people. A curing ceremony was in progress even though it was the middle of the afternoon. While Kasupe lay prostrate, a small group of women sang and a healer worked over him, rubbing his body with sweat and moaning in a rising crescendo punctuated by sharp, high-pitched cries.

From his wife I pieced together what had happened to Kasupe. While out hunting two weeks earlier, he shot at and wounded a small duiker. Giving chase, he ran right into a steel trap set by the Herero for a lion. The jaws closed and tore deeply into his ankle. The pain must have been excruciating. Summoning all his strength, he pried open the jaws of the trap and freed his leg. Bleeding profusely, he staggered back to Dobe and collapsed.

I examined the wound. It was badly infected, wrapped with pieces of rag caked with dirt and blood. Fortunately, no bone seemed to be broken. The healer paused to rest while I peeled off the makeshift bandages, washed the wound, and applied a fresh dressing.

As I sat with him, he seemed to be resting peacefully, and some of the color started to come back into his face. I returned to my camp to unpack.

An hour later, ≠Toma//gwe burst into my hut crying, "/Tontah, come quickly, Kasupe is dying!"

I leapt up and followed ≠Toma//gwe at a dogtrot. Entering the camp, I saw a dramatic scene. Kasupe lay unconscious, totally drained of color, while his wife sobbed and his young children wailed. N!eishi was already entering into a trance and working on Kasupe, rubbing him, moaning and screaming. ≠Toma//gwe soon followed him, and the two old men worked over Kasupe for an hour, pulling out imaginary substances from his body and casting them away, standing up and going to the edge of the camp and speaking to themselves, and talking rapidly to each other in fragments of sentences that I could not understand. When Kasupe started to moan they redoubled their efforts until the air was pierced with shrieks and gurgles. Kasupe seemed to be breathing easier when they finished, but he was still a very sick man.

What had caused the relapse? And what were we to do with Kasupe? The nearest hospital was over 200 miles away. That evening, N!eishi, ≠Toma//gwe, and I sat down to discuss the possibilities.

≠Toma//gwe began. "It is not the leg that is killing Kasupe. I'm not sure, but when I was working on Kasupe I saw dead N≠isa. If not her, then another dead one is trying to kill him."

"How did you see her?" I asked.

---

[1]Some of these topics are also discussed in Katz (1982), Lee (1967), L. Marshall (1962, 1969), and Woodburn (1982). For a major study of Ju/'hoansi-!Kung religious practices, see L. Marshall (1999).

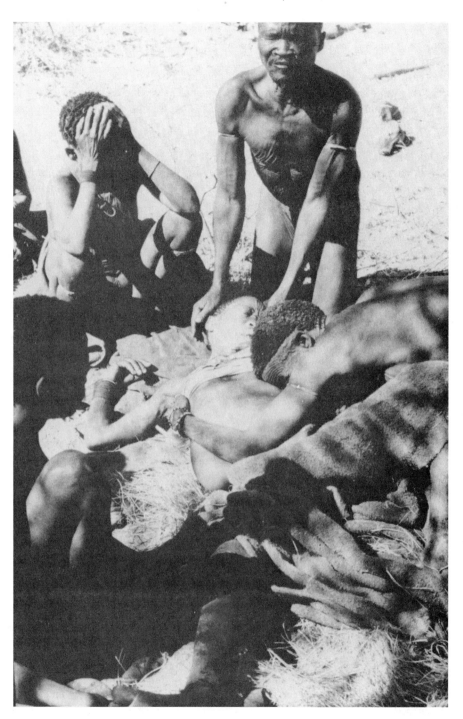

N!eishi and ≠Toma//gwe treating Kasupe on the day of the crisis.

"When we are *!kia* [in the trance state] we always change into something else. We can see things ordinary people can't. Today I saw dead N≠isa near Kasupe with an angry face."

"How do you mean, you 'change into something else'?" I asked.

"Your mind goes blank. You don't feel any pain. The ground seems to be spinning. We are different, a little bit like a ghost ourselves. And if the dead are there we can see them. We call them the *//gangwasi.*"

"Why is it that the dead come back to bother people?" That seemed the next logical question.

"I don't know why N≠isa is bothering Kasupe. When she was alive she was just a normal person, on good terms with Kasupe. But all the dead were good when they were alive. It is when they die that they turn bad.

"Sometimes God himself kills people; sometimes it is the *//gangwasi,*" ≠Toma//gwe continued. "All we can do is try to cure the sick ones. If we fail, then we know that the *//gangwasi* were too strong for us."

I wanted to ask more questions, but I also wanted to get to the matter at hand. "What do you think of Kasupe's chances?"

"We don't know," ≠Toma//gwe replied. "We try to chase N≠isa away, but she just comes back again. We chase her here and she reappears elsewhere."

N!eishi added, "Someone should go to Chum!we to fetch Kasupe's relatives. There are many big healers there among his kin, and it's important that they see him dying and take charge of him. If he dies with us, then his people might blame us."

I replied, "I don't know about *//gangwasi.* I only know that leg wound shouldn't kill a man. I can fix the leg with my medicines, but you will have to handle the *//gangwasi.*"

Both sets of healers did their jobs well. The next day Kasupe sat up and asked for food. The healers saw no signs of N≠isa, and his leg began to heal. Three months later he was hunting again, and he was still living 35 years after (well into his eighties).

What had healed Kasupe? I'm sure it wasn't the penicillin alone. Equally important was the fact that his family and campmates had stuck by him and the healers of the camp had protected his life with their healing energy.

High God–Low God

The Ju/'hoansi have not one origin myth but several. In one version, in the beginning, people and animals were not distinct but all lived together in a single village led by the elephant—K"au and his wife Chu!ko. A large body of myths revolve around the cast of characters inhabiting this village, including jackal, dung beetle, python, kori bustard, and many others.[2] In many of the stories a central character is the praying mantis, a trickster god who is always getting into scrapes and who usually gets caught and punished. The fact that the Ju/'hoan word for mantis is *//gangwa* has led some observers to conclude mistakenly that the San worship the mantis. In fact, the heavenly *//gangwa* is only remotely connected to the mantis.

[2]Biesele (1976, 1993) has made a major collection and analysis of Ju/'hoan myths.

The Ju/'hoansi have two major deities, a high god called //gangwan!an!a (big big god) and by other names, who is sometimes connected with the elephant K"au in the myths; and //gangwa matse (small //gangwa), the trickster god. The Ju/'hoansi volunteered the information that the English word for small //gangwa was Satan. How they made that connection, I do not know.[3]

There are varying opinions about the nature of these two deities. In some myths, the high god is portrayed as good and the lesser god as evil. In others the roles are reversed. Some Ju regard big //gangwa as a creator, remote and inaccessible, and see small //gangwa as the destroyer, the main source of death. Others insist that it is the high god who is both the creator and the killer. Whatever its ultimate source, the Ju do agree that the main agency that brings misfortune is the //gangwasi, the spirits of the dead.[4] Not *all* deaths are caused by the //gangwasi. If someone has lived a long life and died peacefully, they may simply say, "n/ a m a"—heaven ate her or him. But in most serious illness or accidents, //gangwasi are involved.

The healers in trance see the //gangwasi in a variety of forms. To some they look like real people. You can touch them and feel their flesh. To others, they appear like smoke, transparent and ephemeral. One healer described them as having only one leg, standing in midair. Some //gangwasi speak to the healers and give details of why they are there; most remain silent.

How Ancestors Become Enemies

What drives the dead to injure the living? This is a question I asked many Ju. Some said they didn't know why; others said it was in the nature of the //gangwasi to do so. There were a number of ways of propitiating the dead so that their spirits would not come back. Ensuring that they have a namesake in the name relationship (Chapter 5) is one such method, but it doesn't always work. Even spirits with namesakes have been known to bother the living.

For whatever reasons, not all //gangwasi are equally malevolent. Some never come back to make trouble, while others are major sources of misfortune. In a similar vein, some people during life led successful lives relatively free of care, while the lives of others were filled with suffering and misfortune. The Ju/'hoansi themselves were not sure why this was so. There seemed to be conflicting opinions on the question. For example, a man named Kumsa≠dwin (Kumsa "dog") first argued that //gangwasi don't bother those who behave themselves, but later he reversed himself.

"We don't see the //gangwasi," Kumsa said, "but we know that they expect certain behavior of us. We must eat so, and act so. When you are quarrelsome and unpleasant to other people, and people are angry with you, the //gangwasi see this and come to kill you. The //gangwasi can judge who is right and who is wrong.

"But," Kumsa continued, "although //gangwasi watch over people, we feel that people should try to settle their differences among themselves. Because sometimes the //gangwasi try to pick fights among people."

---

[3]There are many puzzling aspects of the High God/Low God dichotomy. In some myths there is only one god, leading me to wonder if the split isn't of recent origin.

[4]For a discussion of this question, see Marshall (1962, 1969, 1999), Katz (1982:34–57), and Guenther (1999).

"Doesn't this contradict what you were saying earlier, that the //gangwasi don't like people who fight?" I asked Kumsa.

Kumsa replied, "No, we have one story. The //gangwasi don't like us to fight, but they also make us fight.

"You see," he continued, "people have different types of //gangwasi. One may have bad //gangwasi, another may have good //gangwasi. People want good //gangwasi so you wake up in the morning and your heart wants to kill meat. Your //gangwa will help you in hunting.

"But you have no choice in your //gangwasi. You can't control them but must accept what they give you."

As Kumsa finished speaking, one of the listeners was visibly skeptical. "I don't know about these questions of good //gangwasi and bad //gangwasi, and not being able to control them. All I know is if I want something of my //gangwasi I just ask for it."

It is not surprising that the Ju/'hoansi hold seemingly contradictory views on these matters. The sources of good and evil and of luck and misfortune have been a topic of speculation of every major world religion. And the answers they give have not been conspicuously more successful than those of the Ju/'hoansi in unraveling the ultimate mysteries of life and fate.

The best answer I received on the question of why the living bother the dead came from Chu!ko, a vigorous woman in her sixties and an experienced healer.

"Longing," she said. "Longing for the living is what drives the dead to make people sick. When they go on the road that leads to the village of the //gangwasi they are very, very sad. Even though they will have food and company and everything they need there, they are not content. They miss their people on earth. And so they come back to us. They hover near the villages and put sickness into people, saying, 'Come, come here to me.' "

Chu!ko's answer made sense to me. She also spoke from experience. Recently widowed after 40 years of marriage, she had nursed her ailing husband for months, going into small trances almost nightly and pleading with the //gangwasi to spare him. Chu!ko's view, corroborated by others, made the process of death a struggle between two loving sets of relatives, one living and the other dead, each wanting the individual for themselves. The dying and those who survived them could take comfort from the sense that, whatever the outcome, the person would be in the bosom of loving kin.

Whatever the nature of their gods and ghosts, the Ju do not spend their time in philosophical discourse in the abstract (except when anthropologists prod them). They are more concerned with the concrete matters of life and death, health and illness in their daily lives, and at this level they have evolved an extraordinarily effective method of social healing based on the principle of n/um.

N/UM AND THE GIRAFFE DANCE

N/um[5] is a substance that lies in the pit of the stomach of men and women who are n/um k"ausi—medicine owners—and becomes active during a healing dance. The

---

[5]The n/um of the healing dance is just one of many forms of n/um. The word has a wide range of meanings for the Ju. N/um can mean medicine, energy, power, special skill, or anything out of the ordinary. Menstrual blood, African sorcery, herbal remedies, a vapor trail of a jet plane, tape recorders, and traveling in a truck at high speeds are just a few of the contexts in which the word n/um is used.

Ju/'hoansi believe that the movements of the dancers heat the *n/um* up, and when it boils it rises up the spinal cord and explodes in the brain. The *n/um* k"au then feels enormous power and energy coursing through his or her body. The legs are trembling, the chest is heaving, the throat is dry. And strange visions flood the healer's senses.

As one healer put it,

> *N/um* is put into the body through the backbone. It boils in my belly and boils up to my head like beer. When the women start singing and I start dancing, at first I feel quite all right. Then in the middle, the medicine begins to rise from my stomach. After that I see all the people like very small birds, the whole place will be spinning around, and that is why we run around. The trees will be circling also. You feel your blood become very hot, just like blood boiling on a fire, and then you start healing.

After a period of disorientation, the healer begins to move unsteadily toward the dance fire. He or she lays trembling hands on the chest and back of a person and begins a series of moaning lamentations punctuated by loud shrieks the Ju/'hoansi call *kow-he-dile*. She or he then moves to the next person and the next, repeating the action until everyone in attendance, men, women, and children, have received supernatural protection. If sick people are present at the dance, the *n/um k"ausi* will pay special attention to them, spending up to an hour working on one person, rubbing back, chest, forehead, legs, and arms with magical sweat. With the very ill, teams of up to six healers work in relays on several parts of the body at once. It is during these trances that the *//gangwasi* appear to the people.

In addition to their ability to see the dead, the healers have other healing skills. They are able to put *n/um* into the bodies of sick people and novice healers in the form of sweat. They can pull (*≠twe*) sickness out of the bodies. Like shamans elsewhere in the world, they describe these substances as having the physical form of needles, arrows, pebbles, and slivers, which only the healers can see. Third, they have the ability to speak to specific *//gangwasi* and argue with them. Lastly, they have a host of secondary skills involving knowledge of dietary prescriptions and prohibitions. As they put it, "we can tell the people how to eat properly."

Though not a central part of their ritual, the Ju men routinely walk in fire and handle live coals without burning themselves. It is mainly the less experienced healers who do this. They walk in fire because, as one told Dick Katz, "Because *n/um* is hot like fire it makes you want to jump in. Because you don't know what is fire and what isn't. But only the young ones without brains do this" (Katz, 1982:122).

How effective are these healing practices? Are the *n/um k"ausi* actually able to heal the sick by pulling out substances and by driving away the spirits of the dead? In thinking about this tricky question it is important to keep in mind that the !Kung healers operate with the same odds that medical doctors do: over 90 percent of all illnesses are self-limiting and would go away even if left untreated. With these kinds of odds to start off, the !Kung healers, like our own, have a high success rate.

The healing dances at which these performances take place are the main ritual activity of the Dobe Ju/'hoansi. They occur from once a month to several times a week, depending on the season, the size of the camp, and other factors. The presence of sickness is not the only reason for dancing. These dances serve a social as well as a sacred function. In fact, they are in many ways like a party—a time for relaxing, socializing, and letting off steam. The sacred and healing purposes of the dance do not seem to be

A healing dance at sunrise.

spoiled by the socializing; in fact, they may be aided by it. The Ju/'hoansi say the stronger the singing, the better the *n/um.*

The sacred dance fire is lit after sundown, and the women singers arrange themselves in a circle around it. Around the women, the men dance, beating a circular path in the sand several inches deep. There is a strict division of labor in the dance. The women sing and tend the fire, and the men dance and enter trances. Occasionally a woman will dance with the men for a few turns, and very occasionally a woman healer will enter a trance. However, the men insist that it is the women who are crucial to the success of the dance. Without their strong sustained singing, the *n/um* cannot boil and the men cannot heal.

The *n/um* songs, sung without words, have beautiful complex melodies. They include several versions of Giraffe and older songs, such as Gemsbok, Eland (my favorite), Mongongo, Rain, and several others. When I first saw Giraffe danced with its intricate melodies and rhythms, I assumed that it was a very old dance, going back beyond the memories of people. I was surprised to learn that, far from being old, the Giraffe Dance was invented by a man named /Ti!kay, who was still alive at Chum!kwe. He gave Giraffe and two other dances to the people after //gangwa had come to him in a dream. The basic dance form, however, must be very old. Prehistoric San rock paintings show people performing the same steps (Lewis-Williams, 1981).

The first few hours of the dance are relaxed and sociable. Then, nearing midnight, one or more men begin to show the signs of trance: glassy stares, intense footwork, and heavy breathing. They start to sweat profusely. The other men call to the women *gu tsiu, gu tsiu*—"pick it up, pick it up," and the women sing louder and more intensely. First one healer and then the others fall into trances and begin to cure. An ordinary dance might continue until two or three in the morning. On a good night the music and the singing will be so powerful that the dance is still going strong as the sun rises. On very special occasions a dance will go all night, right through the next day, and end the morning of the third day.

Becoming a Healer

Every young Ju/'hoan man aspires to become a healer, and a surprisingly large proportion of the men achieve this status. *N/um,* the Ju say, is not the exclusive possession of a few. It was given by //gangwa to all Ju/'hoansi. Almost half of the adult men have achieved the *!kia* (trance) state, and about a third of the women.

In seeking *n/um,* a young man must undergo a long and difficult training process. First he must find someone to train him—his father or uncle if they have *n/um,* or a nonrelated *n/um k"au.* The Ju/'hoansi discourage the very young or immature from seeking *n/um.* They say that achieving the *!kia* state is extremely painful and should not be undertaken lightly. At dances the novices can be seen dancing intensely, staring straight forward and not engaging in the social chatter of the dance. The teacher will usually go into a trance himself and then work on his pupil, rubbing sweat into key centers: the chest, belly, base of spine, and forehead.

But at a certain point one often sees the novices leave the dance and sit down at the edge trying to "come down" and regain their composure. They may reenter the dance, only to step out a few minutes later. I asked N!eishi, an experienced healer, why the novices always stop at this point. He replied, "*N/um* is not an easy thing. It is extremely difficult. As the *n/um* starts to build up inside you, the pain is intense. You are gasping for breath. You feel as if you are choking. The boys are afraid; they fear what will happen to them next."

"What are they afraid of?" I asked. "The pain? The unknown? The *//gangwasi?*"

"Death," replied N!eishi.

The state is indeed painful, as I discovered on my one attempt to enter *!kia.* On further questioning the healers I was able to get a better sense of what they feared. It seems that there is both a psychological and a physical barrier, on the one hand involving maximum physical exertion and on the other an acute fear of loss of control.

What *is* this barrier? I think the best way to understand it is to compare it to "the wall," the phenomenon marathon runners experience around mile 19 of a 26-mile run. You reach a point beyond which it seems physically impossible to go. If you do go on and finish the race, it is because you have tapped into physical and emotional resources you didn't know you had.

Achieving *!kia* for the first time seems to involve a similar kind of breakthrough. The young dancer must punch through his pain and anxiety by force of will to reach a new level of experience. This, I think, is what *!kia* and *n/um* are about. Even the most accomplished healers go through periods of doubt. As one man put it to Dick Katz,

N/um is hot; mine is hot too. Others who say it is not have deceived you. Those without *n/um* may look at those who do *n/um* and say, "Why can't I do like that?" Now if I tell them that it's very painful, they say, "Oh, you're just fooling me. I still want to do *n/um!*" But then when they start, they see how painful it is, and then they stop because they fear it. This is

A !Kung healer working himself into a !kia *state.*

how it was with me. I thought they were kidding me when they told me how painful *n/um* was. I tried *n/um,* and it was so painful that I stopped. And I even stopped going to dances for years because I feared *n/um.* Only after I got married did I try *n/um* again. This time [the pain] again came up in me, but I passed through it, and then *n/um* came to me. Now I have *n/um.* (Katz, 1982:119)

Entering *!kia,* however, is only the first step. Once in the trance, the novice's perceptions become acutely disoriented and his behavior becomes wild and erratic. He will run off into the bush, gashing himself on branches or thorns, or worse, dance through the *n/um* fire itself, showering burning coals in every direction. The healers say that the young ones are still afraid of *n/um;* they can't control it and must be restrained. The teacher, now aided by other men and women, force the young man to lie down. They massage his body vigorously, always from the extremities to the torso, and on the torso towards the stomach, symbolically working the boiling *n/um* back into its resting state in the pit of the stomach. (John Marshall's excellent film on the trance dance, *N/um Tchai* [1969] has a long sequence of a young trancer being aided in this way.)

With time, most of the men overcome their fear of *n/um;* they learn to control its effects and to make it work for them. (About a third of those who achieve *!kia,* however, do not continue on to become healers.) For those who succeed, the path is opened for them to explore new levels of reality and to perform a useful function for the community and for their families. Although they worry that the novice trancers will hurt themselves, parents are delighted when offspring become healers for, as one mother said,

> It is all right when they try to throw themselves into the fire. It shows the *n/um* is strong in them. This is good. If he has *n/um* he can take care of his children. If I am sick he can heal me.

THE WOMEN'S DRUM DANCE

In recent years a new dance has been gaining in popularity among the Ju/'hoansi. Beginning at the turn of the century and centered at the !Goshe waterhole, the Women's Dance, *!Gwah tsi,* has been spreading rapidly. It was unknown to the Marshalls during their Nyae Nyae fieldwork in the 1950s. It reached Chum!kwe during the 1960s, and since then it has taken on the character of a social movement, gaining new converts every year. During the 1980s and 1990s it even exceeded the Men's Giraffe Dance in popularity.

In *!Gwah tsi* the roles of the Giraffe Dance are reversed. Women dance and enter trances, and men play a supporting role, beating complex rhythms on the long drum that is the central symbol of the dance. Dances may be held weekly, and when the new form reaches a settlement, dances may occur nightly as new women join in. Typical dances involve 8 to 12 women, and several drummers working in relays. Two, three, or up to eight women may *!kia* at any one dance. Men enjoy the dance as drummers and spectators, and they may assist the women who enter trances.

Dances begin at nightfall, the sound of the drums summoning the people. The women arrange themselves in a semicircle, with the drummer off to one side. They sing the *!Gwah* songs and accompany the drumming with contrasting hand-clapping rhythms. Instead of dancing in a circle like the men, the women dance in one place with short steps, swaying from side to side. The onset of the *!kia* state is heralded by a bout of intense trembling in the legs. The woman staggers and is held up by the other dancers. After a few minutes the woman collapses into a full *!kia.*

The women say that the *!Gwah* medicine lies in the stomach and the kidneys. When they dance, it rises in two routes, up the chest and the backbone, and when active it lodges in the cervical vertebrae. In *!kia* the woman is rubbed and massaged by the other women, but no healing of the kind commonly seen in the Giraffe Dance occurs in the Women's Dance. This is a major difference between the two forms.

The Women's Drum Dance: !Gwah tsi.

Women entering *!kia* for the first few times seem to experience the same kind of pain and anxiety as the men do, but not to the same degree. They do not run off into the bush or try to fling themselves into the fire. They do behave erratically and thus require supervision. Frequently at this stage the helping women will cover the *!kia* woman's lap with a blanket and change her pubic apron. They say they do this because when a woman falls in *!kia* she is likely to expose herself.[6] The pubic apron of experienced women may be changed as well.

The *!Gwah tsi* is not primarily a healing dance as such, but rather a dance for introducing women to *!kia* and allowing them to go deeper into *!kia* in a supportive context. As one woman put it, "Most of us are just learning to *!kia.* We are new at entering it. It is like school for us. But the older ones do *kowhedile.*"

This is true. After a period of training, many women go on to become healers. At special healings, women healers are now active, performing the laying on of hands and the pulling of sickness and seeing the *//gangwasi,* just as the men do. Often men and women healers work in teams on seriously ill people.

The source of this power, the women claim, is the *!gwah* plant, a short, stiff, unidentified shrub. The roots are chopped up and boiled, and the tea drunk. It is only taken initially and not before every dance. So the active principle of the drug, if any, is not a prerequisite to *!kia.* I suspect that ingesting the infusion has a psychological rather than a psychochemical effect on the initiates.

The Drum Dance appears to have first entered the Dobe area from the east around 1915. The drum itself was borrowed from the Mbukushu, a Bantu-speaking farming

---

[6] *!Kia* experiences may also be symbolically connected with sexual arousal and orgasm.

people living in the Okavango swamps. The co-founder of the Drum Dance was a woman named /Twa, who was still alive in the 1960s. /Twa was generally acknowledged to be the most powerful healer, male or female, in the Dobe area. I interviewed her in 1964.

"The Drum Dance started with the Mbukushu, where my father was working," /Twa said. "The Ju/'hoansi used to build them for the Mbukushu, so when it came here we knew how to make them. The one who was responsible for bringing it here was my husband, /Gau, who was traveling around. We started Drum together."

For years the Drum Dance was confined to !Kangwa and !Goshe, and the main practitioners were /Twa, her two daughters, and the people of !Goshe. Starting around 1960, it began to spread west, reaching /Xai/ xai and Chum!kwe in the mid-1960s. When /Twa died in 1972 at an estimated age of 85, the dance had spread throughout the area and was rapidly supplanting the Giraffe Dance as the major Ju/'hoan ritual. At !Goshe today the women have even begun to admit men as trainees in a modified *!Gwah tsi* that contains elements of both male and female rituals. This mixed dance has also spread to other communities.

Other forms of new rituals appear from time to time among the Ju/'hoansi. A /Xai/ xai man named /Gaugo left the area to work on a contract as a mine laborer in Johannesburg. He experienced a revelation there and rested and brought a highly entertaining new dance form back to /Xai/ xai in 1967. Called Trees Dance, it involves a male leader barking orders in Fanagalong, the mine jargon, at a chorus line of women. The structure and premise of Trees Dance are strongly reminiscent of the famous Mine dances held in the mining compounds on Sundays. /Gaugo's male helpers at the dance are called "Bossboy" and "Foremana." The people of /Xai/ xai danced Trees Dance for days on end in 1967–1968.

THREE MEDICINES: ONE BLOOD

Earlier I mentioned that the Ju/'hoansi, though immersed in their own beliefs, are aware of and receptive to other theories of illness and health. Their Black neighbors, the Herero, Tswana, and Bayei, have well-developed beliefs in sorcery, and the Ju have been struggling to accommodate these within their own explanatory system. They are less impressed with European theories of disease causation, but they have easily accepted the efficacy of European medicines, particularly antibiotics.

/Twan!a, the most charismatic of the Ju healers, told me,

People were created by //gangwan!n!a with different things to use, different skins, and different medicines. The Blacks have their medicine in divination and sorcery, the Europeans have their medicine in pills and steel needles, and the San have their medicine in the form of *kowhedile*. Different medicine, very different ways of living. But when you cut any one of them their blood flows the same color.

During the time of my fieldwork, there had been no Western missionary work among the Dobe Ju/'hoansi, and thus there had as yet been no ideological attack from that quarter on Ju beliefs. The beliefs of the Blacks have offered a far more fundamental challenge to the Ju/'hoansi. Sorcery, the belief in the ability of one person to consciously do harm to another by magical means, explains misfortune in a very

/Twan!a putting n/ um into her pupil Chu!ko.

un-!Kung way. Central to Ju/'hoan belief is the concept of the *//gangwasi* as an external threat. The ghosts attack, and the living must unite to defend themselves. Thus the healing dance involves the whole body of the living in a struggle against an external enemy—the dead. Sorcery (and witchcraft) beliefs, by contrast, seek the source of misfortune *within* the community. A spouse, a kinperson, or a neighbor could be causing illness knowingly or unknowingly. Such beliefs set kin against kin and neighbor against neighbor. They divide the living into mutually suspicious camps and break down the solidarity of the community.

This new explanatory system now competes with the older theory of misfortune for dominance in Ju/'hoan thought. The struggle has put a great deal of strain on Ju social relations. Among the more acculturated Ju there is more interpersonal hostility, especially between the sexes. Beliefs in sorcery affect the Ju/'hoansi in several major ways. Some injuries and illnesses are interpreted to have been caused by Black sorcery. In other cases, Ju have sought out Black diviners who, in return for payment, have diagnosed the source of illness as coming from living relatives of the Ju/'hoansi. For further payment, the diviners will take appropriate countermeasures.

The flow of culture is not just one way. The Blacks are also impressed with Ju healing techniques and believe in their efficacy. Blacks frequently ask Ju healers to do a healing on their sick, and this type of work is usually accompanied by payment in cash or in kind.

That raises an interesting question: When Ju healers diagnose Blacks' illnesses, which theory of disease causation do they employ? Do they see the source of illness in terms of the dead or the living?

There is some evidence that they use both theories. Blacks are not adverse to concepts of misfortune deriving from ancestors. In fact, a new syncretic form of explanation has emerged that combines sorcery and Ju theories. A Ju/'hoan who is ill may accuse a Ju/'hoan neighbor of not propitiating his //gangwasi properly and of allowing them to bring sickness. Thus the source of illness remains the same—the dead—but a new element of human agency is introduced.

This kind of explanation is still not widespread, but it is becoming more common and may indicate a new, privatized theory of disease causation, congruent with new forms of private property and wage earning, where ownership is much clearer and the importance attached to sharing declines.

Another very important aspect of the changing conceptions of health and illness among the Ju/'hoansi is the new professionalism of the healers. /Twan!a was one of the first paid healers. She received goats, blankets, clothing, and money for her healing work with the Blacks. Other Ju healers have followed suit, even traveling to commercial farming areas in Botswana to perform healings for San and Black workers.

But their very success has put new strains on the healers in their relationship to the community. In the past, *n/um* was freely given, and the rewards to the healers were manifold and diffuse. Personal satisfaction, the love and respect of family, and the gratitude of those they had "saved" are some of the positive themes mentioned by healers in interviews. But the interviews contain another theme, a recurrent complaint about other Ju/'hoansi: they are *chi dole* (bad, strange) because they take the medicine for granted and don't pay for successful treatment. ≠Toma zho, a famous /Xai/ xai healer (see Katz, 1982:177–195), made regular trips to the Ghanzi farms to cure and dance because at /Xai/ xai "people haven't paid me anything."

When two cultures come into contact, the problem arises of translating values from one to the other. This translation concerns tangibles—for example, how much tobacco for one antelope hide—but it can also concern intangibles like healing "services." In our discussion of *hxaro* (Chapter 8), we saw how the essence of *hxaro* was to resist the idea of exact equivalences, focusing instead on the value of the *social* relationship with the *hxaro* partner.

Putting a price tag on a healing removes it from the communal sphere. Payment for healing validates the healer in a different way, marking the value of his treatment by price, and the higher the price, the better the treatment. But once the healer has been paid, it is difficult for him or her to turn around and "do it for nothing." When a healing is done for pay, it, in effect, belongs to the individual who paid for it, not to the community at large.

Not all healers share this view, however. Many continue to heal other Ju as they always have, for free. They deplore the fact that some of their fellow healers are holding back.

The Ju/'hoansi are rapidly entering the cash economy (see Chapters 11 and 12). The debate among healers illustrates graphically how individuals attempt to grapple at the level of consciousness with the wrenching changes that accompany the shift from a community-based economy to an economy based on the impersonal forces of the marketplace. It is this theme that we will address in the final chapters.

10/The Ju/'hoansi and Their Neighbors

Starting in the 1920s and especially since the 1950s, the Ju/'hoansi have shared the Dobe area with Herero and Tswana pastoralists. These were tribal peoples, speaking Bantu languages, whose lives were not so very different from that of the Ju. The Herero and Tswana grew crops, kept livestock, and made iron tools. However, their social systems, like that of the Ju/'hoansi, were based on kinship, and neither people had developed markets, monarchs, or elaborate craft specialization.

The Tswana lived in chiefdoms with the beginnings of internal stratification, and the Ju/'hoansi were immediately accorded a position at the bottom of the social scale, but in the Dobe area the San were not enserfed or enslaved; nor were they propelled into the cash economy. (The lively debate on this question is the subject of Appendix B.)

Though subordinate, the San were not simply servants of the Blacks. In the early days, Tswana and Ju men hunted side by side, each with bow and arrows, and in recent years Tswana and Herero women have been observed gathering wild plants alongside Ju women in times of drought.

Since the time of the first Black visitors in the nineteenth century, the Ju/'hoansi have been exposed to several important innovations: the use of metal tools and containers, the smoking of tobacco, and the raising of livestock and planting of crops. They adopted the first two with enthusiasm: iron tools and cooking utensils are universals among the Ju/'hoansi, and everyone smokes tobacco when they can get it. In fact, the two innovations are combined in the Ju's favorite smoking device, an empty rifle shell obtained from the Blacks with tobacco stuffed in one end and a grass stopper in the other. But the more basic economic changes of agriculture and livestock production did not take hold. By 1960 the Ju/'hoansi still remained largely hunter-gatherers without herds or fields. They have, however, established social and economic ties with the Blacks, and these ties are the subject of this chapter.

The chapter introduces the Herero and Tswana, details their interactions with the Ju, and explains how the lives of the Ju/'hoansi have been affected by living as hunters in a world of nonhunters.

INTRODUCING THE HERERO AND THE TSWANA

The Hereros are the largest group of non-!Kung in the Dobe area.[1] They are superb pastoralists, and their cattle herds number in the thousands. They also practice agriculture. They live in dispersed hamlets of two to six houses built around a cattle

---

[1]The Herero are composed of two main branches, the Herero proper and the Mbanderu, or eastern Herero. It is the Mbanderu who comprise the bulk of the Herero population in the Dobe area.

Herero and !Kung women.

kraal. They practice a system of double descent with an individual belonging to both his or her father's and mother's lineages. Women enjoy relatively high status and frequently own and inherit cattle. The women wear a characteristic dress adapted from the early German missionaries: full-length, gaily colored dresses with many underskirts and petticoats and a matching three-cornered headdress or *tuku*.

Speaking a southwestern Bantu language, the Herero migrated south from Angola several centuries ago into what is now central Namibia. Growing strong from a combination of extensive cattle pastoralism and raiding, the Herero were a powerful and populous presence in southwest Africa when the German colonists arrived in the 1880s. But the Germans, through force and trickery, steadily encroached upon the Herero lands. Finally, in desperation, the Herero arose in 1904 and killed some of the colonists. The Germans used this as a pretext for an all-out war of extermination. By the end of 1905, 60 percent of the estimated 80,000 Hereros had been killed by the Germans or had died of thirst in the Kalahari trying to escape the war. Several thousand survived the trek across the desert and sought refuge in the Tswana chiefdoms to the east, in the British sphere of influence. There the Herero survivors rebuilt their herds. It is the descendants of these refugees who form the bulk of the 250 Hereros who now live in the Dobe area. Work on the Herero cattle posts provides a major source of employment for the Ju.

The BaTawana, one branch of the powerful BaTswana chiefdoms, are the overlords of the region. Although numerically small in the Dobe area, they are large cattle-holders and until recently dominated the administrative posts at both the chiefdom and the national government levels. In the Dobe area they live in dispersed hamlets similar to those of the Herero (who in fact adopted their house type from the Tswana). Elsewhere in Botswana, the other Tswanas traditionally live in large towns of up to 20,000 people.

Tswana language, social organization, and, especially, legal code provide models for the Ju/'hoansi and other subject peoples to adopt. The court, or *kgotla,* of the Tswana headman has been an important element in dispute settlement since the 1940s (see Chapter 8).

The first Tswana reached the Dobe area in the 1870s on brief hunting expeditions (see Appendix B). By 1900 the area had been allocated to two powerful Tswana families in a kind of feudal tenure, one receiving the area north of the Ahas and the other the area to the south. Some decades passed before the first Tswana settled in the area.

In addition to these immigrants, there are small numbers of two other Bantu-speaking peoples in the Dobe area: the Mbukushu and the BeYei. Both live in the nearby Okavango swamps and are known collectively by the !Kung as *Goba,* a term generally applied to all non-Herero, non-Tswana Blacks.[2]

Actual settlement of the Dobe area by outsiders only began in the 1920s, and even by 1948, when a headmanship was established, the total number of non-!Kung residents probably was under 50. Since 1950 the numbers have steadily increased. Their presence has affected the Ju in several ways. The Herero and Tswana immigrants have built homesteads, deepened and fenced off the waterholes, hired Ju men as laborers, and in some cases have begun to court and marry Ju women. We will look at each of these impacts in turn.

ECOLOGICAL CHANGE

As the Hereros and Tswana came with their cattle to settle most of the waterholes of the Dobe area, major ecological changes occurred. First, they deepened the wells to ensure a water supply for their stock, and fenced off the deep pits to prevent the cattle from falling in. The !Kung have benefited in some ways from this work: it gives them a cleaner and more abundant water supply. But the presence of cattle has had the effect of lowering the water table and of turning once-verdant *melapo* into dustbowls.

---

[2]American Blacks, interestingly, are classified as Whites by the Ju. Japanese are called Machapani or the "ju/'hoan/onsi" (the San Europeans).

Ecological change: !Kung men watering Herero cattle from a deepened well.

The effect on vegetation and insect life has also been considerable. The cattle and goats have destroyed the grass and leafy shrub cover within a three-kilometer radius of the permanent waterholes, and a cover of thorny runners and bushes has replaced it. Also, each cattle-post has a massive permanent population of houseflies that people learn to tolerate. Farther afield, grass cover and game still persist, and here one can see the northern Kalahari environment as it used to be.[3]

Cattle and goats don't compete directly with humans for edible plant species. Animals cannot ingest, for example, the famous mongongo nut. Much of the Ju/'hoansi vegetable diet remains accessible to them despite the inroads of the cattle. At one waterhole, however, the cattle are a real menace. For reasons unknown, the cattle of /Xai/ xai have developed a taste for human clothing and will eat your laundry right off the line if left untended. Washing is jealously guarded, and some of the Ju have stockaded their camps to keep the marauders away. No one has suggested a plausible explanation for this puzzling phenomenon, which has been the subject of several cases in the tribal court. The local Tswana and Herero believe it is sorcery. The Ju and I were inclined to agree.

WORK RELATIONS

In 1968 there were 4500 cattle and 1800 goats in the Dobe area, and over 95 percent of those were in Tswana and Herero hands. These large herds could not be managed effectively by the Blacks themselves because they were so few in number, and so, many Ju men were brought into service as cowherds. The Ju, usually men between the ages of 15 and 25, but some much older, would work with the cattle owner, take their meals with the Herero family, and sleep in the Herero hamlet. Each worker was given a donkey to ride, a store-bought outfit of shirt, pants, and shoes, and a blanket to sleep on. If he was married, he could bring his wife and family to live with him. The wages, if any, were minimal, but at the end of a year's service, if his work was satisfactory, the herder might receive a female calf of his own as payment. If the calf survived to maturity and proved fertile, the offspring were also his, and with luck they could form the basis of a small herd. Because of high bovine mortality, however, this rarely occurred. The real advantage of employment for the Ju herdsman was not the long-term benefits, which were risky at best, but rather the short-term gain of being able to offer his relatives hospitality at the cattle post.

The Herero and Tswana lived in kin-based societies like the Ju/'hoansi, and they placed a high value on offering hospitality to visitors and neighbors. Every Ju in the Dobe area had a son, nephew, or other relative working for the Blacks, and all the San paid regular visits to one cattle post or another to drink the milk.

The milk is never taken fresh. It is always poured into large gourds or calabashes containing a yogurt-like bacterial culture. It may be taken as whole sour milk, or the

---

[3]In an ironic reference to the prevalence of cattle and their accompanying pests, Edwin Wilmsen titled his book on the Kalahari "Land Filled with Flies" (1989). However, in so doing, Wilmsen ignored the large stretches of the Kalahari, like the Dobe and Nyae Nyae areas, that were cattle-free zones until this century.

cream may be taken off to be churned into butter and the skim sour milk drunk. I found the whole sour milk (in Herero, *kamaihi,* in !Kung, *ku n!um*—literally, ripe milk) a tasty and refreshing drink like buttermilk. An Herero neighbor delivered a bottle of it to our camp every day. The skim milk, by contrast, was sour in the extreme, and only the hardy could enjoy it.

Another benefit of the Herero presence was the distribution of meat. Cattle from the large Herero herds sometimes fell prey to lions, leopards, or wild dogs. Whatever meat could be salvaged from the kill was distributed to the Ju. More frequently, especially in the spring, the cattle would eat an attractive but highly poisonous plant called *mogau* and would die from the effects. The meat was unaffected by the poison, and the Ju received the bulk of it. There were periods at /Xai/ xai when the consumption of beef from this source considerably exceeded the meat produced by the !Kung's own hunting efforts.

Although many Ju men worked for Hereros on the cattle and lived with them for years, few succeeded in becoming pastoralists in their own right. For most, working for the Blacks and being part of a client group was a phase in their lives. After a while they collected their families and possessions and returned to rejoin a parent's camp, a move which sometimes might take them only a few hundred meters away.

For some, the work relation evolves into a kind of clientship, which could be a lifelong relationship. The client and his master live side by side, their children grow up together speaking each other's languages, and for the Ju client a process of deculturation may begin. The Ju may begin to identify more closely with Herero than with Ju/'hoansi. In some cases this kind of co-residence and friendship leads to the marriage of Ju and Blacks.

Ju/'hoansi churning butter at an Herero village.

INTERMARRIAGE

In 1968 a small but significant number of Ju women, about eight in all, were married to Herero and Tswana men. In addition, there were many more cases of Herero and Tswana young men having affairs with married and unmarried Ju women. There were no Ju men married to Black women, although we did hear of a few affairs involving Ju men and Herero women.

Ju women marrying Black men faced a number of problems. First, there was the question of status difference: marrying a Black man was definitely a step up. As one Ju woman put it, "I married our masters." Second, there was the question of translating between the norms of the two kinship systems. How the Herero relatives would accept the Ju woman was one concern, but equal in importance was the question of how the Ju relatives would accept their Herero in-law. Finally, there was the question of the children: Would they be raised as Herero or Ju/'hoansi? Who would decide?

From the Herero point of view, marrying a Ju woman had advantages and disadvantages. Dobe was a frontier area with few amenities. The Herero settlers were far from the main Herero community. It was hard to convince a prospective Herero bride to come out to the Dobe area, far from relatives and friends. The Ju/'hoansi, by contrast, were right there and used to the rigors of bush life. In fact, they found life on a Herero cattle post downright luxurious. Second, marrying a Herero involved elaborate negotiations and the payment of a large bride price; no similar payment was required for a Ju/'hoan bride. Third, the Ju girls in their later teens were attractive and vivacious and were reputed by Ju and Herero boys alike to be good lovers.

But there were disadvantages as well. The Ju girls, though undeniably attractive, were by Herero standards free spirits. Herero gender relations were patriarchal, or at least *more* patriarchal than the egalitarian Ju/'hoansi. Despite their lower status in the eyes of the Herero, the Ju girls were not about to conform to the subservience and deference expected of them by their Herero in-laws. This was often a source of friction between Black husbands and their Ju wives.

The question of bride price was also a double-edged sword. The dilemma it created is discussed by Gutayone, a Tswana man who married a Ju woman and then found unexpected complications.

> When I married /Twa, at first we were very happy together. We loved each other and she worked hard around the house. But later when we had a fight she would go away and live with her people for weeks at a time. We always made up, and continued to live together well, but then I had a terrible thought: if we had children and had a fight, what would stop her from taking the children and leaving me flat? Nothing!
>
> Soon after that the matter came to a head when /Twa became pregnant. But what to do? I discussed it with my family, and my mother suggested we pay her people bride wealth (*bogadi*) for her. This would ensure that any children born would belong to our lineage. But another problem came up, who to give the *bogadi* to? /Twa was an orphan. Her parents and older brothers were dead. In our custom you give it to the lineage (*loshika*) on behalf of the girl's family, but the Ju have no such unit. Each family is independent. /Twa's closest relative was a man named Kumsa, her mother's brother. My father and I went to him and said, "*Mi ≠tum*," using the !Kung term for father-in-law, "today I want to pay you *bogadi* for your child /Twa and for the child in her womb and for any future children."

Kumsa replied, "I don't know what you are talking about. What is this thing? What would I do with cattle? I live in the bush."

I said, "Cows are useful. You can keep them with the herd of the Blacks, who will take care of it for you."

After much talk, Kumsa finally agreed, and we transferred a heifer from our herd to that of a Herero near where Kumsa was living. Later Kumsa sold it and used the money to buy a donkey and a saddle and clothes. But we were satisfied. His acceptance of the cow meant that we had a right to /Twa's children if a dispute ever came up."

Whether Gutayone's fears were justified, I can't say, but his two sons, now in their forties, have both been raised as Tswanas and think of themselves as Tswanas. Both, however, married Ju girls when they grew up. In general, children of these mixed marriages grow up speaking both parental languages, but their identity was firmly with the dominant group. The boys tended to marry Ju girls and the girls tended to marry Herero, but the numbers were too small to make any definite statements.

SWARA AND THE *SARWA*

The BaTswana call all San peoples "Sarwa" or "Basarwa" (people of the west). One area of potential tension in Black-San (Basarwa) marriages, or for that matter, in all interethnic marriages, is the relationship between the husband on the one hand and the brothers and male relatives of the wife on the other. The husband from the dominant group in effect takes a woman away from the subordinate group, a potential bride for some local man. Resentment, open conflict, or worse could ensue unless some special steps were taken to smooth over this tricky relationship.

The Herero and Tswana use a special kinship term, *swara,* to apply to brothers-in-law created by intermarriage. This term and the behavior associated with it have proven so popular that the term is used informally as well for brothers-in-law among Blacks and Ju themselves. *Swara* is a term associated with behaviors of extreme, almost exaggerated cordiality. Greetings are accompanied by jovial handshaking and backslapping, and sometimes include bawdy joking. The term is also used by a Herero with any Ju man whose sister he is sleeping with, the implication being, "This is not just a casual affair, we are almost brothers-in-law." This joking and cordiality is quite out of character for Ju/'hoan brothers-in-law. As we saw in Chapters 5 and 6, the *tun!ga–tun!gama* relationship, referring to wife's brother or sister's husband (man speaking), is an avoidance relationship, not a joking one. Ju men related this way are supposed to show respect, not joviality.

What then is the function of the term *swara?* The widespread use of the term evidently fulfills a need in interethnic relations for defusing the anger between a wife's brothers from the subordinate group and their sisters' husbands from the dominant group. There is, however, an important hidden agenda in the use of this term. The term *swara* is used reciprocally: both Blacks and Ju call each other *swara,* implying that *either man could give his sister in marriage to the other.* When Ju and Blacks call each other *swara* they are sharing a joke: "You gave me your sister today, I may give you my sister tomorrow."

This of course is not true. Despite the apparent reciprocity, the dominant group will not give sisters in return to a subordinate group. It would be unthinkable for a

Herero giving cow's meat from a lion kill to the !Kung.

Herero or Tswana girl to marry a Ju/'hoan boy, and none have so far. Therefore the term *swara* is a mystification hiding a basic inequality behind a show of equality and reciprocity.

But the most fascinating aspect of the *swara* relationship has yet to be mentioned: Where did the term come from? It is not a Ju/'hoan word; nor is it Herero or Tswana. In fact, it does not appear as the basic term for brother-in-law in any African language.[4] The term *swara* is of Afrikaans origin, the language of the Boer settlers of South Africa. It is a direct descendant of the Afrikaans word for brother-in-law, *swaer,* related to the Dutch term *zwager.* This derivation opens a very interesting area of explanation of how the term came into being in the first place. The modern Afrikaners oppose intermarriage with "non-Whites," and until recently a White could go to jail in South Africa for even sleeping with a non-White, but their ancestors did not share this abhorrence of "miscegenation." On the contrary, history tells us that the Afrikaner men actively sought liaisons with San, Khoi, and Bantu women on the frontier. Since both the term *swara* and the associated behavior are not indigenous to either the San or the Herero-Tswana, it is reasonable to assume that the term and the behavior had their beginnings with the Boer frontier settlers of earlier times. Marrying a woman of the local people turns a potential enemy into

[4]In some it appears as a secondary term, but its derivation is the same as for the Ju/'hoansi (see text).

a brother-in-law. And your children tie you together even more strongly, but the tenseness of the situation must be papered over with cordiality. One can imagine the term *swara* traveling down through generations and spreading throughout southern Africa, as men of one society moved into territory held by another. The tension of hostility versus friendship remains in the *swara* tie, as does the remarkable ambiguity between equality/reciprocity on the one hand and inequality/hierarchy on the other.

In the late 1990s the game of soccer became a favorite pastime in the Dobe area. Here local Ju boys and young men from outside on work contracts could play together and defuse some of the tensions of potential competition for the local (Ju) girls (see Chapter 12).

11/Perceptions and Directions of Social Change

Despite their history of contact with Whites and Blacks, the Ju/'hoansi were still relatively isolated when I first encountered them in 1963. They had very hazy notions of the world beyond their periphery. For example, no one I spoke to in 1963 had ever heard of Africa. They were surprised to learn that they lived on a large body of land called Africa. They *had* heard of South Africa, however. They called it *Johanni,* after Johannesburg, the place where the mine laborers went. More striking was the fact that none of the Ju were aware of the Atlantic Ocean, which was less than 800 kilometers (500 miles) due west of Dobe. I asked them if they knew of a body of water that was so large that if you stood on one side you couldn't see the other. After much discussion they pointed north to the Okavango River, rather than west to the Atlantic.

But a third experience brought home to me how unfamiliar the Ju/'hoansi were with the ways of the wider world. In 1964 I hired Koshitambo, one of the most sophisticated and well-traveled Ju/'hoan. He had made frequent trips to Maun, the tribal capital, as a valet to the local headman, Isak; he loved to make jokes in Setswana and Herero; and seemed to be as knowledgeable about the world as any Ju. I agreed to pay him £10 for two months' work, a reasonable sum in those days, and on pay day I handed him an envelope containing two crisp £5 notes. Koshitambo looked puzzled and appeared upset, but I thought nothing of it and went on with my business. Ten minutes passed, and I caught a glimpse of him sitting forlornly at the edge of the camp, the £5 notes in his hand.

"What's the matter?" I asked Koshitambo.

"Oh, nothing," he said, hesitating.

"Yes there is, I can see something is wrong."

"Oh, /Tontah," Koshitambo finally blurted out, "/Tontah, you disappoint me. You said you were going to pay me ten monies, but instead you have paid me only two!"

It took fifteen minutes and all my limited linguistic powers to explain to Koshitambo that those two scraps of legal tender indeed constituted "ten monies" and not just two. The idea of money, of paper money, of different denominations of paper money, and of convertibility all had to be carefully put across before a pale smile broke on Koshitambo's face and he pocketed the money.

Despite the changes, the Ju/'hoansi entered the 1960s with their kinship, productive, and land-tenure systems relatively intact. They gave birth, raised their children, married, grew old, prayed to their gods and buried their dead in ways that

A Ju/'hoan, a Canadian, and
an Herero: an old-style an-
thropological mug shot.

were similar to what they had done for hundreds of years. This is certainly not to say that the Ju/'hoansi had been static or unchanging. Their way of life had its own rhythms of change, and the arrival of the Whites and the longer contacts with the Blacks had introduced many new elements. But the pace of these changes was sufficiently slow that with time they could be absorbed into the existing structures and world view. Their systems did not break under the force of these changes; they bent and adapted.[1]

But in the 1970s the tempo of change accelerated, and new changes kept arriving before the previous ones could be absorbed. The capacity of the Ju to absorb these developments without shattering was being tested to the limit. It is these fundamental changes that we will explore in this chapter.

We will first try to look at the outside world through Ju/'hoansi eyes. How do they perceive the coming of the Blacks and Whites? Then we will explore how they are attempting to adapt to agriculture, wage labor, schools, and changes in land tenure.

---

[1]As noted in Chapter 2 I disagree with the thesis of Schrire (1984) and Wilmsen (1978b, 1981, 1989) that prehistoric contact with herders, some as early as A.D. 1000, fundamentally altered the character of Ju society long before 1900. If true, there should be an abundance of prehistoric evidence of cattle and goat bones in the Dobe area. Such evidence, despite concerted efforts to find it between 1978 and 1992, is almost totally lacking. This topic is explored in detail in Appendix B.

PERCEPTIONS OF THE WHITE MAN

Well into the 1970s the Ju/'hoansi still retained a vigorous sense of themselves as a people and their special status in relation to outsiders. They called themselves *Ju/'hoansi,* "real" or "genuine" people, a term they grudgingly extended to San of other language groups elsewhere in the Kalahari—the Nharo, /Gwi, and !Ko—but not to their Black and White neighbors.

It took over a year of fieldwork before I could speak Ju well enough to find out how the Ju thought of me and the people I represented—the Whites—and where we fit into their scheme of things. The picture was not flattering: very matter of factly, they considered us to be wild animals. One day in late 1964 I was interviewing //Kokan!a, the wise and playful wife of ≠Toma// gwe, about animal classification.

"Wild animals we call *!hohm,*" she said. "Lions, leopards, cats, hyenas, and wild dogs we call *!hohm a tsi*—wild things of the bush. Tswanas, Gobas, Hereros, and Europeans like you, /Tontah, we call *!hohmsa chu/ o,* wild things of the village."

This came as a great revelation to me. "What exactly are the *!hohm?*"

"We call all creatures who are different from us *!hohm* because when they speak we cannot understand a word. *!Hohm a tsi* are the animals that kill people. We don't understand their language either, so we call them *!hohm.*"

"I don't quite understand. Do you mean you don't hear their language?" I asked.

Rakudu, a congenial and very intelligent Ju/'hoan from Mahopa, interjected, "It's not quite so simple. The Blacks and Whites we don't understand at all. But the wild animals of the bush, we can understand them a little. When the *!hohm a tsi* call each other we understand what they say. They are saying, 'Come, come join me in enjoying this food.'"

"We called the Blacks and the Whites *!hohm* long ago because we were afraid of them like we were afraid of wild animals. Today we don't fear them. We call them by their names. *Dama* (Herero), *≠Tebe* (Tswana), */Ton* (European)."

//Koka was right. Listening in on Ju/'hoan conversations, I heard the terms *!hohm* and its singular, *!homa,* used in everyday speech for Whites and Blacks, without derogatory intent. The older fear had been replaced by a familiarity, yet a definite distance remained.

The Ju were fascinated by Western technology, which they called */tondiesi,* White Man's expertise or skill. They loved to ride on trucks most of all, and developed a lively curiosity about how things worked. I once asked Ju to name as many parts of the truck as they could. This proved to be an interesting exercise because the Ju had to assemble vocabulary from several areas—anatomy, dress, and hunting technology—in order to describe the various parts. The headlights were called */gasi*—eyes; and the hood was called the *tsi*—mouth; the tires were the */ gwesi*—shoes or sandals. Gasoline was called *n/ i,* literally vegetable oil or butter; it was also called *!kaitoro,* a derivation from the word *petrol.* Most other parts of the truck were not named at all, or the English-derived names were used. The truck itself was called *do,* the Ju word for metal. Tin cans were also called *do.*

Tape recorders were another source of wonderment for the Ju/'hoansi. They were always asking to listen to tapes recorded at other villages and to *n/ wi e dumsi*—literally, "collect our throats"—so that they could listen to themselves on the tape. One woman even went into trance while listening to a tape of the Women's Drum Dance (see also Katz, 1982:187–191).

Fascination with Western technology: peering under the hood of a Land Rover.

Some forms of Western high technology were the subject of intense discussion. For example, Dobe lay on the flight path for jet planes from South Africa to Angola. Flying so high that they were almost invisible from the ground, the aircraft left vapor trails at 35,000 to 40,000 feet. One day Tsau, a leading /Xai/ xai man, and I watched as a plane came over.

"What *is* that thing up there with the long tail?" asked Tsau.

"It's a 'fly machine,' " I answered, using the term the !Kung used for airplane. "But it is flying so high that you can't see it."

"That's what I thought it was," explained Tsau, in all seriousness. "Some Ju/'hoansi deceived me. You know what they said? That the Whites were sending messages to each other on long rolls of paper. In the south they could take a great roll of paper covered with writing and fire it out of a giant gun. It would stream over to the north and land. Then they would cover it with new writing and fire it back to the south." Never, I thought, had toilet paper been put to such an imaginative use.

Artificial satellites, which had begun to appear in the Kalahari skies after 1957, were also a topic of discussion. Remember that my fieldwork began only five years after the first satellite had appeared. One starry night I was camped in the bush with two men named /Gau, one young and one old, when a Sputnik slowly crossed the sky. As we watched its progress excitedly, I asked each of them what they thought it was.

Young /Gau spoke with feeling, "The elders have told me that when you see a star moving like that it means that war is coming from the west and going to the east."

/Twan!a and other !Goshe people listening to a tape of one of their healing dances.

Not a bad answer I thought, thinking about the Cold War and the arms race. "And what do you think it means?" I asked the older /Gau.

"I don't know what the elders say. They never said anything to me. All I know is when I see something like that I think the Whites sure have powerful *n/um* to make the stars move!"

In less than a decade, the isolation of the Ju/'hoansi disappeared and their perceptions about and knowledge of the outside world changed rapidly. Young men began to travel out of the area to work on mines and farms, and they brought back wondrous tales of far-off places.

The same /Gau who had spoken so gravely of the satellites was a 25-year-old man who had never been farther than 100 miles from home. In July 1964 I hired him to be my assistant on an archeological dig near Lusaka, Zambia, 500 miles east of Dobe. /Gau was eager for the chance to go to some of the world that he had heard about but never seen. He underwent a profound change on the trip. Arriving in Maun, the tribal capital, clad only in a *chuana,* the leather breechclout, /Gau expressed intense embarrassment. I bought /Gau an outfit—khaki shirt, shorts, socks, and shoes. He balled his *chuana* in his fist and heaved it with all his might into the Okavango River, saying, "I'm never going to wear that thing again as long as I live."

"I wouldn't bet on it, /Gau," I said.

The trip to Zambia lasted five weeks. /Gau was exposed to one staggering novelty after another: tarred roads, street lights, running water, and railroad trains were only a few. After three weeks /Gau took to his bed. Whether it was sickness or culture shock I could not tell. But when /Gau returned to Dobe he recovered almost immediately. And soon he was eager to share his experiences with his kin. At the same time, he was awed by the problem of how to put all of this new world into words, how to convey to his listeners a sense of what he saw. Since 1964 many !Kung have made such trips, and the experiences /Gau describes are commonplace, but then it was all, as he put it, "strange and fearful."

We drove and drove and drove and drove, through the country of the Gobas, the Damas, the Tswanas, and then we came to people who were San like ourselves, with our faces and our skin. They even had quivers on their shoulders like us, and yet when they spoke I could not understand a word of them. I had no *!kun!as* in common with them, no kinsmen among them. When we spoke we had to speak in Setswana. Then we left that place and came to a fence that stretched far in each direction. Men with guns and clothing the color of sand opened the gate and let us through. Then a strange thing happened. The road transformed itself. A giant black snake with a smooth back came up, and we rode on his back. He twisted and turned but we always stayed on his back; we never left him. Riding on that snake's back we went as fast as the wind.

We got to a big village of those people and stopped. We were dying of hunger by that time, and /Tontah made us go into a house and sit down on a chair with a table in front of it. A man who was not a relative of /Tontah came and brought food in a dish. There were three different kinds of food on one bowl. We had to eat it in a strange way. A metal thing shaped like a lizard's forefoot was given to me. I had to spear food with it and bring it to my mouth. It was very hard, but I learned to do it. The other things at this table—knives, cups, spoons—we have in our country too.

Metal is everywhere. When you twist metal, water comes out. You sleep on metal. When night comes giant metal flashlights as tall as trees come on and make the black snake's back shine like day. The people of this country refuse night. They reject it and push it back with light. Even in their houses there are flashlights everywhere.

But one creature of metal frightened me the most. It made the ground shake like a giant herd of wildebeest fleeing for their lives. It had one eye living in its face, like a ghost. It was bigger than many elephants, but walked on wheels like a truck. It had its path of metal and no one could make it go left or right. A fire was in its belly and black smoke breathed from its head. When it stopped it vomited people, and then ate more people. /Tontah was not afraid of it and said let's go in it. I refused. Then I said all right but feared it would kill me. I got in and sat still. When it started to move I wanted to get off. /Tontah made me stay on and so, fearing for my life, I lived.

After that I became ill and lay in my bed for many days. /Tontah took care of me and gave European *n/um*. Then /Tontah brought me back to Dobe; the medicine men and women worked me and worked me and revived me. Today I am just like myself again but happy to be alive and happy to be home.

Experiences like /Gau's gave the younger generations of Ju a changed outlook from that of their parents. They came to handle cash with confidence and would speak of the relative merits of Johannesburg, Francistown, and Windhoek as places to find work. New technology such as transistor radios expanded their horizons even further, though by the year 2000 the first computer had yet to reach the Dobe area.

I think it is fair to say that in the 1960s there were genuine disagreements among the Ju on the desirability of change. Many expressed a fondness for their way of life and a love of the *t'si*—the bush. They said that in the bush you can always find food and game; in the bush you are free to live as you please. An equal number of Ju, like young /Gau, expressed a fear and dislike of the bush. The bush is hunger, said one man; it is heat and thirst, said another.

As time went on, more and more Ju/'hoansi shifted to the latter view. They wanted money and the things that it could buy. They wanted donkeys to ride on and goats and cattle. But wanting is one thing, and getting is quite another.

TRANSITION TO FARMING AND HERDING

At the time of my first field trip in 1963, the Dobe area Ju/'hoansi appeared to be full-time hunter-gatherers, with no agriculture or livestock (except at !Goshe). As the fieldwork proceeded, however, a more realistic picture emerged of the "pristine" nature of the Dobe area. I learned that most of the men had experience herding cattle at some point in their lives, and that many men had owned cattle and goats in the past. Further, the Ju were no strangers to agriculture. Many had learned the techniques by assisting Black neighbors, and in years of good rainfall had planted crops themselves. However, because of the extreme unreliability of the rainfall, none of them had succeeded in establishing themselves on an agricultural basis. The same pattern occurred with livestock raising. Men often obtained cattle or goats in payment for working for the Blacks, but only a few families had set themselves up as herders independent of a Black patron.

In all, the Ju planted 10 different crops, including gourds, marijuana, sugarcane, and beans, but by far the most important crops—those planted by 50 or more families—were maize, melons, sorghum, and tobacco. Surprisingly, tobacco was the most frequently planted. It is also the most difficult of the four to grow, requiring deep shade and daily watering. The fact that the Ju/'hoansi devoted so much of their farming effort to a nonfood crop suggests that the motive of increasing their food supply was not uppermost in their minds.

Sorghum was the most successful food crop, and those who planted it enjoyed a 50 percent rate of success, compared to 35 percent for maize. The government's Agricultural Extension Department even distributed bags of drought-resistant sorghum seed to Ju and other marginal farmers during the 1967 and 1968 growing seasons.

Despite these efforts, agriculture continues to be a very risky proposition for the Dobe area !Kung. Only at !Goshe, where the Ju/'hoansi enjoy the patronage of an influential Tswana-Yei cattleman, has agriculture begun to provide a significant proportion of the subsistence.

Unlike farming, livestock production is an economically viable adaptation in the Kalahari, and it continues to be the economic mainstay of Botswana. Some form of small-scale herding represents the main hope for the future development of San communities. During 1967–1969 only about 100 head of cattle and 155 goats were owned by Ju in the Dobe area, representing about 2 percent of the cows and 8 percent of the goats in the district (see Chapter 10). Only six Ju families owned the minimum number of livestock to form a viable herd, and of these, only one man had set up with his family as independent farmer-herders. Most of the other people let their animals run with the herds of their Black neighbors.

A goat herd is easier to manage, and several families have built kraals and assembled small herds consisting of their own goats and those of their relatives. These families put the children of the camp to work herding and watering the goats while

/Xashe milking a cow from his
new herd, 1980.

the adult members combine farming with gathering and hunting. These are the modest beginnings of animal husbandry among the Ju on their own, not as employees or clients of Black masters.

The possession of a herd of goats or cattle, or of a field of maize and melons, puts Ju farmer-herders in a difficult position. First, their mobility is restricted by the need for daily supervision of the animals. It is not as easy for family members to go on an extended foraging trip or to pay visits to relatives at distant camps. Someone must always remain with the animals. Second, there are daily tasks to be performed, and the children are pressed into service. Draper (1976) has described how the children in the sedentary !Kung villages are put to work tending the animals or helping with chores, a contrast with their carefree life in the bush camps. A more subtle change noted by Draper (1975) concerns the separation of men and women in daily work and the confining of the latter much closer to home. In bush camps both women and men go far afield in the food quest. In village life, the men maintain their mobility, following the herds, but the women become housebound, with more of their time spent alone with their children and less with peers on common productive tasks. Perhaps the beginnings of the subordination of women can be glimpsed here in the reorganization of household work loads around the demands of farming and herding (see Lee, 1975).

The Case of Debe and Bo

There is a great deal of tension between those families of Ju/'hoansi who have begun to farm and herd and their relatives who continue the foraging life. There are real
contradictions between the organization and ideology of farming and the organization and ideology of foraging. The most important of these is the contradiction between *sharing,* or generalized reciprocity, which is central to the hunting and gathering way of life, and the *saving,* or husbandry of resources, which is equally central to
the farming and herding way of life. As we saw in Chapter 4, the food brought into a
Ju/'hoansi camp is shared out immediately with residents and visitors alike; for
herders to do the same with their livestock, or farmers with their harvested grain,
would quickly put them out of business.

How people grappled with these contradictions on the ground was very interesting.
Sometimes they made surprising choices. For example, there were two enterprising Ju
men at Mahopa, one named Debe, the other Bo. Debe assembled a small herd of goats
and cattle and appeared to be on his way to becoming a successful herder. But when
meat was scarce his relatives would visit from /Xai/ xai, and under heavy social pressure, Debe would slaughter one goat after another until after several years he sold or
gave away his remaining herd, saying that the responsibilities were too heavy. Debe
was also successful as a farmer, but his relatives always seemed to appear on his
doorstep right at harvest time to consume his harvested crops. Later he tried to enlist
the help of his relatives in building a larger field so that they could plant crops together
for all of them to eat. But they were so reluctant that Debe in disgust *hired* a Black for
wages to help him clear the land and build the brush fence—the first case we know of
in which a San paid wages to a Tswana. Oscillating between exhorting his kinfolk to
help him farm and hiring an outsider, Debe seemed to be caught in the contradictions
between a communalistic and an individualistic style of work relations.

The second man was Bo, the leader of the only group whose members have established themselves as independent farmer-herders. Bo took great pride in his herd of six
cows and his fields of maize and melons, and he emphasized to all who would listen
that he was on his own and not under Black patronage. Bo was also a rational man, and
when his many kinsmen and affines came to his hamlet to share in his good fortune,
he fed them a fine meal, offered his fire for overnight, and sent them on their way the
next morning with a handful of his home-grown tobacco. Bo knew that nothing could
put him out of business more quickly than the arrival of kin on extended visits, so he
sent them on their way. The effects of this were striking: people spoke of Bo as stingy
and far-hearted; he became feared, and there were mutterings that he had learned techniques of sorcery from Black diviners. So Bo became a successful but very isolated
farmer-herder. Finally, in 1970, Bo had had enough. He sold all his cattle and other
stock for cash, packed his things, and walked across the border to settle at Chum!kwe
(now spelled Tjum!kui) in Namibia. It was factors such as these, and not simply ecological limitations, that were preventing more Ju from moving into farming and herding during the 1960s and 1970s. But even more dramatic changes were on the horizon.

WAGE WORK AND MIGRANT LABOR

During the period 1900–1979, migrant labor in the gold fields of South Africa was
a main source of income for hundreds of thousands of African men drawn from

Lesotho, Swaziland, Mozambique, Botswana, and as far away as Angola and Malawi. In some areas half the adult men are away in the mines at any given moment.

This practice reached the Dobe area in the late 1950s. By 1968, 15 Dobe area men, about 10 percent of the adult male population, had made the trip to Johannesburg; eight of them had made two or more trips, and one man had signed on for five of the nine-month tours of duty. Men reported wages of between R12 and R18 per month (then equal to 18 to 25 American dollars), but from this total were deducted the worker's off-hours canteen and bar bills, so that when the Dobe area workers were paid off at the end of their contracts, most brought home only between R25 and R40 in total.

In order to go to "Johanni," Dobe area men had to walk out 100 kilometers to the main road at Nokaneg and hitch a ride north to the Witwatersrand Native Labour (Wenela) recruiting depot at Shakawe. After receiving a cursory medical examination, they would wait along with 150 other men for the weekly flight to the mines. At Johannesburg they were sent to one of the 40 or so giant Rand gold mines. The shorter men were classified for surface work at lower pay; the taller and huskier ones were chosen for the more dangerous and better-paid underground work. Returning home after nine months' work, the men were paid off in Shakawe, where a variety of home-brew joints and prostitutes were waiting to relieve them of part of their pay. Many returning workers have brought gonorrhea back to the Dobe area as a result. (By the time of the AIDS crisis of the 1990s this migrant labor system had stopped.) With the rest of their money the men purchased clothes, shoes, saddles, blankets and yard goods, and sometimes donkeys to make their way back to the home area.

The system of remitting mine wages back to families in the rural areas was unknown among the Dobe San. There was no post office, and neither the workers nor their wives could read or write. Instead, the !Kung had developed a standard method for translating the values gained through wage work back into significant values in the *hxaro* exchange system.

When young Bo returned to !Kangwa in September 1968, he was dressed to kill in fedora, plaid shirt, undershirt, sport jacket, long pants with cowboy belt, underpants, new shoes, and socks. Over the next few days his wardrobe dwindled as each item of clothing appeared in turn in the costume of a friend or relative. By the third day Bo himself was strolling around dressed only in his undershirt and his leather *chuana.* Bo had given away his entire wardrobe in the *hxaro* network, and we enjoyed seeing one of his kinsmen appear in fedora and *chuana,* another in sport jacket and *chuana,* and so on.

In 1967 the first store opened in the Dobe area, at !Kangwa, operated by Greek traders. Housed in the first modern building ever constructed in the !Kangwa Valley, the store sold mealie meal, soap, kerosene, clothing, saddles, and dry goods at inflated prices and purchased cattle from the Herero at reduced prices. The San had few, if any, cattle to sell, but five young men were hired for wages to tend and water the purchased cattle. The pay was only R6 to R8 per month ($8.40 to $11.20), but even this small amount has had a major impact in a world without cash.

The major impact of the store on both the San and their Black neighbors came from a single store-bought commodity—sugar. Sugar is the prime ingredient in the potent home-brewed beer (actually a form of mead) that is the centerpiece of a new culture that has sprung up around the !Kangwa store. The beer, called *khadi,* is a clear

One hundred fifty miles north of Dobe is the recruiting depot for migrant laborers to the South African mines.

amber beverage that looks and tastes like a sparkling hard cider. It is made from brown sugar and *Grewia* berries, with fermentation induced by a mixture of bee earth, honeycomb, and honey called *seretse*. A number of Ju women have set themselves up as beer entrepreneurs, buying the sugar at the store and selling the product at 5 cents ($.07) a cup. The Ju are scrupulous businesswomen. They do not give drinks on credit, and even close kin are charged the full price for each drink. However, after the day's business is done the same women are seen sharing their wild plant foods in the traditional Ju way with their "customers" at the evening meal.

The new Ju culture is based on selling and drinking beer and listening (and dancing!) to hit tunes from Radio Botswana on transistor radios. Ju drinking behavior resembles that of their Herero and Tswana neighbors, whose women also brew and sell beer. Drinking is confined to the hottest hours of the day, beginning at ten in the morning and continuing to late afternoon. The hot sun overhead must speed the alcohol's effect, because most people are thoroughly drunk by two in the afternoon. Ju drinking parties are loud and rowdy, with shouting and laughter that can be heard a good distance away. Sometimes they take a nasty turn and fights break out, like the brawl at !Kangwa in which a mine returnee gave another man a blow with a club that fractured his skull. The situation is even worse at Chum!kwe across the border in Namibia, where frequent injuries and even deaths occur as a result of Saturday night (and day) brawls.

Many Ju/'hoansi were appalled by the new way of life. They expressed fear at the effects of drinking on people's behavior; the loss of control, the fighting, and the neglect of daily tasks were seen as signs of the breakdown of the fabric of society. Stories were told and retold, with a mixture of glee and apprehension, of the bizarre behavior of people under the influence. A man named ≠Toma had stepped out of a drinking hut to urinate and had blithely relieved himself into a Herero woman's cooking pot filled with meat. In the uproar that followed, he narrowly escaped a thrashing by the woman's husband. A case was brought in the headman's court, but ≠Toma disclaimed all responsibility, saying that *he* would never do such a thing; it was entirely the fault of the beer. The headman was not persuaded by this argument and fined him a goat for the outrage.

Incidents like these were widely discussed and helped convince many Ju at the other waterholes that !Kangwa was an evil place, one to be avoided. The Ju/'hoansi of the interior had entered the 1960s in their isolated areas with their group structures and productive systems intact. Through the decade, the Dobe area became open to outside penetration, starting with the building of the Chum!kwe settlement in 1960 and continuing with the opening of the !Kangwa store and its home-brew supplies in 1967. The arrival of the anthropologists in 1963 and their continuous residence from 1967 to 1971 also had its effect. But a 1960 visitor returning in 1970 would have had no great difficulty in recognizing the Ju/'hoansi he knew before. More store-bought clothes, more babies, and more donkeys and goats were in evidence, but the basic pattern remained the same. The 1970s, however, brought new challenges that threatened to change fundamentally the basic pattern of Ju/'hoansi existence. The power to make decisions about their lives and future was shifting from within the community to agencies outside the Dobe area and not under their control.

THE FIRST SCHOOL

The Botswana government announced plans in 1968 to build a primary school at !Kangwa, and the school opened its doors in January 1973. The school, a two-room, single-story structure, had two teachers and offered Standards I to IV. The first class consisted of 55 Herero and Tswana students aged 5 to 10, all enrolled in Standard I. The medium of instruction was Setswana, and the curriculum was the standard one for Botswana: reading, writing, math, English, music, art, and Bible study.

Of the 60 or so Ju children of school age, *not a single one enrolled in January 1973*. When I spoke to them in July of that year, Ju parents claimed that the R3 ($4.50) annual school fee was too high for them. When I observed that R3 per year was not an outrageous amount for people who brewed beer and sometimes worked for wages, they responded that in addition to the fees, each child had to purchase an obligatory school outfit consisting of shoes, underpants, sweater, shirt, and short pants for the boys; shoes, underpants, sweater, and dress for the girls, costing R15 to R17 at the local store, plus the weekly cost of the laundry soap to keep all the clothes clean. This sum put the cost of schooling out of the reach of all but a few Ju families. For those who *could* pay for the fees and the outfits, there remained yet another problem of equal magnitude: how to feed and care for the children in !Kangwa five days a week for eight months of the year. Even though the children would receive a nutritious school lunch, how was the rest of the family to forage for sufficient food in the immediate vicinity of !Kangwa, which already had a resident population of 63 Ju? Ju life depended on mobility, a demand that stood in direct conflict with the school's requirement of regular attendance.

The new school at !Kangwa, 1973.

Ju parents had other objections. Especially at waterholes west and south of !Kangwa, parents expressed concern that the school was located at the village where the heaviest drinking took place. They feared their children might be beaten or neglected if they were left in the care of !Kangwa relatives. Parents also objected to the corporal punishment meted out by the schoolmaster. A fifth reason given by some parents concerned reports from relatives who had children in the school at Chum!kwe, across the border in Namibia. According to these reports, schoolchildren there were growing up to be disrespectful and contemptuous of their parents, even *za*ing them, a form of verbal sexual insulting expressly forbidden between parents and children (see Chapter 8). Finally the Ju/'hoansi were disturbed by the lack of sympathy for their culture expressed by the schoolteachers. Ju children were forbidden to speak their own language on school grounds, and no attempt was made in the curriculum to value Ju/'hoan culture and heritage. It wasn't until later years that this policy changed for the better (see Chapter 12 and Postscript).

In short, the Ju/'hoansi were faced with a real dilemma. They had many good reasons for being suspicious of the school and its impact on their lives, yet if the children did not gain some literacy skills, they would find themselves severely disadvantaged in the rapidly evolving world of land claims, jobs, and international conflict that surrounded them. The central government was creating laws that would increasingly have a direct impact on Ju/'hoan lives, and unless the San could read and interpret these laws and make the appropriate responses, their way of life would be in danger. The ability to read and write, therefore, was becoming an even more important skill than hunting in the struggle for survival.

GOVERNMENT AND THE FUTURE

Like their notions of other elements in the outside world, the Ju/'hoansi's ideas of government and the state were relatively hazy in 1963. *Horomenti* was their word for the government, an amalgam in their minds of Tswana and British overlords, with the British paramount. The only two individuals in high office they could name before 1963 were *Mogumagadi,* Mrs. Elizabeth Pulane, the ruling regent of the Batawana tribe and widow of the late paramount chief Moremi, and *Mosadinyane,* an affectionate Tswana nickname for Queen Victoria. There was some question over whether Queen Victoria and Queen Elizabeth were one and the same person. Apart from the occasional government patrols, almost the first direct contact the !Kung had with the central government was when the trucks announcing the pre-Independence elections arrived in mid-1964. I was struck by the spectacle of these "primitive" democrats being carefully instructed by means of a film on what elections were about and how to mark a ballot. The !Kangwa district voted solidly for the ruling Botswana Democratic Party, the electoral symbol of which was the *Dumkra,* an automobile jack.

After Independence in 1966, their member of the legislative assembly, Mr. Kwerepe, occasionally visited the district. From an aristocratic Tswana family, he was reputed to own *mafisa* cattle near !Kangwa. When I met him in 1967 he had just returned from a trip to the United States, where he had had lunch with Robert Kennedy. He was extolling the virtues of the American model of development through private enterprise, a model that was later put into practice in Botswana in the form of the Tribal Grazing Lands Policy (TGLP).

The TGLP provided a mechanism for taking land out of communal tenure and putting it into what amounted to freehold tenure in order to encourage more businesslike farming and ranching practices. Until Independence, the great bulk of Botswana's land had been held under a tribal form of tenure. In this system the paramount chief of each of the eight Tswana tribes doled out parcels of land to senior Tswana lineage heads to allocate grazing and agricultural rights. Effectively, it was a form of communal tenure; no land taxes or grazing fees were paid, and no one could appropriate a piece of land for his own exclusive use. In the Dobe area, this tribal tenure coexisted with the Ju/'hoan *n!ore* system: foragers and herders shared the waterholes and the space around them.

With Independence came a plan to rationalize the country's cattle industry, to take land out of tribal tenure and allocate it to individuals and syndicates on 50–99 year renewable leases. The lessees would survey and fence the land and would limit their herd sizes to the number of animals that could be supported in line with modern range management techniques. The plan's proponents, like Mr. Kwerepe, hailed it as the start of a new era in scientific and profitable animal production. But, like the Enclosure movement in seventeenth-century Britain and similar movements in many other Western countries, the Tribal Grazing Land Policy was a means of transforming inalienable communal land into valuable real estate, the leases for which could be bought and sold. It threatened to transform the people who lived on that land from independent hunters and herders into tenants and landless squatters.

To the government's credit, safeguards were installed to prevent the too-rapid takeover of tribal land by unscrupulous speculators. Land boards were set up in each district to screen every application before deed and title were granted. In spite of the safeguards, the Ju of the Dobe area and other San were at a great disadvantage under the new legislation. Lacking schooling, they were quite out of their depth in the legal complexities of land board negotiations. Also, it was impossible for them to make the frequent trips to Maun to attend the land board hearings.

With the start of the 1970s, the future of the San and their role in society became a topic of discussion within the higher levels of the government. Liberal, Western-trained Batswana and expatriate civil servants saw the San, now called the *Basarwa,* as in some ways analogous to the native peoples in places like Canada and the United States. They lived on the margins of society, were socially stigmatized, and had less opportunity for advancement than did the great majority of their fellow citizens.

In 1974, the government established the Basarwa Development Office (BDO). The BDO's job was to count the Basarwa, find out what their special needs were, and offer grants to local authorities for their welfare. In the North West District, where Dobe was located, the Ju/'hoansi received three forms of aid: scholarships to attend primary school, aid for well-digging, and agricultural extension advice. The effects on the Dobe area were striking. By 1976–1977, over 70 Ju children had enrolled in the two area schools, one at !Kangwa and the other at /Xai/ xai. After a series of name changes, and in order to remove any association of this agency with a single ethnic group, the BDO became the RADO, Remote Area Dwellers Office, and ever since, the Dobe Ju/'hoansi and other Botswana San, some 58,000 of them, have been known as "Rads."

Craft marketing was another important development for the Ju/'hoansi. For many years the Ju had produced some ostrich-eggshell bead necklaces for the tourist trade. They were purchased by European traders from Ghanzi for ridiculously low prices. Fifteen cents was paid for a string that took two days of work to produce. The traders then resold them for ten times the amount. The government-owned craft marketing board, Botswanacraft, was thus a boon to the Ju and to many other rural people. They paid the craftspeople two-thirds of retail for everything they bought.

Income from craft production quickly rose to become the major source of cash in the Dobe area, an influx to the community of $300 to $500 a month.

Unfortunately, the influx of cash also caused a boom in beer-making at !Kangwa, and the practice spread to other centers. Drunkenness, squabbling, and neglect of nutrition increased in frequency and caused a crisis in the school program. Several parents withdrew their children from the school, fearing for the children's safety.

Well-digging was another area of emphasis by the Remote Area Dwellers Office. By 1977, 20 applications had been received from Dobe area Ju/'hoansi for digging permits. But here again, things didn't turn out as planned. Despite the efforts of the RADO, 15 of the applications were tied up in red tape by local land boards, and only 5 were approved. Of these, at only one, the well at Dobe itself, were the Ju/'hoansi successful in striking water.

The greatest successes have been recorded in agriculture and stock raising. By the early 1980s, the number of cattle in Ju hands had increased dramatically, and over 50 Ju agricultural fields had been registered with the land board. In 1980 I estimated that at least a dozen Ju families had herds of sufficient size to provide a substantial proportion of their diet. And six Ju families owned steel ploughs, a device that made agriculture possible on a greatly expanded scale.

Yet even these successes brought with them new social problems. The breakdown of sharing, the appearance for the first time of wealth differences, and a tendency toward the subordination of women were all trends that could be discerned in embryo as the Ju/'hoansi entered the last two decades of the twentieth century.

On a trip to Dobe in 1980, I visited my old friend /Xashe. It was his father, ≠Toma// gwe, who had first greeted me at Dobe Pan 17 years before (Chapter 1). His *tsu* N!eishi had made me his "son." /Xashe's daughter //Koka, now in her twenties, had been my "betrothed" (see Chapter 6).

The people of the Dobe waterhole had prospered. We were greeted with much affection, and /Xashe showed me around his new semipermanent village of well-constructed mud-walled houses that he had built with his two middle-aged brothers and an older sister. Then we visited the kraal, where I counted 19 cows and calves in the family herd, a very respectable herd size, well above the minimum for herding self-sufficiency. /Xashe and I talked over old times as his daughter //Koka, who was now happily married to a man from Chum!kwe, played her portable record player, blasting out the latest hit tunes from Johannesburg. We walked over to a smaller kraal, where his teenage son was leading 60 goats out to browse. The cows and goats of other Dobe hamlets could be heard through the trees heading out to pasture.

In a quiet glade away from the village we sat down to smoke our pipes. /Xashe, always a thoughtful person, seemed to be in an even more somber mood than usual. I asked him what was the matter.

After a long pause he replied, "It's all these people of Dobe. There are so many of them now, and all these goats, and all the cows, and all the things. And everyone has trunks full of clothes and blankets. And we argue all the time. Sometimes I wonder if we wouldn't be better off if we had stayed like we were when you first came here."

"*Mi≠tum,*" I replied, using the term we had shared many years before, "*mi≠tum,* I don't know, I honestly don't know. You may be right. But whatever you and I feel, this is your life now. You can't go back."

12/The Ju/'hoansi Today

Over 20 years have passed since that fateful conversation with /Xashe. Changes that /Xashe saw so clearly in 1980 have continued to gather momentum. There is more cash circulating in the Dobe area but also more poverty. Sharing has declined further and interpersonal conflict, fueled by alcohol, seems even more frequent. The government now offers more services in the area but also controls their lives more tightly. Outside forces are seeking to control the economic resources of the Dobe area—water and grazing—and the Ju/'hoansi are mobilizing to resist. The experience of the Ju/'hoansi in the 1980s and 1990s has paralleled that of band and tribal societies worldwide. Like other foragers they are becoming part of the modern "world system."

This chapter updates the changes in Ju/'hoansi life and documents their continuing transformation from (relatively) isolated foragers to peasants coping with the demands of the state, of investment capital, and of development. Anthropological studies began in the Nyae Nyae in 1951 and in the Dobe area in 1963 (see pp. 11–14). But even as these studies were in full swing, the ground was shifting and the pace of change was accelerating; earlier in Nyae Nyae, and later in Dobe. To bring the story up to the present, this chapter will deal first with the Dobe area and second with Nyae Nyae. Chapter 13 goes on to make some observations on changing anthropological practice and to draw some conclusions about the lessons the Ju/'hoansi can teach us.

A traveller returning to the Dobe area in the 1990s would notice the changes even before he or she arrives. The 90-mile road from Nokaneng, once considered the worst in the district if not the whole country, was upgraded. The deep sand and heavy going remain, but a trip that used to take eight hours in four-wheel drive was reduced to three. Eight miles before !Goshe one saw the first borehole, owned by a private ranching syndicate, and the first of many if powerful cattle-barons have their way.

!Goshe itself, the first village, hasn't changed much, though a borehole has replaced the pitwells, and the homesteads of mud-walled houses look prosperous. Ten miles further brings you to !Kangwa and here the changes *are* dramatic. !Kangwa, or Qangwa, the capital of the Qangwa district (population 1000) has become an administrative and services center with close to 300 inhabitants (compared to 108 in 1964). I counted at least 25 salaried officeholders in the 1990s, compared to three in the 1960s. Today !Kangwa boasts an expanded school with eight grades and a student hostel, a four-bed clinic with a birthing wing, a police station, an agricultural extension office, and a large storehouse for drought relief food distributions. Other amenities include a dirt-and-gravel airstrip, a piped water system to standpipes, and a radio-telephone link to the capital (that sometimes works). There are several small stores and home-brew parlors; the latter, filled from morning on with raucous patrons, lend an air of frontier gaiety to the scene.

Twelve miles further west, along a new road, we come to the Dobe waterhole itself, and while the changes here are less dramatic than at !Kangwa, they still offer surprises. Three decades of cattle grazing have turned the Dobe pan into a dustbowl. Gone are the rich groves of berry bushes; the goats have browsed them out. Water for humans and cattle comes from a borehole drilled in the 1990s. The scale of Dobe has expanded considerably, from one or two small camps in the 1960s to eight large semipermanent villages in 2000. Herero live here now, as well as Ju/'hoansi. In a fenced compound built for government business, a mobile clinic is held monthly. Located strategically near the border crossing, Dobe has become an important transit point and stopover for visitors to and from Namibia. In fact, the village closest to the fence receives so many visitors that everyone calls it "Dam //ga si-"—"the place you drop your hat." With a population of 165 (up from 35 in 1964), Dobe is now the third-largest village in the Qangwa District and is in line for a school and clinic of its own in the next few years.

DOBE: THREE DECADES OF CHANGE

In 1963 three-quarters of the Dobe area Ju/'hoansi had been living in camps based primarily on hunting and gathering, while the rest were attached to Black cattle-posts. In the Dobe area of 1963–1964 there had been a virtual absence of the institutions associated with the state and the mercantile economy; there were no trading stores, no schools, no clinics, no government feeding programs, no boreholes or airstrips, and except for the tribal headman, clerk, and constable, no resident civil servants. By 1992 all these institutions were in place and the Dobe area people were entering their third decade of rapid social change; they had been transformed in a generation from a society of foragers—some of whom herded and worked for others—to a society of small-holders who eked out a living by herding, farming, and craft production, along with some hunting and gathering.

Some of the more significant developments can be briefly recapped. In 1965 a fence was built along the Botswana/Namibia border, dividing the Dobe area from the adjacent Nyae Nyae and limiting movement between the two. Foragers had to climb the fence in order to reach food on the other side, and this affected use of about 30 percent of their foraging area. In 1967 the first store opened at !Kangwa, making goods available to the Ju/'hoansi, who at the time, had almost no money to buy anything.

In 1973 the first school was opened at !Kangwa, followed by the second school at /Xai/ xai in 1976. During the 1970s most Ju/'hoansi started to build semipermanent mud-walled houses around cattle kraals. Most of the cattle in their herds were loan cattle or *mafisa*. In the mid-1970s the first borehole was drilled, primarily to serve the school and the growing administrative structures at !Kangwa village. In 1978, as the result of a prolonged drought, feeding programs were instituted for all the Ju/'hoansi residents of the Dobe area as well as some of the Hereros. Feeding eased hardship but at the same time sharply increased the dependency of the Ju/'hoansi on the central government.

In the same year South Africa upgraded its counter-insurgency warfare in South West Africa, and in 1979 some Dobe Ju/'hoansi men crossed the border to join the

Government officials registering voters at Dobe in 1964 on the eve of Botswana independence.

South African Defense Force (SADF) in its fight against the South West African People's Organization (SWAPO) (Lee and Hurlich, 1982).

In 1980 a clinic staffed by a nurse was opened at !Kangwa. Through the decade the clinic was upgraded and its links were improved to outlying communities. With the building of two airstrips and the inauguration of a radio link with Maun, it became possible for doctors to fly in and to evacuate seriously ill people to a hospital.

In the early 1980s game laws were tightened; the exemption for bow hunters was abolished and they were required to purchase an expensive (for them) license; as a result hunting declined. For most of the decade most Ju/'hoansi lived on government rations supplemented by herding, farming, and foraging. The formation of the Village Development Committees (VDCs) around the same time gave some Ju/'hoansi a nominal voice in local affairs, though the emerging local (Herero) elites often disregarded their opinions.

LIFE IN THE 1990S

Let us look at the Dobe area in the 1990s in more detail according to some of the categories discussed in previous chapters. In settlement patterns, Ju/'hoansi villages now look like other Botswana villages. The beehive-shaped grass huts are largely gone, replaced by semipermanent mud-walled houses behind makeshift stockades to keep out cattle. Villages ceased to be circular and tight-knit. Twenty-five people who lived in a space 20-by-20 meters now spread themselves out in a line-village several hundred meters long. Instead of looking across the central open space at each other the houses face the kraal where cattle and goats are kept, inscribing in settlement pattern a symbolic shift from reliance on each other to reliance on property in the form of herds (Yellen, 1990c).

Weekly distribution of food from international donors to remote area dwellers at !Kangwa, 1987.

Marked changes could also be seen in the way the Ju/'hoansi made a living. Hunting and gathering, which provided Dobe Ju/'hoansi with 85 percent of their calories as recently as 1964, now supplies perhaps 30 percent of their food. The rest is made up of milk and meat from domestic stock, store-bought or government-issue mealie meal, and vast quantities of heavily-sugared tea whitened with powdered milk. Foraged foods and occasional produce from gardens makes up the rest of the vegetable diet. For most of the 1980s, government and foreign drought relief provided most of the food. So much was available that surplus was often fed to dogs.

Changes in health and nutritional status have been striking. In the medical world the !Kung San had been famous for having very low serum cholesterols, low blood pressures that do not rise with age, and a general absence of heart disease (Truswell and Hansen, 1976:165–194; Truswell, Kennelly, Hansen, and Lee, 1972). Restudies in the late 1980s of the same population indicate that cholesterol counts and blood pressures at all ages are higher, and cases of hypertension and heart disease have been reported (Kent and Lee, 1992; Hansen et al., 1994). Adoption of a diet dominated by refined carbohydrates, heavier smoking, alcohol consumption, and changes in lifestyle are all factors implicated in producing these changes.

During the 1980s the food handouts almost became a way of life, so when the government cut off general food distributions, the Dobe people were shocked and angry. They had become dependent on the weekly handouts and didn't know where to turn. It was an open question how they would respond to the cut-off, but they did bounce back—and in unexpected ways. For example, in mid-1987 there was a revival of hunting; men who hadn't hunted for years took it up again, and younger men who had never become skilled with bow and arrow hunted from horseback with spears.[1] In the first week of July 1987 five eland were killed, more than had been taken in the previous year. The possession of horses was the key to hunting success. One old couple sold six of their cows to buy one horse and then sent young men out to hunt for them. Subsequently food distribution was resumed but stricter criteria were instituted, leaving an atmosphere of uncertainty about the government's intentions.[2]

Of particular significance economically has been their relations with their Herero neighbors. As early as 1900 some Ju/'hoansi had been involved in boarding cattle for wealthy Tswana (Lee, 1979:76–82). The institution of loan cattle or *mafisa* is well established all over Botswana (Hitchcock, 1977). By 1973 about 20 percent of Ju/'hoansi families had some involvement as *mafisa* herders and the numbers were increasing. However, in the 1980s people had become bitter about *mafisa:* they complained that cattle promised in payment for services rendered—usually one female calf per year—were not being paid, and without these beasts it was difficult to start one's own herd. Coupled with the withdrawal of government rations the lack of *mafisa* had soured some Dobe Ju/'hoansi about their prospects in Botswana.

The people saw what was happening in Namibia where a nonprofit foundation, the Nyae Nyae Development Foundation of Namibia, was helping the Ju/'hoansi drill boreholes for extended family groups and helping them obtain cattle. Dobe area Ju/'hoansi wanted their own boreholes and a Norwegian government overseas development agency was favorably disposed to financing the project. But a Kalahari Peoples Fund proposal for five to eight boreholes, strongly supported by the people of the Dobe area, was blocked by the Botswana Government, a decision indicating that the government's once liberal policies toward the Remote Area Dwellers/Basarwa were assuming an increasingly regressive character.

The unofficial grounds given for rejecting the borehole proposal in 1987 was that the anthropological presence in the Northwest District was promoting "ethnic favoritism." But the anti-San attitude was reflected in other areas as well. In 1990–1991 three ranches in the Ghanzi District to the south, earmarked for settlement by Remote Area Dwellers (mostly Bushmen), were taken by the government and turned over to private interests. After many protests, local and international, the status of these ranches remains in doubt (Hitchcock and Holm, 1993). Government plans tabled in 1992 indicate further disturbing trends: a policy of wholesale dispossession of the San that is so drastic that it has alarmed human-rights advocates in Botswana and internationally (Mogwe, 1992).

In the late 1980s some Dobe people started a movement to leave Botswana and cross the fence to their relatives in Namibia, and by 1992 some had actually made the move. As Komtsa from Mahopa said of the Botswana government in October, 1991, (for the source of the following quotes see note 7, p. 181).

> We don't want a government which treats us like the woman who ate meat but only smeared her child's mouth with fat. When someone came to ask if the child had been fed she said "Don't you see the fat around his mouth?" But in fact he was hungry.

---

[1]The revival of hunting was encouraged by the government in connection with wider conservation measures. Aerial game censuses showed that game was plentiful, so individuals—both men and women—were issued permits to kill one male and one female per year of many species of large game.

[2]For this and other information about conditions in the Dobe area in the early 1990s, I thank Jeffrey Kurland, Megan Biesele, and Eric Wood who visited Dobe-Nyae Nyae in 1991–1992.

!Kung San Works staff on a crafts-buying trip to /Xai/ xai in 1987.

While uncertainty about land continues to dog the Dobe Ju/'hoansi, some compensating developments have brightened this generally gloomy picture. Craft production, introduced earlier (see p. 165), has taken a major step forward. The *!Kung San Works* and its successor organizations are purchasing increasing volumes of Dobe Area crafts, primarily from Ju/'hoansi but also from Herero. This has had the effect of pumping considerable cash into the Ju/'hoansi economy, from a level of $300–$500 per month before the marketing scheme, to $2000–$3000 per month at the peak of the scheme. Unfortunately there were still not many opportunities for productive investment of the proceeds in infrastructure such as plows, bicycles, cattle, or horses. While some large stock was purchased, a distressing amount of income was absorbed in buying beer, brandy, home-brew materials, bags of candies, and the ubiquitous sugar, tea, and powdered milk product Nespray, called "Nes" by the Ju/'hoansi. Itinerant "hawkers" from Maun have been quick to capitalize on the Ju/'hoansi appetite for alcohol. They always seemed to arrive in a village immediately after the *!Kung San Works* payroll vehicle has left.

Schooling and the problems of youth have been a particular area of concern. When the first school opened, at !Kangwa, some Ju/'hoansi parents overcame initial reluctance and registered their children, scraping together the money for fees and the obligatory school uniforms (pp. 162–163). Most Ju/'hoansi, however, ignored the school or withdrew their children when the latter objected to being forbidden to speak their own language on school grounds or to the mild corporal punishment that is standard practice in Botswana schools. Even when Ju/'hoansi parents insisted that their children stay in school, the children often failed to attend classes and walked back to their home villages. Recently attempts have been made to set up a hostel for Ju/'hoansi children near the school where they can have a home away from home (the school itself has no residential facilities) but absenteeism remains a major problem in the 1990s.

In spite of these obstacles, at least four of the Dobe area students went on to secondary school in the 1980s. But even for these students—the first to get this far in the educational system—the road has not been easy. While troubles with the law and with alcohol have plagued the graduates, as of this writing, two hold teaching jobs in Namibia and one, Royal /O/oo, played a crucial role in Ju/'hoansi empowerment there (see pp. 187–188). The fourth, Chiqo Nxauwe (the only woman), was working in Maun, in the 1990s seeking higher education and struggling with the issue of racism against San. As she wrote:

> ... I am down here in Botswana trying to find out how I can get educated but it is really difficult; everything needs money to continue with my education at private secondary [school]. So I tell you my problem. Maybe you can help me with something or ideas. Royal and Benjamin are at Namibia working there because of the problems of money and racism in Botswana. . . . (Chiqo Nxauwe, personal communication, 13 May 1992)

For the large majority of Ju/'hoansi with no or little schooling, the job prospects are poor, and a life of odd jobs combined with heavy drinking is not uncommon. It was a bitter irony of underdevelopment that in the mid-1980s many youths were attracted to Namibia where jobs in the South African Army were the only ones available.

Far more successful was the second and smaller of the two schools, at /Xai/ xai. There, a progressive headmaster, wisely incorporating many elements of Ju/'hoansi culture into the curriculum, was rewarded with strong parental and community support for the school and a low absentee rate. The /Gwihaba Dancers, a troupe of /Xai/ xai schoolchildren, drew national attention in 1986 (see Postscript).

In the long run, Dobe area Ju/'hoansi face serious difficulties. Under the 1975 TGLP policy, when wealthy Tswana have wanted to expand cattle production they form borehole syndicates to stake out ranches in remote areas. With 99-year leases that can be bought and sold, ownership is tantamount to private tenure. By the late 1980s the borehole drilling was approaching the Dobe area. Therefore if the Dobe Ju/'hoansi do not form borehole syndicates soon, with overseas help, their traditional foraging areas may be permanently cut off from them by commercial ranching. In the year 2000, through the efforts of KPF and the Kuru Development Trust, the borehole scheme was successfully reinstated (see below).

The Subordinate Land Board in the area has for a long time in essence ignored the Ju/'hoansi, and they are deeply skeptical about their chance to participate in it as citizens of Botswana. As Xumi from /Xai/ xai told a meeting in late 1991:

> They always talk about "Batswana," but where are "Basarwa" supposed to be in that? . . . The Land Board is what they use to take our land away from us.

His relative Tshao added

> The reason is that we're Ju/'hoansi. The ones who are black call themselves "the owners of gardening," and they run the Land Board. Those of us who are Ju/'hoansi are not represented. . . . They say that we're Batswana but don't mean it. The only ones on the Land Board are Black people.

Chiqo Nxauwe (center) and other San students at Okavango Secondary School, Gomare Botswana, 1987.

NYAE NYAE: A STRUGGLE FOR SURVIVAL

In comparison to Dobe, the situation of the Nyae Nyae people across the border in Namibia has been even more difficult. While the Dobe people had to meet the challenges of declining foraging, sedentarization, and the cold immersion into a market economy, the Ju/'hoansi of Nyae Nyae had to deal with even more: massive resettlement, the imposition of apartheid, the loss of most of their land base, militarization, and finally the triumph and trauma of Independence and post-Independence Namibia.

If the Dobe Ju/'hoansi had largely been left to their own devices in a policy of benign neglect, the Nyae Nyae Ju/'hoansi were subjected to a policy of forced acculturation. The story begins on Christmas Day 1959, after the Marshall family had completed their anthropological research, when a South African administrator arrived in Nyae Nyae to assemble the Ju/'hoansi at the town of Tjum!kui (Chum!kwe). They were attracted by promises of wage work, agricultural training, and medical care, but what they found was very different.

For over two decades 900–1000 Ju/'hoansi were herded together under the watchful eye of South African authorities and missionaries, while weekly shipments of government rations supported the settlement. These rations were supplemented by some wage work, and by occasional trips out—further and further from the artificial center as time went on—for bush foods. The enforced idleness and unaccustomed crowding took a heavy toll; home-brew parties, social problems, and family violence became a regular feature of life at Tjum!kui. One Ju/'hoan woman described life there this way:

> People ate well but . . . sometimes people were eating when others had no food. So they
> began to fight. When we first started . . . we ate well but got paid only five pounds [$10 per

month]. We could buy a lot with that, at the store the minister built. The only problem was anger: the Ju/'hoansi fought with each other . . . And then the laws got tough . . . And they'd take them to jail, where they'd just sit. And they beat them in jail. And when the laws were fully grown, people were going often to jail . . . That's what we've seen at Tjum!kui.

Ironically it was after decades of forced settlement, rising alcohol consumption, and government paternalism that South African filmmaker Jamie Uys (pronounced "ace") came to Tjum!kui to film what turned out to be a worldwide hit. In a cruel caricature of reality, the feature film *The Gods Must Be Crazy* (1984) portrays the Ju/'hoansi as pristine hunter-gatherers so "untouched" by "civilization" that the mere appearance of a Coke bottle upsets the equilibrium of the society.

John Marshall's film *N!ai: The Story of a !Kung Woman* (1980) is a useful antidote to the distortions of *The Gods*. It documents the militarization, anomie, and alcohol-induced brawling that characterized Ju/'hoansi life at Tjum!kui: it even contains a telling sequence of the filming of *The Gods*.

South Africa had ruled the territory of Namibia (South West Africa) under a League of Nations mandate since capturing it from Germany back in World War I. When it became clear after World War II that South Africa was intent on imposing the apartheid system there, her occupation was declared illegal by the United Nations, and in August 1966 the South West African Peoples' Organization started military action to liberate the country. Until 1978 the war zone was far from Nyae Nyae, but in that year the South African Defense Forces (SADF) upgraded their counter-insurgency measures against SWAPO and began to recruit Nyae Nyae men into the army. Ultimately the 201 Battalion had about 700 Ju/'hoan soldiers,[3] making the Ju/'hoansi one of the most heavily militarized peoples in Africa.

The SADF recruitment campaign brought contradictory responses. On the positive side, the men were happy to finally have "work" (if you could call it that) and good pay; thousands of Rand (in the 1980s, 1 Rand = 40 cents U.S.) poured into Tjum!kui and other communities every month. On the negative side, the people were sharply divided on the morality of the war and which side to support (many Ju/'hoansi quietly supported SWAPO, and some soldiers even tried to warn SWAPO units of impending attacks.[4] ≠Toma, one of the Marshalls' main informants, said in 1978:

SWAPO won't kill us. We're good with SWAPO and good with these soldiers too. SWAPO will shoot the soldiers' airplanes. The soldiers will bring the fighting here. We're good people. We'd share the pot with SWAPO. But these soldiers are the owners of fighting. They fight even when they play, and I fear them. I won't let my children be soldiers, the experts at anger. The soldiers will bring the killing. This I know. (Volkman, 1983:50).

Gradually ≠Toma's view won out as it became clear to the Ju/'hoansi that the promises of the SADF were hollow ones; disillusionment became a major theme of

---

[3]Most of whom were Angolan !Kung, not from Nyae Nyae or the Dobe area.

[4]Also of interest was the reactions of anthropologists to the militarization of the Ju/'hoansi-!Kung. Some saw it as an unjust manipulation of a politically unsophisticated group to serve the ends of apartheid (e.g. Lee and Hurlich, 1982). Others saw the recruitment as a perfectly acceptable way of bringing the !Kung into the "modern world," with the army providing good pay, technical training, and even specially down-sized uniforms for the diminuitive !Kung, according to one anthropologist (quoted in Kolata, 1981).

discussions among Ju/'hoansi concerning SADF involvement: As one Nyae Nyae man recounted:

> We thought our young men were being offered a job of work, like any other job. The only difference was the salaries were much bigger. But we came to see it was a job of anger, and of killing, and of deception. The SADF said they were helping us against SWAPO but we found out we were helping them instead. SWAPO never did anything to us. Most of us have asked our children to come home.

Since engagements with "the enemy" were infrequent, far more destructive was the sudden wealth in the hands of so many young men away from their families. Alcohol consumption increased dramatically and payday brawls became more deadly. In a two-year period in 1978–1980, John Marshall recorded seven homicides, compared to an estimated four cases for the previous decade (cf. Marshall, 1984; Marshall and Ritchie, 1984).

THE PLASTIC STONE AGE

Even while the war was going on with all its dislocations, a new threat emerged in the 1980s from a different quarter. The Department of Nature Conservation within the South West African administration was pushing strongly to have the Nyae Nyae area declared a game reserve from which all development, including livestock, was to be excluded. A few Ju/'hoansi, for their part, were to dress up in traditional clothes, dance, and sell curios to the wealthy tourists who were to flock in droves to the spectacle.

The Ju/'hoansi were appalled by this scheme and opposed it vehemently. As G≠Kao Dabe said:

> Is it right that we should still be wearing loincloths? [Eating well] is a good thing, but it doesn't mean our women should have to expose their stomachs and buttocks again by wearing skin clothing . . .

To Ju/'hoansi the scheme represented an ironic about-face. First the government had done everything it could to wean them away from bush life; now they were pushing them back into it! But the people were well aware that their traditional way of life had been seriously compromised, and their future lay not in being props in what John Marshall labelled a "Plastic Stone Age," but in building up their herds and fields to establish themselves as small-holders with a mixed economy of foraging, farming, and wage labor. They also wanted clear rights to any revenues produced by the wildlife of their area or its products. In the game reserve scheme, by contrast, trophy hunting and tourist revenues would be siphoned off into central government coffers. After years of opposition and protest, locally and in international media, the South African scheme was dropped (Volkman, 1986).

INDEPENDENCE AND AFTER

The Ju/'hoansi and their allies won this victory in part because by 1988 the tide was turning in Namibia against South Africa; the SADF had suffered a serious military defeat at the hands of Angolan-Cuban forces at the battle of Cuito-Carnevale. Finally in 1989, the United Nations forces (UNTAG) entered the territory and implemented the long-awaited U.N. plan for Namibian Independence. With U.N. peacekeepers in place, the people of Namibia could finally express themselves freely and SWAPO won a clear majority in September 1989 elections. The Nyae Nyae area had voted strongly for SWAPO.

The independent nation of Namibia came into being in March 1990. Often heard at Independence and after was the Ju/'hoan phrase "Namibia !'oahn!" (Namibia's free!). Choosing "!'oahn" to express freedom connotes "broken open to reveal what's good inside," and "cleared up," as of cloudy weather (M. Biesele, personal communication). Western media had widely (and wrongly) predicted reprisals against the Bushmen for their participation in the South African war machine. Reprisals did not materialize, in part because some elements of *all* Namibia's ethnic groups had contributed soldiers to the SADF, and in part due to vigorous affirmative action policies pursued by SWAPO President Sam Nujoma. Nevertheless the most destructive aspect of the war for the Ju/'hoansi was the setback they received as "Bushmen" in taking their places in postwar nationbuilding. They had to overcome the negative effects of both the propagandizing they had received and the stereotyping (as collaborators) they had undergone.

Fortunately, with the war over and the troops demobilized, SWAPO worked hard to foster a spirit of reconciliation in Namibian society, determining to put the past behind and focus on the tasks of reconstruction. But despite the rejoicing at the end of 75 years of South African rule, Independence for the Ju/'hoansi was a mixed blessing. Namibia faced an uncertain future. For all intents and purposes the new nation was broke, without developed energy sources, its minerals systematically extracted, and its former patron, South Africa, disappearing over the horizon. The hasty retreat was thrown into relief by the hundreds of demobilized Ju/'hoan soldiers, their livelihood suddenly vanished, lounging around their home communities with a great deal of time on their hands.

At the same time, neighboring ethnic groups began to cast an envious gaze in the direction of the open spaces of "Bushmanland"—its grasslands having been protected from overgrazing by the logic of the apartheid system. Now that apartheid was gone, the neighbors reasoned, they could move in with all their cattle, and in 1990–1991 an advance guard of several families with hundreds of cattle settled at Ju/'hoansi waterholes in southern Bushmanland.

THE NYAE NYAE FOUNDATION AND THE FARMERS' CO-OP

With all these forces arrayed against them, the Nyae Nyae Ju/'hoansi have had a major ally in the form of the Nyae Nyae Development Foundation of Namibia (NNDFN), based in Windhoek. Founded by anthropologists and filmmakers John Marshall and Claire Ritchie in 1981,[5] the foundation has lobbied hard in the capital, Windhoek, and internationally to preserve the Ju/'hoan land base and community organization. Rather than "speaking for" the Ju/'hoansi, the Foundation has tried to facilitate Ju/'hoan voices directly reaching governments, donors, and the media. Another of its tasks is the promotion of literacy in Ju/'hoan and English so the people can

---

[5]Formally chartered in 1986 as the Ju/wa/Bushman Development Foundation (JBDF).

control their own communications in future. The spelling "Ju/'hoansi" and the title of this book is a direct outgrowth of these literacy efforts (cf. Dickens et al. 1990).

The Foundation was a response by anthropologists to concrete initiatives by the Ju/'hoansi in the late 1970s and early 1980s. Life in Tjum!kui was becoming more and more dysfunctional, and the people were becoming more and more aware that if they did not re-occupy the traditional areas they had left to join the Tjum!kui settlement, they would lose them to Nature Conservation or other settlers one day.

So in the early 1980s, tiring of the incessant squabbling, hunger and uncertainty at Tjum!kui, small groups of Ju/'hoansi began to move away to reestablish themselves on their traditional *n!ores*. By 1986 eight such groups totalling 140 people had reoccupied waterholes 15–30 miles from Tjum!kui; by November 1992 over 30 of these "outstations" had established themselves. Drawing upon private donations and later international agencies, the NNDFN was able to provide funds to the newly formed Ju/wa Farmers' Union (later known as the Nyae Nyae Farmers' Cooperative, or NNFC, and today [2001–2002] known as the Nyae Nyae Conservancy or NNC) to drill boreholes and purchase small herds of cattle to sell at subsidized prices to these re-formed *n!ore* groups (Ritchie, 1989).

Even with the Foundation's aid, the road to a semblance of self-reliance for the Nyae Nyae Ju/'hoansi has not been easy. Before Independence, the Farmers' Cooperative had to fight interference from the South African bureaucracy that still ran Namibia. The Ju/'hoansi's small boreholes and cattle-posts existed at that time in the middle of what was still regarded by the administration as a vast game reserve. Between 1983 and 1986 lions decimated the herds of cattle; and elephants, seeking water, broke down several borehole pumps. At one village the elephants were so destructive that the community had to erect an electrified fence to keep them away from the wind pump and dam. Artificially protected by Nature Conservation for tourism, lions were characterized by some Ju/'hoansi as the "dogs" of Nature Conservation, kept alive to do their bidding, which in the eyes of the Ju/'hoansi, was to generate tourist revenues for outsiders and kill Ju/'hoan livestock.

THE LAND QUESTION: A VICTORY FOR THE JU/'HOANSI

Despite all these uncertainties, the future of the Nyae Nyae people and their land took a significant step forward with the convening of the national Land Conference in Windhoek in June–July 1991. The Farmers' Co-op and the NNDFN came to the conference armed with legal opinions, maps surveying the hundreds of traditional *n!ores* (territories) into which Nyae Nyae was divided, a complete set of by-laws and constitution for the NNFC in Ju/'hoansi and English, position papers, and other documents. The delegation was accompanied by lawyers, interpreters, and a press kit. Two television documentaries about the Nyae Nyae people and their plight had been made with the support of the Swedish government. The most effective components of the NNFC presentation were a graphic map plotting 200 *n!ores* and a detailed discussion of the traditional *n!ore* tenure system and how it was being adapted creatively to the tasks of economic development. It urged that any land law that came into force should acknowledge these forms of tenure and their legitimacy.

Given only five minutes to present their brief, the Farmers' Cooperative leadership worked hard to distill their position about land in Nyae Nyae and other communal lands in Namibia down to its essentials. "Royal" Kgau /O/oo, their English–Ju/'hoan interpreter from Botswana,[6] set out their six-point summary:

1. Farmers should not be allowed to overgraze their own land and then move to other people's land and ruin it.
2. Namibia is now free and open but permission must be asked from local residents by anyone wanting to resettle.
3. It is not good for the land to have too many cattle: better to take good care of a few cattle, offtake the rest, and use the proceeds to establish water points and support the health of the land.
4. The land we have is today reduced and we must protect it as best we can. Those who live on land and know it well are its best protectors.
5. In the case of Nyae Nyae, taking care of land means that some must be set aside for wild animal breeding and some for wild plant collecting.
6. If we protect our land, it will support many more of our people, for example those who were taken to the Gobabis farms as slaves and those who went to South Africa with the SADF (NNDFN Internal Document July 1991).

Royal's presentation received a standing ovation from the conference delegates, and in the end the conference adopted most of the recommendations put forward by the NNFC, which was a major victory for the Ju/'hoansi. Immediately after the conference ended the Minister of Land, Resettlement, and Rehabilitation issued a statement that the *n!ore* system had been accepted by his Ministry as the basis for land allocation in Nyae Nyae, and that it would also be used, with local modification, in other areas of Namibia where Bushmen and other foraging peoples were living.

The effects of the Land Conference have continued to unfold: in August 1991 Sam Nujoma, President of Namibia and head of SWAPO, visited Eastern Bushmanland and instructed local authorities to respect Ju/'hoan land rights. Most important, the regional commissioner issued an edict that paved the way for the NNFC to negotiate the peaceful removal of the neighboring pastoralists who, with their large herds of cattle, had illegally occupied southern Bushmanland in the euphoria and confusion following Independence. The removals were successfully and peacefully concluded in December 1991, setting an important precedent for traditional authorities and longtime inhabitants in communal lands all over Namibia.

Not all the political problems have come from the outside. In setting up the Farmers' Cooperative, the Ju/'hoansi have had to delegate authority and act *collectively* for the first time, a difficult task for people who prided themselves on their egalitarianism (see pp. 58, 110–111). Through their elected leaders they have had to speak with one voice, not as members of one kin group or band. The leadership of the Co-op has crisscrossed Nyae Nyae dozens of times by truck and on foot holding interminable meetings. A recurrent theme has been how the Ju/'hoansi can meet the challenges of economic and political change without losing their cultural ethos or

---

[6]"Royal," a nickname he had chosen himself, was one of the four Botswana high school students who had overcome great odds to make their way in life, and also to help their people (pp. 172–173).

"soul." As in other former hunter-gathering groups, holding on to the land is the key to developing both a mixed economy and a unified voice. As one elected officer of the Co-op said:

> Land is something you don't divide. It's where your mother and father gave birth to you. All those little things your parents teach you to find and eat, things like g/ /uia and g/o!'o, all those things nourish you while you grow up. When your parents die, you have children yourself, and pass on what you know. What you know is your n!ore: you don't divide it.

Speaking of how the Co-op can help Ju/'hoan people change, the new chairman encouraged this group by saying:

> Look: if you're poor, you're weak, you have very few things—new ideas might defeat you. But things just naturally defeat you if you let them! If we work together with the Farmers' Co-op we will gradually succeed. You have to keep trying day after day to be strong. . . . We have to gather together everyone who has something in his heart to say. Everyone must speak the truth in his heart or he will get sick. But let's make sure that after we talk, the Farmers' Cooperative can speak about our land with one voice.

Becoming successful, or even viable, pastoralists and farmers—given the area's perennial ecological problems—would be difficult enough. But to be suddenly thrust into this brave new world after 30 years of colonial paternalism compounds the problem. The atmosphere of struggle and uncertainty is powerfully conveyed in John Marshall's film *Pull Ourselves Up or Die* (1986) and Marshall, Ritchie, and Biesele's trilogy *Death By Myth* (1992) as well as in Biesele and Weinberg's book *Shaken Roots* (1990).

The Nyae Nyae Ju/'hoansi are struggling against long odds to establish themselves as herder-foragers and as citizens in a modernizing state. But the legacy of decades of colonialism and forced acculturation is a bitter one: chronic drinking bouts and anomie are manifest; in the SADF days soldiers would think nothing of hiring a truck to drive them 250 miles to Grootfontein for cases of beer and brandy. Today such easy money is long gone. The 30 outstation communities vary widely in their economic well-being and sense of identity, from bustling villages of 50 to rural slums on the edge of hunger. It is too early to tell whether the battle for self-reliance will be won by the Ju/'hoansi of Nyae Nyae. However, if empowerment is the key to survival, then the Land Conference and its followup *do* offer a modest basis for optimism.

What has been the impact of all this on the Ju/'hoansi of neighboring Botswana, the subject of most of this book? The experience of the NNDFN and the NNFC in Namibia highlights the urgent need for similar organizations across the border. In November 1991 the Dobe and /Xai/ xai Ju/'hoansi, along with Bushmen of other linguistic groups to the south, held a joint meeting with the NNFC, and one of the outcomes is that the Botswana people were mobilizing for action. Through the 1990s they addressed international agencies in Gaborone directly for emergency aid to drill boreholes, so that they could apply as syndicates for grazing land—even if they have no cattle—before they are boxed out of the last land available. In the experience of the KPF and NNDFN, they will need strategic help from outsiders— transport and communications—in order to achieve this. Gaborone is 800 *miles—*

The Executive of the Nyae Nyae Farmer's Co-op and Dr. Megan Biesele and Richard Lee at a meeting in Windhoek, Namibia.

not 800 kilometers—from Dobe. Until the land base is secured the future of the Dobe area Ju/'hoansi will hang in the balance.[7]

JU/'HOANSI AT THE MILLENNIUM: PROGRESS AND POVERTY

In the first decade of the twenty-first century, the people of Dobe continue to travel the road away from their hunting and gathering past and toward an uncertain future. On our most recent visits to Dobe village in 1999 and 2001, both Megan Biesele and myself noted some major changes. First, the long and twisting 90-mile road to the village had been vastly improved, with travel time cut from 6–7 hours to 2.5. At Dobe waterhole, something new had emerged; the 150 residents were living

---

[7]All the remarkable quotes in this chapter from Ju/'hoan speakers, with the exception of Chiqo Nxauwe's (p. 173) and /Toma's (p. 175), were recorded in the field and translated by Megan Biesele in her capacity as professional documentarian for the Nyae Nyae Farmers' Cooperative. In comparison with more conventional anthropological data, these quotes represent privileged communications that could have been gathered in no other way except through Biesele's involvement in a people's grassroots movement. This illustrates the quality of the insights possible through the kind of anthropological engagement discussed in more detail in Chapter 13, pp. 196–197.

Dobe people returning to the village from a day's work on a government road improvement project (1999).

in eight hamlets drawing their water from a new borehole, engine, and water tank. But the space in front of the borehole had created a sort of "downtown" where people congregated. The pride of the village though, was a soccer field, where teams of local and outside youths played a daily pickup game. Nearby, a preschool had been set up to give students two years of preparation before attending the main primary school as boarders, in !Kangwa 20 kilometers away. Dobe had become more cosmopolitan with a dozen outsiders resident: there were border guards patrolling the Namibian frontier two kilometers to the west, as well as veterinary officials, teachers, and construction workers.

On the downside, home-brew sellers, formerly confined to !Kangwa, had brought their trade to "downtown" Dobe, bringing daily drinking parties and social dysfunction. Dobe's most traumatic experience, however, had been in 1996 when a districtwide outbreak of bovine pleuro-pneumonia (which, it should be noted, is *not* mad-cow disease or foot-and-mouth disease) had necessitated destruction of the entire cattle population of the Northwest District. Some 300,000 head were slaughtered, including several thousand in the Dobe area, and their carcasses buried by bulldozers. Ju/'hoansi who were slowly building up their herds since the 1970s, lost everything. Although herd owners were compensated, the process of rebuilding herds has been slow.

The central borehole and water tank at "downtown" Dobe.

The daily soccer game at Dobe where both local and outside players defuse tensions and enjoy recreation.

Ecologists however, were heartened at the welcome relief of pressure on the fragile ecosystem by the sudden withdrawal of bovine biomass. The new situation refocused attention on a prime pre-existing "asset" of the Dobe area: the still-abundant game populations. The creation of Wildlife Conservancies, under

The new Community Based Game Management Project at /Xai/ xai posts their boundary marker on the road not far from Dobe.

Botswana's Community-Based Natural Resource Management Programs (CBNRM), is an effort to combine environmental conservation with economic development. Small-scale wildlife conservancies have sprung up throughout Africa, 28 in Botswana alone. At /Xai/ xai, south of Dobe, the Thlabololo Development Trust (TDT) also known as the (CTT), originally with Dutch overseas assistance, has created a wildlife management area controlled by the Ju/'hoansi. The Trust caters to tourists who want to experience Ju/'hoan life and see game, while limited subsistence hunting and gathering by Ju themselves is allowed. The TDT had revenues of P400,000 (About $80,000 US) in 1999–2000.

The Ju of Dobe are in the process of setting up a similar wildlife conservancy under the guidance of the Kuru Development Trust, a successful Botswana-based NGO with funding from Germany, the Netherlands, Scandinavia, and the European Union. In preparation for the Conservancy, a land use and mapping project was instituted at Dobe, making the most thorough study of local ecology since the intensive research of the 1960s. The Land Use Study has demonstrated the feasibility of the Kalahari People's Fund initiative of the 1980s to drill a series of boreholes on Dobe's outer margins. Now successfully revived, the plan will resettle Ju families and secure their

The new branch office of the Kuru Development Trust under construction in "downtown" Dobe, July 1999.

land against the threat of land encroachment by Tswana cattle syndicates. As of April 2001, the Trust's name was changed to the Tocadi Development Trust and two bore-holes had been successfully drilled. The careful groundwork of the renowned development anthropologist, Dr. Robert Hitchcock, of the University of Nebraska, has been a key to implementation of these plans.

Across the border in Namibia, the 1990s Ju/'hoansi of Nyae Nyae have traveled a similarly rocky road of triumphs and failures. After the independence of Namibia and the successful National Land Conference, there was much discussion of development options for the people of Nyae Nyae. After feasibility studies sponsored by the Nyae Nyae Development Foundation, the Nyae Nyae Wildlife Conservancy was set up in 1995. It was the result of a bold initiative called the "Living in a Finite Environment" (LIFE) Project, funded by USAID, that sought to combine conservation, game management, tourism, and rural economic development.

In 1996 the Tsumkwe Lodge opened, offering tours to selected Ju/'hoan villages and, for the first time in the area, lodge-style accommodations. The Nyae Nyae Farmers' Cooperative launched its own eco-cultural-tourism program around the same time.

The early 1990s had been a stormy period for the Farmers' Cooperative and its funding source, the Nyae Nyae Development Foundation. Infighting among Foundation personnel over conflicting philosophies of change and management styles had mirrored dissension within the Cooperative itself. In a dramatic move in 1996 the Ju/'hoansi asked Foundation personnel to withdraw to Windhoek and leave running of the Co-op to the Ju themselves. After a general shakeup of both organizations non-Ju staff were cut back and Ju took over all management positions. The results have been mixed. Despite the efforts of the LIFE project and the NNDFN, the 37 Nyae Nyae villages continue to vary widely in viability. In a recent study, Polly Wiessner evaluated the subsistence levels of a sample of villages and found over one-third were experiencing a serious shortfall in food supply (Wiessner, 1998). At the Co-op's Baraka headquarters, vehicles have been rolled and rendered undriveable. Recently the Nyae Nyae Farmers' Co-op renamed itself the Nyae Nyae Conservancy in recognition of the importance of Community-Based Natural Resource Management (CBNRM) for the future of the Ju/'hoansi.

The Village Schools Project has been one of the bright spots in Nyae Nyae. The VSP offers three years of preschool training in their own language and in English for 6–8-year-olds to prepare them for the government primary school at Tsumkwe. Initiated by the Nyae Nyae community with the support of Megan Biesele and others in the Nyae Nyae Development Foundation in 1990, the project has assisted hundreds of Ju children with the culture shock of the transition from village life to life in an African residential school.

Small Victories

To give some life to these broad accounts, let us look at the lives of several individuals. Chu!ko N//auwe (Chiqo Nxauwe), the lively young woman from Bate, had been the first female student from the Dobe area to reach high school. Graduating from a junior secondary school in 1989, Chu!ko was hired as a clerk-interpreter in the !Kung San Works, a craft-buying operation in Maun. After completing several years in that post she then taught school at /Xai/ xai, before going to nursing school to train as a family planning educator. Now in her early thirties, with two children (though no husband) Chu!ko has taken the post of family planning educator attached to the !Kangwa Clinic. She dispenses birth control advice and holds workshops to explain their options to rural women, the first Dobe area woman to hold such a high-status position. Recently Chu!ko has added AIDS education to her job description.

The Gods Must Be Crazy (1984) was filmed on location in the Nyae Nyae area by South African director, Jamie Uys (pronounced "Ace") in 1978. Along with its sequel (1990), it became the highest-grossing non-U.S. film of all time. The role of "the Bushman" was played by /Gaq'o, a 30-year-old Ju man from Tjum!kui (Tsumkwe). Portrayed in the press kit as a leather-clad hunter-gatherer, /Gaq'o in fact had never hunted and was employed in the Tjum!kui primary school as a cook (Davis, 1996:90–91)! Despite the films' grossing over $100 million U.S., Uys paid /Gaq'o only the equivalent of U.S. $2,000. The arts and film community of South Africa protested this scandalous underpayment, and before his death Uys gave /Gaq'o $20,000 U.S. plus a monthly stipend. With the money /Gaq'o built a western style house on the main street of Tjum!kui, where he can still be seen by backpacking tourists on the porch, spending time with his family.

The roller-coaster life of Kgau Royal /O/oo mirrors the ups and downs of the Ju/'hoansi from the 1960s to the 1990s. Born in 1964 (I was present at his birth) Kgau grew up in a close-knit, though unconventional family. His father had been a good hunter while his mother and older sisters had participated in the new home-brew economy at !Kangwa. Displaying a keen intelligence as a child, Kgau was among the very first Ju/'hoan children to attend !Kangwa school after it opened in 1973. By 1985 the youthful-looking Kgau had made it to Maun Junior Secondary School, the first Ju from the Dobe area to do so. After graduation his excellent English got him many jobs

Chiqo Nxauwe, the Family Health Educator with her son, at the !Kangwa Clinic,
Botswana (1999).

working as an interpreter with government offices, visiting anthropologists, and filmmakers. His personal life was stormy, however, with changing jobs and a succession
of girl friends. After Namibia's 1989 move to Independence under the democratic
leadership of SWAPO, Kgau /O/oo emigrated to the new nation to answer the demand
for educated English speakers. There he made his mark in the Nyae Nyae Farmers
Co-op as the presenter for the Nyae Nyae position paper at the National Land Conference (see p. 179), as spokesperson at international fora, and as Namibian President

Children at the Bushman "location" at Tjum!kui (Tsumkwe) Namibia. Urbanization comes to the Ju/'hoansi.

The Honourable Royal Kgau /O/oo (standing left), Ju/'hoan member of Namibian parliament, and his family, with R. B. Lee (standing second from right), August 2001.

Sam Nujoma's personal interpreter when he toured Bushmanland. His language skills were key in his co-authoring with Megan Biesele the book *San* (Biesele and /O/oo, 1997).

Despite these successes, Kgau's personal life, like so many of his generation and background, continued to be unstable. Yet after 1997 Kgau Royal /O/oo made a dramatic personal turnaround. Elected to the post of Traditional Tribal Authority at Tjum!kui, he stopped drinking and devoted himself fully to the welfare of his

The elected headman at Dobe. //Kau, jokingly expresses the tensions and frustrations of his office, being pulled in all directions.

constituents. His third wife, Paula, from an Angolan !Kung family displaced by the war, was a major influence in setting him straight. News of his good work spread, and in 1999 he was summoned to Windhoek by President Nujoma. The Namibian constitution permits the president to appoint members of Parliament from under-represented marginalized minorities. Nujoma offered Kgau the seat and he accepted. Now Kgau /O/oo sits in national Parliament, owns a home and car in Windhoek, and stays in touch with his constituents in Tjum!kui by fax and cell phone.

REGIONAL DEVELOPMENTS: MANDELA AND AFTER

The 1990s saw tumultuous changes in the political landscape of southern Africa: the Independence of Namibia, followed closely by the release of Nelson Mandela from prison in 1990 and his coming to power in South Africa's first democratic elections (in 1994). The Ju/'hoansi speak of the recent era as the time of "//xabe" or "opening up," as new political and cultural spaces opened up for San peoples. The founding of the Workgroup for Indigenous Minorities of Southern Africa (WIMSA) as an important umbrella group based in Windhoek has created a forum at which leaders from Dobe, Tsumkwe, Baraka, and many other communities can come together to get a sense of common problems and lobby for change. WIMSA delegations have traveled to Geneva, London, Stockholm, and New York and have received very sympathetic hearings from governments and NGOs. Wildlife Conservancies and schools programs are just two of the kinds of grassroots programs receiving international support. More information on WIMSA and many other southern African Indigenous organizations can be found at the Kalahari Peoples Fund website (http://www.kalaharipeoples.org).

Kgau Royal /O/oo (left), the Member of Namibian Parliament for Tjum!kui (Tsumkwe) District meets with a constituent in his district.

THE CHALLENGE OF HIV/AIDS

In 1994, after successfully surviving the hardships of long-running regional wars, the legacy of colonialism, and the horrors of the apartheid system, the peoples of southern Africa looked forward to a bright future after the coming to power in South Africa of Nelson Mandela's government. For the first time, non-racial democracy had been achieved throughout the region. However, a new and ominous threat was already disrupting the lives of first thousands and then millions in South Africa, Botswana, Namibia, and other countries.

Today the countries of southern Africa have the highest rates of HIV/AIDS in the world. U.N. figures for June 2000 show a seropositive rate among adults of 19.54 percent in Namibia, 19.94 percent in South Africa, and a staggering 35.8 percent in Botswana. The epidemic threatens to undo the development gains of recent decades and cause incalculable hardship and suffering among the ordinary peoples of the region. In certain districts in Botswana life expectancy has already fallen from 55 to 37. In parts of KwaZulu-Natal, one-half of all adults are carrying the virus.

Geographically the Ju/'hoansi are located in the heart of the world region hardest hit by AIDS. How has the AIDS epidemic affected the Ju/'hoan people? As late as 1987 there were no cases of AIDS reported from Dobe or Nyae Nyae and the peoples of the region wondered if the disease would somehow bypass them. By the mid-1990s however, cases began to appear; both areas now have many. Although reliable figures are lacking, there may be between 50 and 100 HIV-positive individuals, in a population on both sides of the border of about 2,500 Ju/'hoan people. Although this figure may seem high, it is not. Compared to levels in cities, towns, and along truck routes elsewhere in Namibia and Botswana, the incidence of the

Young Ju/'hoan men and women at the Tjum!kui "location." Home-brew sellers and "she-beens" have become a point of transmission for HIV.

disease is quite low, between 3 and 6 percent HIV positive compared to national averages of 20 to 35 percent.

Since 1996 Professor Ida Susser, of the City University of New York, and I have been studying social and cultural aspects of the AIDS epidemic in Namibia and Botswana. In the course of this work we have traveled widely and interviewed men and women in urban and rural settings (Susser, 2000; Lee, 2001). In Africa AIDS is primarily a heterosexual disease; transmitted mainly through unprotected vaginal intercourse. The most effective means of preventing transmission is condom use. For a variety of cultural and economic reasons, abstinence and/or strict monogamy do not appear to be viable solutions. Recognizing the realities of the situation, governments and international agencies have made condoms widely available for free through clinics and health posts. For example at Tjum!kui, Namibia, the international organization Health Unlimited as well as the government clinic both distribute condoms.

The problem is that despite the known dangers, nationally many Namibian men object to the use of condoms. Men view the condom as implying unfaithfulness and become angry if the issue is raised. This has placed Namibian women in a very difficult situation. Here a striking contrast has emerged in how young Ju/'hoansi women negotiate sex compared to women in other Namibian ethnic groups. Among Ovambo and Damara women, if a husband or boyfriend does not want to use a condom, they say there is little they can do about it for fear of being abused or abandoned. In our interviews, Ju/'hoan women by contrast, told us that whether to have sex with a man is their decision and is not being forced on them. One said she would not agree to sleep with a man unless he used a condom, while other girls expressed caution in entering into any kind of liaison.

There is a remarkable link here to Ju/'hoan women's long-noted sense of empowerment and high status relative to men (see Chapter 6). It has proven to be a valuable defense in the fight against AIDS and certainly contributes to the lower HIV-positive rates noted for the Ju/'hoansi. This contrast highlights the high status of Ju women, noted in the more "traditional" past (Draper, 1975), and evidently this sense of autonomy has proven crucial to their avoidance, so far, of the most devastating effects of the AIDS crisis.

Unfortunately, that is not the whole story. Not all Ju women are as thoughtful and prudent as were our informants. There are pockets both in Namibia and Botswana where young Ju women participate in the drinking culture of shebeens and home-brew establishments catering largely to men from outside the communities. These liaisons have created points of entry for HIV infection and from these AIDS "hot spots" the virus may spread to the wider community.

One of the initiatives currently underway by the Kalahari Peoples Fund is to produce AIDS education kits appropriate to Ju/'hoan language and cultural values. The KPF is convinced that such materials must be part of all future development work and included in every project from well-digging to schooling to natural resource management. WIMSA (the Workgroup for Indigenous Minorities in Southern Africa) has endorsed these initiatives and is extending them to other indigenous groups. The next decade will be crucial in whether the Ju and other San communities are able to develop the coping skills that will enable them to survive in the Age of AIDS. More information on this work will be posted on the Kalahari Peoples Fund website (http://www.kalaharipeoples.org).

13/Anthropological Practice and Lessons of the Ju/'hoansi

As one of the most thoroughly documented and cross-examined foraging societies in anthropological history, and as the darlings of the mass media, the Ju/'hoansi–!Kung have come to occupy a special place in the scholarly and popular imagination as a rich source of models and speculation on past human society. But as we have seen in Chapter 12, with each year the leather-clad, bow-and-arrow wielding Ju/'hoansi look less and less like hunter-gatherers. Their remoteness and desert location, so long effective barriers to colonization, no longer protect them. The cash nexus, poverty, class formation, bureaucratic control, and media manipulation, as well as anomie and alienation, are all part of the daily lives of the Ju/'hoansi–!Kung people in the 1990s and 2000s. Like other foragers they have become increasingly drawn into the world system.

The changes have been so far-reaching and so rapid that many anthropologists and others have failed to absorb the implications, and this has resulted in a curious schism or division in scholarly and popular perceptions of them.

One school of thought, labelled "traditionalists," attempt to deal with the changes by ignoring them. They see today's dire circumstances and frankly, liked the Ju/'hoansi better "the way they were," when they dressed in skins and foraged for a living. Refusing to acknowledge the passing of the old ways, these anthropologists seem determined to focus exclusively on foraging behavior either to build models of the evolution of human behavior, or to perpetuate the romantic image of the "noble savage," even in the face of contradictory evidence. The film *The Gods Must Be Crazy* is an obvious example of this tendency; however, some contemporary models in evolutionary ecology fall into this error, too.[1]

But another school of thought, sometimes labelled "revisionist," has attempted to come to grips with the changes in the opposite way; they see in the Ju/'hoansi's current poverty and exploitation, evidence not of novelty, but of continuity with the past. They argue that the Ju/'hoansi are not hunters and gatherers at all in the conventional sense. Ju/'hoan people have been dominated for centuries; thus their recent foraging ways are part of a culture of poverty and can bear no resemblance to the ancestral cultures of the Later Stone Age (e.g., Wilmsen, 1989; cf. Gordon, 1992; Lewin, 1988).

---

[1]Not all such models can be so characterized; but those that treat foragers as isolates and exclude consideration of a broader social context are out of touch with today's realities. One widely cited study of "optimal foraging" for example, barely acknowledged that the foragers in question, whose behavior was the basis for elaborate model-building, spent the greater part of their year living sedentary lives on store-bought rations on a mission station.

I am convinced that neither the traditionalist nor the revisionist position can do justice to the realities of Ju/'hoan life today, or in the past. Indeed, one of my goals in this book has been to bring together these shattered perceptions and to restore to the Ju/'hoansi a semblance of coherence. To the revisionists I would argue that the dire conditions of today's Ju/'hoansi cannot simply be projected onto their entire history. In fact recent research has found evidence for a degree of viability and autonomy for Ju/'hoansi as foragers in the last century and well into the 1960s (Chapter 2, pp. 18-22, and Appendix B). And to the traditionalists I would point out that the Ju/'hoansi didn't stop being a people when the last hunter laid down his bow and picked up a transistor radio. The Ju persist as a people, embattled and struggling, but a people nonetheless with a strong sense of themselves.

When anthropologists struggle to respond to the dramatic changes in Dobe and Nyae Nyae life, and in the lives of other band and tribal peoples, they are grappling with still larger issues concerning "science," "humanism," and the ethics of fieldwork. Many of the principles that were once taken for granted are now up for grabs. At stake is the broader question of whether a "science-oriented" research strategy with its roots in the eighteenth-century Enlightenment constitutes an adequate basis for the practice of anthropology in the year 2000 and beyond. The Enlightenment, embodied in the ideals of the French and the American (and Russian) revolutions, saw science and democracy as two elements of a program of human emancipation. Scientific progress and political reform were supposed to be the twin bases for liberating the human potential. But things haven't always worked out that way, and many are asking whether this long-potent combination of research strategy and political rallying cry can still do service in the age of the "end of history" and postmodern disillusionment?

There are two responses to this problem: some reject science on political grounds while others, equally sincere, reject political commitment on "scientific" grounds. Practically speaking, both tendencies question the idea that an "objective," "hands-off" science will actually solve the world's problems, and both lead in different ways to an attitude of disengagement. In the discipline of anthropology at large, responses have varied widely: some don't even acknowledge that there is a problem and carry on as if nothing were amiss: the science as business-as-usual attitude of the traditionalists. Others see the changes as so catastrophic that they are grounds for rejecting all previous understandings, leading toward the dark postmodern visions of the revisionists (Lee, 1992a).

But these are not the only possible outcomes. Some anthropologists reject neither science *nor* political engagement; they seek to combine science with a sense of political and ethical awareness which, in current jargon, has been called reflexivity. By and large the members of both the Marshall and the Harvard Kalahari research groups have avoided either of the extremes. In different ways they have been cognizant of change while recognizing continuities and have tried to combine the methods of science with a recognition of changing political realities.

Most of the original researchers have maintained a degree of focus, continuing to remain active in research and advocacy among the Ju/'hoansi into the 1990s and 2000s. Lorna Marshall, at age 100, recently completed her second monograph on Nyae Nyae Ju/'hoansi belief and ritual (L. Marshall, 1999). John Marshall's ongoing filmmaking has won international acclaim (Kapfer, Petermann, and Thoms, 1991).

Many of the Harvard group continued to do field research in the Kalahari into the 1980s and 1990s. Megan Biesele, Nicholas Blurton-Jones, Alison Brooks, Pat Draper, Henry Harpending, Nancy Howell, Richard Katz, Richard Lee, the late Marjorie Shostak, and John Yellen have all made one or more trips to the area in the period 1984–2000.

Former students such as Robert Hitchcock, Elizabeth Cashdan, Jim Ebert, Helga Vierich, and Jacqueline Solway have produced theses and articles on Kalahari research and have gone on to productive careers in their own right (Hitchcock, 1977, 1982; Cashdan, 1987, 1990; Ebert, 1979, 1989; Vierich, 1982; Kent and Vierich, 1989; Solway, 1990). All their studies have attempted, in different ways, to document the pace of change and its impacts.

My own way of approaching the San has changed over the years and these changes have taken me away from the position I started with. I no longer believe that studies of contemporary hunter-gatherers are primarily a tool for understanding the evolution of human behavior. Understanding hunter-gatherer ecology, however important, is not enough. One has to both build on it and transcend it by looking at adaptation in a much broader sense, including the internal dynamics of foragers and their articulation with wider political economies. This has led to a shift in my thinking, away from an emphasis on hunting and gathering as modes of subsistence and toward the broader concept of Communal Mode of Production (Lee, 1988, 1990a, 1992a; Leacock and Lee, 1982; Lee and Daly, 1999).

A second change has to do with moving away from hunter-gatherers as an "object" of study and toward research as a more collaborative exercise, in which anthropologists consciously give way, allowing the people to take over direction of research and set the agenda in terms of their own priorities. While this is a still unrealized goal for many of us, some anthropologists have moved further in this direction.

An excellent illustration of this change in research strategy can be found in the San research. For some anthropologists, the magnitude of the dislocations experienced by the San has made it morally impossible to continue as before: some researchers have become actively committed to an anthropology of "grassroots" development. Starting in Botswana, Robert Hitchcock has become an internationally known advocate of the rights of indigenous peoples (e.g., Hitchcock, 1988; Morris and Hitchcock, 1992; Hitchcock and Holm, 1993). Also, John Marshall's and Megan Biesele's years of involvement with the Nyae Nyae Development Foundation of Namibia (along with Claire Ritchie) has brought them into a very different relationship with the Ju/'hoansi, one not envisioned by the premises of anthropological research current in the 1960s.[2] Yet even here, many of the traditional ethnographic field methods—collecting genealogies, land-use surveys, and analysis of political processes—remain vital to the work of the NNDFN (Biesele et al., 1989; Biesele and Weinberg, 1990; J. Marshall and C. Ritchie, 1984).

The Foundation's basic approach has been to provide strategic support to a peoples' movement, the Nyae Nyae Farmers' Cooperative, now known as the Nyae Nyae Conservancy. The anthropologists concerned have made available to development

---

[2]An early move in this direction was the formation 30 years ago of the Kalahari Peoples' Fund, a nonprofit foundation based in Austin, Texas.

John Marshall (center), co-founder of the NNDFN, and Tsamkxao Toma, President of the Nyae Nyae Farmers Cooperative (second left) meet with village elders and friends from Dobe.

workers, government bodies, and the people themselves—via the Cooperative—all the social, cultural, and ecological understandings built up by research since the time of the Marshall expeditions (1951ff) and reinforced by the long friendship between the Ju and the Marshall family. Clearly this approach involves more than collecting data and publishing results: it has involved a radically new communication process pursued over years, in tandem with the peoples' own grassroots organization.

Megan Biesele's work with the Foundation from 1987–1994 illustrates the changing role of the anthropologist. Drawing on her skills as a folklorist and student of Ju/'hoan traditional ideology, she sought to expand further their already rich and nuanced traditional concepts of land use and social organization and apply them to new settings and new challenges. While other researchers carried out the censuses and land-use surveys, much of Biesele's work has consisted of attending the frequent Co-op meetings and transcribing and translating recordings of these meetings. These transcripts have documented the growth of political self-awareness and the establishment of a Ju/'hoan voice in Namibian national politics. Biesele worked closely with Royal O/oo and the Co-op leaders to develop the brief presented to the Namibian National Land Conference of June 1991 (see Chapter 12, p. 179).

As any reader of this book will have learned, the Ju/'hoansi have always been eloquent and perceptive. But this eloquence and perceptiveness has only recently extended to a grasp of the realities of current national politics, as this statement by Oza !Amace, a former northern !Kung, at a recent NNFC meeting shows:

> It looks to outsiders like Ju/'hoansi have no sense. People who can write have come to see those who can't write as being *behind*. Let's make sure our children go to school and learn to write. Today our people have no work, and try to make a living by selling bows and arrows and tortoise shells. . . . But we have to begin to work with other Namibian people

to find a way to live. . . . It seems that the people holding the paper-sticks [pencils] are the ones who have the say over everything, and we who have no pencils are behind. . . . The Black people and the colored people all have been to school and have pencils and have sense and have things to eat, but not the Ju/'hoansi.[3]

The Ju/'hoansi in these transcriptions do not appear as uniformly heroic and insightful; along with eloquent calls to action, there are notes of despair, confusion, and "false consciousness," reflecting the complex cross-currents in Ju/'hoan life in the 1990s and 2000s.

In situations such as these with the rapid emergence of political consciousness, what can an anthropologist's role be? The role of listener—while people hash out their own problems—may be a large part of it. John Marshall has called this work "a kind of cultural therapy," providing a forum for the exploration of nontraditional political and social issues. Is this to be the anthropology of the future, or at least one version of it? The point at which science and reflexivity meet is perhaps the most compelling feature of this combination of advocacy research with long-term field work in anthropology.

The Nyae Nyae Development Foundation's novel philosophy and goals have been seen by some as a model for anthropology in the future; but others have argued that this is not "science" but "advocacy" and by becoming advocates the scholars forever lose their objectivity. This is a serious charge. Dealing with crises as "advocates" or "intervenors" clearly alters the work of anthropologists, but what is the alternative, if what is at stake is the final loss of a secure land base, the loss of which would foreclose any possibility of future self-determination?

To the anticipated charge of conventional science that such intervention creates distortion, I would agree with Biesele's response that human subjects have always been conscious and active on their own behalf; only the *degree* of their involvement in research has varied. We would argue that knowledge produced in a situation where people are fully involved is different, perhaps, but no less important. If anything, it is clearer and more vital.

THE CHANGING IMAGE OF THE JU/'HOANSI

In recent years anthropologists have watched with dismay as their traditional subjects, the world's so-called "primitive" societies, have been disappearing with the speed of light. Group after group has been settled, censused, inoculated, administered, and put to work in the fields, sweatshops, and factories of the New World Order. The very idea that anthropologists as recently as the 1950s or 1960s could have spent their time with people who dressed in skin clothing and hunted and gathered for a living is actually a source of embarrassment for many of our colleagues. They seem to take a perverse pride in the fact that the world system has penetrated every nook and cranny and that now even the Ju/'hoansi are wearing Levis and drinking Coke.

Others take a different view: for these observers it is a source of astonished delight that the Ju/'hoansi and others like them could have resisted the steamroller of

---

[3]This quote has an interesting background. It is from a meeting taped entirely by Farmers' Co-op workers and intentionally not attended by Foundation staff. The tape was furnished to Megan Biesele, with permission, for transcription and translation for the Cooperative's and the Foundation's archives.

modernity for so long. In the 2000s observers remain amazed at the creative persistence of Ju/'hoan culture in the face of massive outside pressure.

It is these divergent views that underlie the schism in perceptions of the Ju/'hoansi discussed at the outset (pp. 193–194), what I have called the "crisis in hunter-gatherer studies" (Lee, 1992a). For some partisans in these often-heated debates there seems to be only two alternatives: either the Ju/'hoansi are totally pristine, or if not, they must be totally dominated. But why does living in the present mean that a people must be totally divorced from their past? Modernity and the market are powerful and pervasive; but they are not *that* powerful or *that* pervasive. The Ju/'hoansi are enduring but not unchanging; they are adapting to the world system as fast as they can. Their newfound political and technical skills augment a formidable array of knowledge and practices inherited from their foremothers and forefathers: their language, kinship and naming systems, rituals and mythology, subsistence practices, and above all, their ironic sensibility are the firm bases on which they are constructing their future.

What accounts for the ongoing vitality of the Dobe and Nyae Nyae Ju/'hoansi and of so many "indigenous" peoples like them? It is obvious that there is no simple answer to this question. However, I am persuaded that one of their "secret weapons" for survival is their adherence to a communal mode of production, an ethic of sharing and egalitarianism; put simply *it is their ability to reproduce themselves as a society while limiting the accumulation of wealth and power.* Their commitment to egalitarian politics and reciprocity gives them a tremendous source of strength and persistence. Communal relations of production are a widespread and well-documented phenomenon, found among the Ju/'hoansi and a number of hunter-gatherers in a wide variety of historical settings. They are also found among many "tribal" peoples with mixed economies of foraging and horticulture, among former foragers in peripheral capitalism, as well as in some peasant societies (for example, Andean Peru).

It is unfortunate that for many North Americans the term "communal" conjures up associations with "communism" and that this reflex reaction, a product of the Cold War, has led many people to avoid considering the underlying meaning of the concept at all. But as I have pointed out elsewhere (Lee, 1990a) *primitive* communist societies have almost nothing in common with the heavily bureaucratic and authoritarian state structures of the twentieth century "actually existing Socialism." In fact they are the precise opposite of the planned, centralized, media-saturated mass societies of the twentieth century—East *and* West.

If we agree for the moment on the *existence* of communal relations of production in diverse non-industrial settings, the next question is how is it to be explained? Briefly, these societies operate within the confines of a metaphorical "ceiling and floor": a ceiling above which one may not accumulate wealth and power and a floor below which one may not sink. These limits on both aggrandizement and destitution, on upward *and* downward mobility, are maintained by powerful social mechanisms, such as "insulting the meat" and other levelling devices (Lee, 1990a:242–245). "Eating Christmas in the Kalahari" (see Appendix A) is a classic example of these levelling devices in action. Such societies therefore have social and political resources of their own and are not just sitting ducks waiting to adopt the first hierarchical model that comes along.

This is not to imply that these non-state, communally-based societies lived in a state of perfect equality. Hunter-gatherers may exhibit some differences in wealth and

/Twin!a and Kasupe enjoying a good joke at Dobe in 1987.

power and they are certainly *not* nonviolent. I prefer to follow the argument developed by Harriet Rosenberg in her research on !Kung aging and caregiving, set out in Chapter 7. Rosenberg uses the term "entitlement" to account for the ways in which !Kung elderly were cared for by relatives and nonrelatives alike, such that no one, not even childless people, would be denied access to support in old age. This was part of a general phenomenon in !Kung society in which everyone claimed, and was recognized as being "entitled" to, the necessities of life, by right of being a member of the society.

> !Kung elders do not see themselves as burdens. They are not apologetic if they are not able to produce enough to feed themselves. They expect others to care for them when they can no longer do so. Entitlement to care is naturalized within the culture. Elders do not have to negotiate care as if it were a favor; rather it is perceived as a right. (Rosenberg, 1990:29)

Fortunately in the wider world there are signs that people in key places are learning the lessons and recognizing the value of the world of the "primitive." There are signs of convergence between the Ju/'hoan agenda and the changing perspectives among international development agencies, governments, aid workers, media, and scholars. There is recent growth of interest in the notions of "small is beautiful," of "tribal wisdom," and "biodiversity," as seen on the cover of *Time,* the pages of *Cultural Survival Quarterly,* the *Millennium* television series, the Rio Earth Summit and in "green" grassroots politics everywhere (Eaton, Shostak, and Konner, 1988; Durning, 1992). The United Nations declared 1993–2003 the "Decade of Indigenous People," and in 2000 Pope John Paul publicly apologized to the world's indigenous peoples for historic injustices committed by the Catholic Church (along with apologies to other oppressed minorities).

Two specific examples may illustrate this point. Long ignored or downplayed, the communal mode of production has recently made a comeback of sorts and has become a serious subject of study. Theories of common property management are now being debated at the World Bank, and by aid agencies, lawyers, social scientists, and development workers in many parts of the world. One sign of this interest is the formation of an organization called the *International Association for the Study of Common Property,* which meets annually in various world centers. The association argues that since many systems of property management and land tenure work this way, and work quite successfully, it makes sense to try to understand them.

A second instance of this new awareness is the worldwide attention and sympathy indigenous peoples in the United States, Canada, Australia, and the Third World have received; the voices of the marginalized are beginning to be heard in the councils of state. To take just one striking example: for the first time in Canadian history aboriginal people were given full status at a constitutional conference in August 1992. Three members of the native delegation were Inuit (Eskimo) women from Arctic Canada, one of whom—Rosemary Kuptana—grew up in a tent with her hunting and gathering parents. The three played important roles in the drafting of new Canadian constitutional proposals, leading the press to call them the "new mothers of Confederation."

All these signs offer some indication that the wheel may be turning in favor of the preservation of "small peoples," not as museum specimens, but through their recognition as repositories of invaluable knowledge regarding plants, animals, and localities, and as living embodiments of alternative ways of being. As the world enters the new millennium, the two most pressing issues are first, how to rediscover "democracy" and a "just" society, and second, how to find ways of living in balance with our finite resources. The lessons of the Ju/'hoansi and other indigenous peoples offer insights on both these questions and challenge the current complacencies. Their newfound recognition is a cause for optimism. Let us take heart: ecological and cultural diversity may still have a place on this planet.

Postscript / The /Gwihaba Dancers

It would be far too early to count the Ju/'hoansi out of the running in the struggle for dignity and viability. Some of the resilience and adaptability that struck so many observers of their life in the 1960s and 1970s is evidenced in the ways the Ju/'hoansi of one small village are adapting themselves to the new order of things. This is a story about a school, some parents and teachers, and a group of students.

As discussed in Chapter 11, schooling came late to the Dobe area Ju/'hoansi. The first school opened at !Kangwa in 1973 and even today it has still not become an integral part of Ju lives. For a long list of reasons, the absentee rate remains high and parents and children of several outlying communities continue to regard the school with suspicion.

The second school, which opened at /Xai/ xai in 1976, proved to be more successful. The /Xai/ xai school was in many ways no different from others in the remoter parts of the country: three or four classrooms plus teachers' housing and a kitchen for the lunch program, all without electricity in a compound fenced to keep out cattle. Classes began at seven and ended at one, with younger grades holding early morning classes outdoors, since inside the unheated classrooms it was often close to freezing.

But in other ways, the /Xai/ xai school was different. In innumerable small ways, the Tswana headmaster, Mr. Seelapilu, encouraged Ju/'hoan participation and the parents and children of this small community of 300 rewarded his efforts with an attendance rate for Ju children of over 90 percent. In the recess and afterschool chatter, one could hear Ju children's games being played as well as Tswana and Herero games, and Ju/'hoan language was freely spoken. Elsewhere we noted that headmasters would often punish such usage in a misguided policy of assimilation.

In 1986 Harriet Rosenberg and I, along with our daughter Miriam, were en route to /Xai/ xai after an absence of several years. I had lived there for 14 months in the 1960s and knew many of the people well. Among other goals, Harriet and I were curious to see how Mr. Seelapilu's ongoing experiment in multicultural education was faring. We also wanted to see /Twan!a, a dynamic young grandmother who had given Harriet her Ju/'hoan name (/Twa) and adopted her as a !kuma (see Chapter 5). Grinding along in the heavy sand down an isolated road, we began to make out over the roar of the engine the sound of a large vehicle and some high-pitched, muffled but melodious sounds we could not identify. In the thick bush we could see nothing, so we drove on. Gradually the sounds grew louder and we could distinguish singing voices in the distance. Suddenly around a bend came a five-ton pickup truck with a load of /Xai/ xai schoolchildren—both Ju/'hoan and non-Ju/'hoan—singing lustily in beautiful three-part harmony. Excitedly we stopped; on board we could see the children of many of our old friends. The children, it turned out, were on their way to the annual competition of traditional culture, which brought singers, musicians, and performers together from all over the North West district. The group had decided to call themselves the "/Gwihaba Dancers" after the famous caves (p. 1), now a national monument,

The /Gwihaba Dancers at /Xai/ xai, July 1987.

east of /Xai/ xai. Better yet, the chaperone on board and general cheerleader for the 14 children was none other than /Twan!a herself! We hoisted Miriam up onto the back of the truck to greet her "mother" and the youngsters. After a warm exchange of greetings we wished them good luck and continued on to /Xai/ xai.

For several days the people of /Xai/ xai waited expectantly, eager for news of the children. With no two-way radio or telephone link to the outside, the only sources of news were passing vehicles or the national news service of Radio Botswana; they interrogated truckers and kept glued to their radios, but there was no news. Finally after four days we heard the same truck sound in the distance and the same joyful singing: the troupe was returning to /Xai/ xai. All ran down to the schoolyard to await their arrival. As they approached, /Twan!a was shouting something we couldn't make out and gesturing rapidly with her forefinger in the air. Finally we got it; she was yelling (in English) "We're number one!! We're number one!!" The /Gwihaba Dancers had won first prize in a field that included performing groups from more than 20 schools.

The village was ecstatic: winning this competition was something like winning the Little League World Series and was especially sweet for one of the smallest schools from one of the most isolated villages in the entire District. That night the children were the center of attention in every /Xai/ xai household as every detail of their triumph was discussed around the family fires. The next morning the villagers assembled in the schoolyard while the children, aged 9 to 14, put on a special performance of their winning number, the Lion Dance.

As the girls and boys made their grand entrance, dancing out in single file, one was struck by the beauty of their costumes, the traditional Ju/'hoansi-style leather garments hand-beaded and sewn by the mothers from the hides of antelope especially

Ju/'hoan and Herero dancers of the /Gwihaba Dance Troupe.

hunted by the fathers and older brothers of the schoolchildren. But most impressive was the fact that several of the troupe members were Herero, yet they were wearing the traditional Ju/'hoan karosses and singing the traditional Ju/'hoan songs along with the other children. In the context of Kalahari ethnic and class differences this was a powerful and moving gesture of respect for the Ju/'hoansi and their culture.

The singing was electrifying and the choreography flawlessly executed. The dance was an interesting amalgam of traditional Ju/'hoan dance forms and elements introduced by the troupe's coach, the school's music teacher. The mixture of traditional Ju/'hoan themes with the music teacher's imagination was hokey but effective. It managed to convey drama and intensity while retaining a sense of cultural coherence and fun.

The girls sat singing and clapping in the center while the boys danced around their circle in tight formation. One of the boys, carrying a wooden gun, pretended to stalk another boy dressed in a costume suggesting a lion's mane. The "lion" pranced and threatened, the "hunter" bore down relentlessly. The wounding of the lion started a long death scene in which the lion sank slowly to the ground as the singing became stronger and stronger. At the climax the lion fell dead.

It was a stunning moment. The crowd burst into cheers and applause, followed by several encores. In the hubbub and congratulations that followed the performance, the headmaster, Mr. Seelapilu, was particularly pleased. It was he who had encouraged the dance troupe and had patiently nurtured the spirit of tolerance that pervaded it. For his vision and commitment, we felt the triumph was as much his as it was the children's. Finally, after several minutes of exuberant whooping and hand-shaking, Seelapilu turned and shouted to no one in particular, "This will show the nation that the Mosarwa is a person!"

Winning the district competition entitled the dancers to enter the regional and higher-level competitions where the caliber of performances would be even higher, and they resolved to go. Without voicing our thoughts, Harriet and I wondered at their chances, given the pervasive discrimination against San people in Botswana. And we

As the music teacher looks on, the /Gwihaba Dancers perform their winning number.

assumed that even without other victories, the community would at least have the District prize to cherish in years to come. We were wrong on both counts: the community did not rest on its laurels, and the ethnic chauvinism did not prove to be an insuperable barrier. The saga of the dancers continued.

Having won the following week at a regional competition in Maun as well, the /Gwihaba Dancers went on to the capital, Gaborone, and entered the *national* dance festival. This was the ultimate challenge, with the stiffest competition from dozens of the best performing groups drawn from elite high schools in the large towns of eastern Botswana. No one dared predict what would happen next.

Back in /Xai/ xai, they didn't have to wait for the truck to come back from the capital, which was 800 miles away, because a bulletin came over the national news broadcast that a group of schoolchildren from /Xai/ xai known as the /Gwihaba Dancers had won first prize at the National Festival of Traditional Culture!

The now-famous youngsters were acclaimed throughout Botswana and they became a featured part of the entertainment program accompanying the celebrations later that year of the twentieth anniversary of Botswana's Independence.

Was this an anomaly, we wondered, to the general trend of assimilation of the San to conditions of poverty and marginality that seemed to be the fate of so many indigenous people around the world? Or was this a sign of a change of direction, of a new current of tolerance in the relations between dominant cultures and ethnic minorities? In a landscape (and not just in Botswana) strewn with the debris of racism and intolerance, the story of the /Gwihaba Dancers offered a counter-example of hope; Tswana teachers, working with Ju/'hoansi parents, and teaching Herero and Ju/'hoansi children—creating a tradition of harmonious cultural relationships. Or, it could be just a brief moment with no portent—whose larger meaning will be lost in the sand without a trace.

Headmaster Seelapilu congratulates the /Gwihaba Dancers.

A 2001 FOOTNOTE:

The /Gwihaba Dancers disbanded early in the 1990s. However, one remarkable development followed the Dancers' earlier triumphs. By the mid-1990s "Bushman/Basarwa" dancing had become the rage among Tswana high school students. All-BaTswana dance troupes were formed at elite high schools and Basarwa songs, dance steps, and costumes were meticulously copied by affluent teenagers.

It is not clear whether any benefit will return to the peoples whose cultures are being appropriated. But if as the saying goes, "imitation is the sincerest form of flattery," the people of Botswana are paying the Ju/'hoansi a big compliment.

Appendix A/Eating Christmas
in the Kalahari[1]

The Ju/'hoan knowledge of Christmas is third-hand. The London Missionary Society brought the holiday to the southern Tswana tribes in the early nineteenth century. Later, native catechists spread the idea far and wide among the Bantu-speaking pastoralists, even in the remotest corners of the Kalahari Desert. The Ju idea of the Christmas story, stripped to its essentials, is "praise the birth of White Man's god-chief"; what keeps their interest in the holiday high is the Tswana-Herero custom of slaughtering an ox for their Ju neighbors as an annual goodwill gesture. Since the 1930s, part of the San's annual round of activities has included a December congregation at the cattle-posts for trading, marriage brokering, and several days of trance-dance feasting at which the local Tswana headman is host.

As a social anthropologist working with the Ju/'hoansi, I found that the Christmas ox custom suited my purposes. I had come to the Kalahari to study the hunting and gathering subsistence economy of the Ju/'hoansi, and to accomplish this it was essential not to provide them with food, share my own food, or interfere in any way with their food-gathering activities. While liberal handouts of tobacco and medical supplies were appreciated, they were scarcely adequate to erase the glaring disparity in wealth between the anthropologist, who maintained a two-month inventory of canned goods, and the Ju, who rarely had a day's supply of food on hand. My approach, while paying off in terms of data, left me open to frequent accusations of stinginess and hard-heartedness. By their lights, I was a miser.

The Christmas ox was to be my way of saying thank you for the cooperation of the past year; and since it was to be our last Christmas in the field, I was determined to slaughter the largest, meatiest ox that money could buy, insuring that the feast and trance dance would be a success.

Through December I kept my eyes open at the wells as the cattle were brought down for watering. Several animals were offered, but none had quite the grossness that I had in mind. Then, 10 days before the holiday, a Herero friend led an ox of astonishing size and mass up to our camp. It was solid black, stood five feet high at the shoulder, had a five-foot span of horns, and must have weighed 1200 pounds on the hoof. Food consumption calculations are my specialty, and I quickly figured that bones and viscera aside, there was enough meat—at least four pounds—for every man, woman, and child of the 150 Ju/'hoansi in the vicinity of /Xai/ xai who were expected at the feast.

Having found the right animal at last, I paid the Herero £20 ($56) and asked him to keep the beast with his herd until Christmas Day. The next morning word spread

[1]From "Eating Christmas in the Kalahari," by Richard Borshay Lee, with permission from *Natural History,* December 1969; Copyright the American Museum of Natural History, 1969.

among the people that the big solid-black one was the ox chosen by /Tontah for the Christmas feast. That afternoon I received the first delegation. Ben!a, an outspoken 60-year-old mother of five, came to the point slowly.

"Where were you planning to eat Christmas?"

"Right here at /Xai/ xai," I replied.

"Alone or with others?"

"I expect to invite all the people to eat Christmas with me."

"Eat what?"

"I have purchased Yehave's black ox, and I am going to slaughter and cook it."

"That's what we were told at the well but refused to believe it until we heard it from yourself."

"Well, it's the black one," I replied expansively, although wondering what she was driving at.

"Oh, no!" Ben!a groaned, turning to her group. "They were right." Turning back to me she asked, "Do you expect us to eat that bag of bones?"

"Bag of bones! It's the biggest ox at /Xai/ xai."

"Big, yes, but old. And thin. Everybody knows there's no meat on that old ox. What did you expect us to eat off it, the horns?"

Everybody chuckled at Ben!a's one-liner as they walked away, but all I could manage was a weak grin.

That evening it was the turn of the young men. They came to sit at our evening fire. /Gaugo, about my age, spoke to me man-to-man.

"/Tontah, you have always been square with us. What has happened to change your heart? That sack of guts and bones of Yehave's will hardly feed one camp, let alone all the !Kung around /Xai/ xai." And he proceeded to enumerate the seven camps in the /Xai/ xai vicinity, family by family. "Perhaps you have forgotten that we are not few, but many. Or are you too blind to tell the difference between a proper cow and an old wreck? That ox is thin to the point of death."

"Look, you guys," I retorted, "that is a beautiful animal, and I'm sure you will eat it with pleasure at Christmas."

"Of course we will eat it; it's food. But it won't fill us up to the point where we will have enough strength to dance. We will eat and go home to bed with stomachs rumbling."

That night as we turned in, I asked my wife Nancy: "What did you think of the black ox?"

"It looked enormous to me. Why?"

"Well, about eight different people have told me I got gypped; that the ox is nothing but bones."

"What's the angle?" Nancy asked. "Did they have a better one to sell?"

"No, they just said that it was going to be a grim Christmas because there won't be enough meat to go around. Maybe I'll get an independent judge to look at the beast in the morning."

Bright and early, Halingisi, a Tswana cattle-owner, appeared at our camp. But before I could ask him to give me his opinion on Yehave's black ox, he gave me the eye signal that indicated a confidential chat. We left the camp and sat down.

"/Tontah, I'm surprised at you; you've lived here for three years and still haven't learned anything about cattle."

"But what else can a person do but choose the biggest, strongest animal one can find?" I retorted.

"Look, just because an animal is big doesn't mean that it has plenty of meat on it. The black one was a beauty when it was younger, but now it is thin to the point of death."

"Well, I've already bought it. What can I do at this stage?"

"Bought it already? I thought you were just considering it. Well, you'll have to kill and serve it, I suppose. But don't expect much of a dance to follow."

My spirits dropped rapidly. I could believe that Ben!a and /Gaugo just might be putting me on about the black ox, but Halingisi seemed to be an impartial critic. I went around that day feeling as though I had bought a lemon of a used car.

In the afternoon it was ≠Tomazho's turn. ≠Tomazho is a fine hunter, a top trance performer, and one of my most reliable informants. He approached the subject of the Christmas cow as part of my continuing education.

"My friend, the way it is with us Ju/'hoansi," he began, "is that we love meat. And even more than that, we love fat. When we hunt we always search for the fat ones, the ones dripping with layers of white fat: fat that turns into a clear, thick oil in the cooking pot, fat that slides down your gullet, fills your stomach and gives you a roaring diarrhea," he rhapsodized.

"So, feeling as we do," he continued, "it gives us pain to be served such a scrawny thing as Yehave's black ox. It is big, yes, and no doubt its giant bones are good for soup, but fat is what we really crave, and so we will eat Christmas this year with a heavy heart."

The prospect of a gloomy Christmas now had me worried, so I asked ≠Tomazho what I could do about it.

"Look for a fat one, a young one . . . smaller, but fat. Fat enough to make us //gom ('evacuate the bowels'); then we will be happy."

My suspicions were aroused when ≠Tomazho said that he happened to know of a young, fat, barren cow that the owner was willing to part with. Was ≠Tomazho working on commission, I wondered? But I dispelled this unworthy thought when we approached the Herero owner of the cow in question and found that he had decided not to sell.

The scrawny wreck of a Christmas ox now became the talk of the /Xai/ xai waterhole and was the first news told to the outlying groups as they began to come in from the bush for the feast. What finally convinced me that real trouble might be brewing was the visit from /N!au, an old conservative with a reputation for fierceness. His nickname meant "spear" and referred to an incident 30 years ago in which he had speared a man to death. He had an intense manner; fixing me with his eyes, he said in clipped tones:

"I have only just heard about the black ox today, or else I would have come here earlier. /Tontah, do you honestly think you can serve meat like that to people and avoid a fight?" He paused, letting the implications sink in. "I don't mean fight you, /Tontah; you are a White man. I mean a fight between Ju/'hoansi. There are many fierce ones here, and with such a small quantity of meat to distribute, how can you give everybody a fair share? Someone is sure to accuse another of taking too much or hogging all the choice pieces. Then you will see what happens when some go hungry while others eat."

The possibility of at least a serious argument struck me as all too real. I had witnessed the tension that surrounds the distribution of meat from a kuku or gemsbok kill, and had documented many arguments that sprang up from a real or imagined slight in meat distribution. The owners of a kill may spend up to two hours arranging and rearranging the piles of meat under the gaze of a circle of recipients before handing them out. And I also knew that the Christmas feast at /Xai/ xai would be bringing together groups that had feuded in the past.

Convinced now of the gravity of the situation, I went in earnest to search for a second cow; but all my inquiries failed to turn one up.

The Christmas feast was evidently going to be a disaster, and the incessant complaints about the meagerness of the ox had already taken the fun out of it for me. Moreover, I was getting bored with the wisecracks, and after losing my temper a few times, I resolved to serve the beast anyway. If the meat fell short, the hell with it. In the Ju/'hoan idiom, I announced to all who would listen:

"I am a poor man and blind. If I have chosen one that is too old and too thin, we will eat it anyway and see if there is enough meat there to quiet the rumbling of our stomachs."

On hearing this speech, Ben!a offered me a rare word of comfort. "It's thin," she said philosophically, "but the bones will make a good soup."

At dawn Christmas morning, instinct told me to turn over the butchering and cooking to a friend and take off with Nancy and spend Christmas alone in the bush. But curiosity kept me from retreating. I wanted to see what such a scrawny ox looked like on butchering, and if there *was* going to be a fight, I wanted to catch every word of it. Anthropologists are incurable that way.

The great beast was driven up to our dancing ground, and a shot in the forehead dropped it in its tracks. Then, freshly cut branches were heaped around the fallen carcass to receive the meat. Ten men volunteered to help with the cutting. I asked /Gaugo to make the breast bone cut. This cut, which begins the butchering process for most large game, offers easy access for removal of the viscera. But it also allows the hunter to spot-check the amount of fat on the animal. A fat game animal carries a white layer up to an inch thick on the chest, while in a thin one, the knife will quickly cut to bone. All eyes fixed on his hand as /Gaugo, dwarfed by the great carcass, knelt to the breast. The first cut opened a pool of solid white in the black skin. The second and third cut widened and deepened the creamy white. Still no bone. It was pure fat; it must have been two inches thick.

"Hey /Gau," I burst out, "that ox is loaded with fat. What's this about the ox being too thin to bother eating? Are you out of your mind?"

"Fat?" /Gau shot back, "You call that fat? This wreck is thin, sick, dead!" And he broke out laughing. So did everyone else. They rolled on the ground, paralyzed with laughter. Everybody laughed except me; I was thinking.

I ran back to the tent and burst in just as Nancy was getting up. "Hey, the black ox. It's fat as hell! They were kidding about it being too thin to eat. It was a joke or something. A put-on. Everyone is really delighted with it!"

"Some joke," my wife replied. "It was so funny that you were ready to pack up and leave /Xai/ xai."

If it had indeed been a joke, it had been an extraordinarily convincing one, and tinged, I thought, with more than a touch of malice, as many jokes are. Nevertheless, that it was a joke lifted my spirits considerably, and I returned to the butchering site, where the shape of the ox was rapidly disappearing under the axes and knives of the butchers. The atmosphere had become festive. Grinning broadly, their arms covered with blood well past the elbow, men packed chunks of meat into the big cast-iron cooking pots, 50 pounds to the load, and muttered and chuckled all the while about the thinness and worthlessness of the animal and /Tontah's poor judgment.

We danced and ate that ox for two days and two nights; we cooked and distributed 14 potfuls of meat, and no one went home hungry and no fights broke out.

But the "joke" stayed in my mind. I had a growing feeling that something important had happened in my relationship with the Ju/'hoansi, and that the clue lay in the meaning of the joke. Several days later, when most of the people had dispersed back to the bush camps, I raised the question with Hakekgose, a Tswana man who had grown up among the Ju, married a Ju girl, and who probably knew their culture better than any other non-Ju/'hoan.

"With us Whites," I began, "Christmas is supposed to be the day of friendship and brotherly love. What I can't figure out is why the Ju went to such lengths to criticize and belittle the ox I had bought for the feast. The animal was perfectly good, and their jokes and wisecracks practically ruined the holiday for me."

"So it really did bother you," said Hakekgose. "Well, that's the way they always talk. When I take my rifle and go hunting with them, if I miss, they laugh at me for the rest of the day. But if I hit and bring one down, it's no better. To them, the kill is always too small or too old or too thin; and as we sit down on the kill site to cook and eat the liver, they keep grumbling, even with their mouths full of meat. They say things like, 'Oh this is awful! What a worthless animal! Whatever made me think that this Tswana rascal could hunt!' "

"Is this the way outsiders are treated?" I asked.

"No, it is their custom; they talk that way to each other too. Go and ask them."

/Gaugo had been one of the most enthusiastic in making me feel bad about the merit of the Christmas ox. I sought him out first.

"Why did you tell me the black ox was worthless, when you could see that it was loaded with fat and meat?"

"It is our way," he said, smiling. "We always like to fool people about that. Say there is a Ju/'hoan who has been hunting. He must not come home and announce like a braggart, 'I have killed a big one in the bush!' He must first sit down in silence until I or someone else comes up to his fire and asks, 'What did you see today?' He replies quietly, 'Ah, I'm no good for hunting. I saw nothing at all [pause] just a little tiny one.' Then I smile to myself," /Gaugo continued, "because I know he has killed something big.

"In the morning we make up a party of four or five people to cut up and carry the meat back to the camp. When we arrive at the kill we examine it and cry out, 'You mean to say you have dragged us all the way out here in order to make us cart home your pile of bones? Oh, if I had known it was this thin I wouldn't have come.' Another one pipes up, 'People, to think I gave up a nice day in the shade for this. At home we may be hungry, but at least we have nice cool water to drink.' If the horns are big, someone says, 'Did you think that somehow you were going to boil down the horns for soup?'

"To all this you must respond in kind. 'I agree,' you say, 'this one is not worth the effort; let's just cook the liver for strength and leave the rest for the hyenas. It is not too late to hunt today, and even a duiker or a steenbok would be better than this mess.'

"Then you set to work nevertheless, butcher the animal, carry the meat back to the camp, and everyone eats," /Gaugo concluded.

Things were beginning to make sense. Next, I went to ≠Tomazho. He corroborated /Gaugo's story of the obligatory insults over a kill and added a few details of his own.

"But," I asked, "why insult a man after he has gone to all that trouble to track and kill an animal and when he is going to share the meat with you so that your children will have something to eat?"

"Arrogance," was his cryptic answer.

"Arrogance?"

"Yes, when a young man kills much meat he comes to think of himself as a chief or a big man, and he thinks of the rest of us as his servants or inferiors. We can't accept this. We refuse one who boasts, for someday his pride will make him kill somebody. So we always speak of his meat as worthless. This way we cool his heart and make him gentle."

"But why didn't you tell me this before?" I asked ≠Tomazho with some heat.

"Because you never asked me," said ≠Tomazho, echoing the refrain that has come to haunt every field ethnographer.

The pieces now fell into place. I had known for a long time that in situations of social conflict with Ju/'hoansi I held all the cards. I was the only source of tobacco in a thousand square miles, and I was not incapable of cutting an individual off for non-cooperation. Though my boycott never lasted longer than a few days, it was an indication of my strength. People resented my presence at the waterhole, yet simultaneously dreaded my leaving. In short, I was a perfect target for the charge of arrogance and for the Ju tactic of enforcing humility.

I had been taught an object lesson by the Ju/'hoansi; it had come from an unexpected corner and had hurt me in a vulnerable area. For the big black ox was to be the one totally generous, unstinting act of my year at /Xai/ xai, and I was quite unprepared for the reaction I received.

As I read it, their message was this: There are no totally generous acts. All "acts" have an element of calculation. One black ox slaughtered at Christmas does not wipe out a year of careful manipulation of gifts given to serve your own ends. After all, to kill an animal and share the meat with people is really no more than Ju/'hoansi do for each other every day and with far less fanfare.

In the end, I had to admire how the Ju had played out the farce—collectively straight-faced to the end. Curiously, the episode reminded me of the *Good Soldier Schweik* and his marvelous encounters with authority. Like Schweik, the Ju/'hoansi had retained a thoroughgoing skepticism of good intentions. Was it this independence of spirit, I wondered, that had kept them culturally viable in the face of generations of contact with more powerful societies, both Black and White? The thought that the Ju/'hoansi were alive and well in the Kalahari was strangely comforting. Perhaps, armed with that independence and with their superb knowledge of their environment, they might yet survive the future.

Appendix B

The Kalahari Debate: Ju/'hoan Images of the Colonial Encounter

The Kalahari Debate, also known as Kalahari revisionism, sprung up in the late 1980s and early 1990s, and has been a topic of discussion among anthropologists ever since (e.g., Barnard, 1992b; Endicott and Welsch, 2001:214–223; Grinker and Steiner, 1997:246–92; Tomaselli, 1999). What is at stake in the Kalahari Debate is the question of who the San peoples are historically—autonomous foragers or dependent serfs. The position taken in this book is that the Ju/'hoansi of the Dobe area, despite recent changes, show an unbroken history as independent hunters and gatherers that can be traced back far into the past (Lee and Guenther, 1993; Solway and Lee, 1990). The "revisionists" argue that the Nyae Nyae and Dobe area Ju/'hoansi have been bound into regional trade networks and dominated by distant power holders for centuries. In this view they were not even hunters in the past but cattle-keepers, or servants of cattle people, raising the possibility that the Ju/'hoansi's unique cultural features of sharing and egalitarianism come not from their hunting and gathering traditions, but rather from being outcasts, at the bottom of a social hierarchy (Wilmsen, 1989; Wilmsen and Denbow, 1990).

Curiously, until recently, neither the revisionists or their opponents had bothered to systematically ask the Ju people themselves for their views of their own history. How do the Ju/'hoansi interpret their past and how does that picture square with the evidence from archaeology and history?

Map 1 shows the southern African subcontinent in the nineteenth century and the position of the Nyae Nyae-Dobe area within it, straddling what is now the Botswana/Namibia border. North-South Line A-B, dividing the region into eastern and western halves, highlights an interesting aspect of population geography, both in precolonial times and in the present, namely that 90 percent of the human population lived in the *eastern* half. Western southern Africa was and still is a sparsely populated region with widely scattered settlements remote from one another.

Beginning in 1986–1987 when the revisionist debate began to heat up, I started to ask Botswana Ju elders focused questions about the time they refer to as *n//a k'aishe* or "first time" (Lee, 1998). The goal was to elicit collective memories of their pre-colonial past, a time we could date historically to the pre-1870s. Subsequently I returned for two more periods of interviewing, in 1995 and 1997, with informants from the Nyae Nyae and Cho/ana areas of Namibia. Now there are five major areas of Ju settlement represented in the oral history accounts. In this discussion, I will draw on three bodies of evidence on the Nyae Nyae-Dobe area Ju/'hoansi: their own oral histories, archaeology,

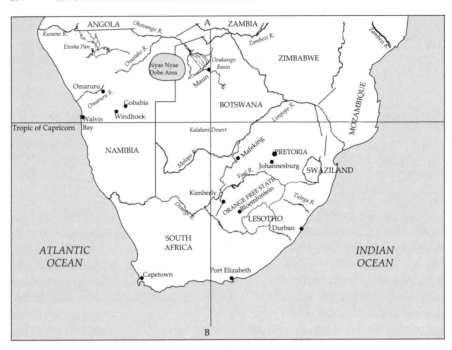

Map 1.1 The Nyae Nyae-Dobe area in southern Africa.

and ethnohistory. Map 2 is a close up of the Nyae Nyae-Dobe area showing some of the places and sites mentioned in the text.

ORAL HISTORIES

During my fieldwork in the Dobe area starting in the 1960s, the Ju/'hoansi were acutely aware that they were living under the gaze and control of the Tawana chiefdom and, beyond it, the British colonial authority. However in speaking of the area's past, Ju/'hoansi informants spoke of their own autonomy in the nineteenth century as a given: they were foragers who lived entirely on their own without agriculture or domesticated animals.

The existence of many Later Stone Age archeological sites in the Dobe area with thousands of stone artifacts and debris, supports this view. But left unexplained is the presence on these same sites of small quantities of pottery and iron, indicating Iron Age presence or contact with Iron Age cultures. The Ju/'hoansi themselves explain the presence of these goods in terms of their long-standing trade relations with riverine peoples. On the other hand, Kalahari revisionists have argued that these archeological traces are proof positive of domination of the Dobe area by Iron Age peoples and the incorporation of the Ju/'hoansi into a regional polity (Wilmsen, 1989; Wilmsen and Denbow, 1990). Wilmsen has further argued that people labeled Bushmen had raised cattle in centuries past:

> [I]n this century . . . an overwhelming majority of peoples so labeled have pursued a substantially pastoral way of life in symbiosis with, employed by, or enserfed to Bantu-speaking cattle owners . . . this is equally true of earlier centuries. (Wilmsen, 1989:1)

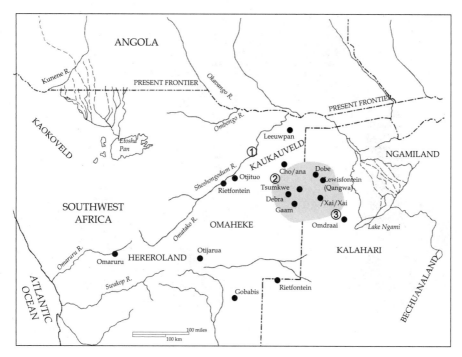

Map 2. Early colonial contacts near the Nyae Nyae-Dobe area: locations of (1) Schinz (1886), (2) Müller (1911–1912), and (3) Baines and Chapman (1868). See also Chapter 2.

Remarkably, in all the voluminous writings on the Kalahari Debate (summarized in Barnard, 1992b), neither side had systematically investigated how the Ju/'hoansi themselves articulate their own history.

An Interview with Kumsa N±whin

Kumsa n≠whin, a 70-year-old Dobe man, was a former tribal policeman and famous healer I interviewed in 1987. I began by asking him if long ago his ancestors had lived with cattle.

"No," he replied. "My father's father saw them for the first time. My father's father's father did not know them. The first non-San to come to the region were Europeans, not Blacks. We worked for them, got money and obtained our first cattle from the Tswana with that money. The Whites first came to !Kubi [south of Dobe], killed elephants and pulled their teeth [i.e., ivory]. In the old days the Ju/'hoansi also killed elephants with spears for the meat. At least 15 men were required for a hunt. They dumped the tusks [they didn't have a use for them].

"The Whites came by ≠dwa-/twe [lit. "giraffe-horse" [i.e., camels]. The Whites had no cattle, they had horses and camels. 'Janny' came from the south. Another one made a well at Qangwa [also called Lewisfontein]. My father said 'Oh, can water come out of there?' They used metal tools but not engines. This well is not used today. They spoke Burusi [Afrikaans]."

Richard Lee collecting Ju elders' oral histories of the life of their ancestors in pre-colonial times.

I asked, "Before the whites came did you know 'Ju sa jo' [Black people] here?" His response was unequivocal: "No. We only knew ourselves. Ju/'hoansi exclusively."

"But when the Blacks did come, who was first?"

"The first Black was Mutibele, a Tswana, and his older brother, Mokgomphata. They came from the east following the paths made by the Whites going in the opposite direction. They were shown the waterholes by Ju/'hoansi including my father /Twi. They were shown the killing sites of the elephants, where the bones lay, the sites where Whites killed. And they said 'Oh, the whites have already got the n!ore [territory] from us.' Then [Mutibele's] father claimed the land and all the Ju/'hoansi on it, but he deceived us."

"How did he deceive you? When the Tswana claims he is master of you all, do you agree?"

"If he was the master, he didn't give us anything, neither clothes nor pots, or even one calf. The Europeans had given the Ju/'hoansi guns. When the Tswana saw this they decided to give guns to other Ju/'hoansi, so that they could hunt eland and giraffe."

Later in the conversation I explored the nature of San–Black interactions in the precolonial period. What had they received from the Blacks?

"When I was young," Kumsa replied "we had no iron pots. We used the clay pots of the Goba. We couldn't make them ourselves."

"Then how do you account for the fact that there are many potsherds on old Ju/'hoansi sites around here?"

"Our fathers' fathers and their fathers' fathers got them from the Gobas. They would trade for them with skins. The Gobas didn't come up here. They stayed where they were [on the rivers] and we went to them. This went on for a very long time [so that is why there are so many potsherds]."

"We [always] got two things from them: iron and pots. If you go to Danega today you will find the right earth. But the Gobas didn't come here. We always went to them."

--*

Kumsa's statements are congruent with a model of autonomy. Others had also made the point that a long-standing trade existed with riverine peoples *in which the Ju did the travelling.* It would be hard to argue that the Blacks could dominate the Dobe area without any physical presence, but I suppose it is not impossible. The trading trips made by the Ju to the east and elsewhere would certainly account for the presence of Iron Age materials on the Dobe area sites. In fact Polly, Wiessner (1990; 1993) has argued that the levels of iron and pottery found on Dobe area Later Stone Age (LSA) sites can be accounted for by *hxaro* trade, a traditional form of delayed exchange still practiced by the Ju/'hoansi that historically has been a vehicle for long-distance trade (see Chapter 8).

One suggestive point was Kumsa's intriguing statement that the pre-colonial Ju hunted elephant but discarded the tusks; remarkable because it indicates that the Dobe Ju/'hoansi were hunting elephant for subsistence and were not part of a mercantile *or* a tributary network, since in either case elephant ivory would have been a prime valuable item.

Also interesting is Kumsa's rather dismissive view of the Tswana as overlords. For Kumsa the criterion for being a chief [lit. in San, "wealth-person"] is giving away in this context, not exercising power *per se.* The Europeans were chiefs because they gave guns, the Tswana were "deceivers" because in Kumsa's terms they claimed chiefly status but gave nothing (see pp. 223–225 for contemporaneous European views of the encounter).

A !Goshe Commentary on the Early Days of Contact

/Ti!kai-n!a, aged 80 at the time of the interview (1987), and /Ti!kai-tsau ("tooth") age 63, were two of the leading men of !Goshe, 16 kilometers east of Qangwa, and the easternmost and most economically "progressive" of the Dobe area villages. !Goshe is the jumping-off point for travel to the east, and the village has kept Tswana cattle since the 1910s. With their strong ties to the east where most Blacks reside, !Goshe people, by reason of history and geography, are the most attuned to links to "Iron Age" peoples.

"Certain Europeans in Gaborone," I began, "argue that long ago you Ju/'hoansi, [that is] your fathers' fathers' fathers' fathers had cattle. Do you agree?"

"No! Not a bit!" was the younger /Ti!kai's emphatic answer. "Long ago our fathers' fathers' fathers' fathers, the only meat *they* had was what they could shoot with arrows. We only got cows from the Tswana."

I persisted. "But when you dig holes deep down beneath where you live, you find pieces of pottery. Where did they come from?"

"Oh those pots were our own work!" replied the elder /Ti!kai. "Our ancestors made them. They would put them on the fire and cook with them. But since we got iron pots from you Europeans we lost the knowledge of pottery making."

Shifting the topic, I asked, "What about iron?"

"We got that from the Mbukushu," said /Ti!kai. "But we learned how to work it ourselves. . . . You stick it in the fire, heat it up, and hammer it. . . . We did it ourselves. We saw how the Gobas did it and we learned from them."

"Where did you get the iron itself from?"

Their answer surprised me. "The Europeans," said /Ti!kai. "The Tswana and Gobas didn't have it. They also got it from the Europeans."

I had to disagree. "But," I said, "in the oldest abandoned villages of the Gobas, iron is there. Long before the Europeans came."

At this point the older /Ti!kai intervened. "Yes! /Tontah is right. Long ago the Mbukushu had the pieces of iron that they worked."

The younger /Ti!kai turned to the older and asked, incredulously, "Well, where did they get the iron from?

Matter-of-factly, the older man replied, "From the earth."

Much discussion followed on this point. The younger man was unconvinced that the Gobas had iron before the Europeans, but old /Ti!kai stuck to his story.

Shifting topic again, I asked, "Long long ago, did your fathers' fathers' fathers' fathers practice *//hara* [farming]?"

There was no disagreement on this point. "No, we didn't. We just ate the food that we collected from the bush."

The older /Ti!kai added, "When I was a boy we had learned about *//hara* from the Tswanas. They showed us how [to do it]."

The !Goshe interviews corroborate the account of Kumsa on the absence of cattle and agriculture before the twentieth-century arrival of the Tswana. They add detail on Ju/'hoan understandings of the history of pottery and iron use. In the first case they spoke of Ju manufacture of pottery, whereas other informants spoke of it as only imported. In the second case there was an intriguing difference of opinion. There was agreement that iron was imported from the Gobas but only in the recent past, but some believed that iron was so recent that the Gobas only obtained iron *after* the arrival of the Europeans, a view that we were to encounter elsewhere.

N!ae and /Kunta at Cho/ana

Another round of oral history interviews took place in 1995 at Cho/ana, a former Ju/'hoan waterhole, 65 kilometers northwest of Dobe, now located in Namibia's Kaudom Game Reserve. The informants were N!ae and her husband /Kunta (/Tontah) one of my namesakes (see Chapter 5). Cho/ana has long been known to historians as a meeting point for Ju/'hoansi from several regions. It was a convenient water hole for Ju/'hoan parties engaged in *hxaro* trade to meet.

In tracing the earliest history of the place, /Kunta saw the original owners as Ju/'hoansi, not Blacks or any other ethnic group. In the beginning, asserted /Kunta, only Ju/'hoansi lived here; there were no Gobas. Ju people would come from Nyae Nyae and from the north, to do *hxaro* here. It was a waterhole that always held water. People from the South (Nyae Nyae) would bring */do* (ostrich eggshell beads). People from the North brought */an* (glass beads). In /Kunta's words, "*Hxaro* brought them together."

A point of emphasis in our interviews was the question of whether the Gobas made trips to the interior to trade or to make their presence felt. /Kunta was emphatic: "No, [they didn't come to us] we went to them. We saw pots on their fires and wanted them, so they gave us some."

"And what did you give them in return?"

"We gave Gobas /do in exchange for pots."

The interior Ju/'hoansis' proximity to Iron Age peoples on their periphery and the use of iron as a marker of Iron Age overlordship has been a particular point of emphasis for the revisionists. I was anxious to hear /Kunta and N!ae's views of the precolonial use of iron and its source.

"Did your ancestors have !ga (iron)?

"Are you joking? we didn't know !ga. If we needed arrows we used ≠dwa (giraffe) or n!n (eland) bones.

"Who gave Ju/'hoansi the iron?"

"We visited north and east and saw this wonderful stuff for arrows and knives; we asked Gobas for it and got some. It was very valuable; when others saw it their hearts were sad because they didn't have it; they wanted it so badly they would even fight other Ju for it. Parties went north to seek it; Gobas gave it to them in exchange for steenbok and duiker skins and other things."

"Where did Goba get iron from?"

Without hesitation /Kunta replied, "From the European."

"Are you saying that before Europeans came Gobas had no iron?"

"Yes, they had no iron."

--*

It is interesting that informants see iron coming ultimately from Europeans; they saw the appearance of iron and Europeans in their areas as so close in time that iron was associated with Europeans. While it is true that the amount of iron on Nyae Nyae-Dobe LSA sites is miniscule, it is striking that the long history of Iron Age occupation on their periphery, for example at the Tsodilo Hills with radiocarbon dates as early as 500 A.D., doesn't have much resonance with the Ju/'hoansi informants. When they did obtain iron from the Gobas, it was clearly an item of trade and not a marker of overlordship. In any event the very (post-European) recency of the trade in iron challenges the revisionist view of a deep antiquity of Ju/'hoan subservience.

Discussion

In all interviews there was repeated insistence that no Gobas or any other Blacks occupied their area or even visited prior to the late nineteenth century; several spoke of the Gobas' preference for staying on the river and avoiding the dry interior. All these accounts illuminate the pragmatic and matter-of-fact approach of Dobe and Nyae Nyae area people to questions of history. These, after all, are questions of the most general nature and the accounts agree closely, not only about the autonomy of the area from outside domination but also about the absence of cattle and agriculture in pre-colonial times (though not of pottery and iron). There are interesting divergences of opinion on whether pottery was imported or locally made, and on whether the Gobas had iron before the Europeans. Taken together these accounts along with others (see, for example, pp. 18–22; as well as Lee, 1979:76–78; L. Marshall, 1976:52–58) constitute a fair representation of mid and late twentieth-century Ju/'hoan views of their forbearers' nineteenth-century history of autonomy.

One other indication of the Ju sense of their history is the largely positive self-image of their past. They see themselves as actors, not victims, and this contrasts with the negative self-imagery expressed by other San people, (such as Hai//om or Nharo views of their present and past (Widlok, 1999; Guenther, 1986:13–15, 232–233).

Ostrich eggshell bead necklaces have been a major item of Ju/'hoan exchange for centuries and are still being manufactured today, both as a local valuable and for the tourist trade.

Despite their proxmity, the Iron Age cultures of the Tsodilo Hills appear to have had minimal impact on the precolonial Ju/'hoansi of Nyae Nyae and Dobe.

Iron tools, once an extremely valuable item of external trade, are now manufactured locally by Ju smiths from abundant scrap metal.

ARCHAEOLOGICAL TIE-INS

The oral history interviews in both 1995 and 1997 accompanied archaeological excavation, designed to link archaeology with the knowledge that was part of the living tradition of the Ju/'hoansi. Professor Andrew Smith of the University of Cape Town started excavating a rich Later Stone Age archaeological site at Cho/ana, which provided a continual stimulus for oral history as new and interesting materials came to light in the excavations. The Ju informants' comments provided a valuable adjunct to the archaeological work (and vice versa). They identified plant remains, made tentative suggestions regarding fragmentary bone materials, and provided a social context in which the material could be interpreted. For example, the elders described a kind of white glass bead as one of the earliest of the European trade goods obtained through intermediaries to the north. A few days after the interview, precisely such a bead was found in a sealed level in association with an LSA industry.

But the most stunning confirmation of the direct late nineteenth-century encounter between people with advanced stone-working skills and colonialists was a piece of bottle glass (mouth and neck) showing signs of delicate micro-retouching that the South African Later Stone Age is famous for. This gave a further indication of the persistence of LSA stone-working techniques into the colonial contact period.

The oral history's insistence on the absence of cattle and Blacks in the interior was confirmed by the complete lack in the archaeological record of the presence of domesticated animals or of non-Ju/'hoan people in the area prior to the latter part of the nineteenth-century. The results obtained demonstrated the efficacy of this kind of collaborative research. The archaeological evidence is set out in more detail in Smith and Lee, 1997.

COLONIAL CONSTRUCTIONS OF THE JU/'HOANSI

Turning to the third body of evidence, what light do ethnohistoric documents shed on these Ju accounts of their own past? Do they support or contradict Ju accounts of relative autonomy? In general, the few historical accounts we do have support the Ju/'hoansi view of autonomy. (Mathias Guenther and I have analyzed a fuller range of the travel literature in detail elsewhere; see, for example, Lee and Guenther, 1993).

One of the earliest detailed accounts of the Nyae Nyae-Dobe Ju/'hoansi comes relatively late when Hauptman Müller, a German colonial officer, traveled through the Nyae Nyae area in 1911. Müller offers some unusually detailed observations on the situation of the Nyae Nyae-Dobe area Ju/'hoansi some 30 years after colonial trade had been established. In Müller's account (1912) the area remained remote and inaccessible. His visit was the first to the interior from the west in five years.

Most telling is Müller's ethnographic description of the bushman inhabitants of this stretch of land he calls "virginal" [jungfräulich] (1912:536–541). He depicts their state as "noch uberuhrt von aller Zivilisation, in alter Ursprunglichkeit" [still untouched by all civilization in their old pristine state]. He reports with amusement how European objects such as matches and mirrors were unknown to them, as well as the camels of his troopers, which startled them and caused the women to grab their

*Excavations of the famous trade entrepot, at Cho/ana, Namibia in 1995–1997 revealed a
rich Later Stone Age (LSA) culture that persisted up to the colonial contact period of the late
nineteenth-century (photo, Andrew Smith).*

children and scatter into the bush (1912:533). However, he did find them using such
things as wooden bowls, glass and iron beads, copper rings, and "Ovambo knives,"
all obtained through trade with Black neighbors.

Of particular interest is Müller's descriptions of the Bushmen themselves. In his
account they were well nourished and relatively tall, thanks to an ample diet of meat
(hunted with bone-tipped arrows) and a variety of wild plants. There is no mention in
Müller's account of any resident cattle or Bantu-speaking overlords, though
BaTswana were visiting the area during his stay. For Müller the association of the
Nyae Nyae Bushmen with the BaTswana was not ancient; it was of recent date and
was based on trade and assistance rendered at the latters' hunting expeditions. The
Bushmen were rewarded with gifts for their services and the relationship with the
hunter/herders is described as equitable and friendly:

> The Bushmen seem, however, to be good friends with the BaTswanas. When I asked a
> Bushman if it didn't bother him that the BaTswanas were killing off so much game every
> year he said "Yes, but we are getting presents!" (Müller 1912:535; translated from original
> German by Mathias Guenther)

Müller's is one of the earliest accounts to be based on actual reports of what he observed, as distinguished from second-hand accounts at a distance. And the preceeding short quotation is among the very first to cite the actual words of a Ju/'hoan person.

--*

To sum up this section, both German and Ju/'hoan testimony are consistent and mutually supportive. The detail presented by Müller and the others (such as Hans Schinz and James Chapman; see Chapter 2) attests to five propositions that accord closely with statements made by the Ju/'hoansi themselves:

1. The relative isolation of the Nyae Nyae-Dobe area from the West and the low volume of European traffic, 1880–1911
2. The absence of cattle in pre-colonial Ju subsistence
3. The absence of Bantu overlords or tributary relations
4. The relatively favorable terms of trade between Blacks and San
5. The relatively good foraging subsistence base and nutritional status of the San

These lines of evidence argue the case that the views of the Ju/'hoansi about their historical autonomy are not sharply at odds with the ethnohistoric sources.

Hunter-Gatherer Discourse and Agrarian Discourse

Both the Ju oral histories and the German and other historical texts are cultural constructions, and yet, how are we to account for the correspondences between these two bodies of evidence? Why do they corroborate one another? To argue that both are careful fabrications still leaves open the question of why they agree so closely. One would have to invoke conspiracy or coincidence, in either case a tough sell. Surely it would be more reasonable to assume that they agree because they are describing the same reality. If Kumsa's, the two /Ti!kai's, N!ae and /Kunta's and others' collective accounts of the Ju/'hoansi autonomous past gibe so closely with those of European eyewitnesses such as Müller, then on what grounds rests the view of the historic Ju/'hoansi as enserfed pastoralists? And why has this view gained such currency in anthropological circles?

A more fruitful approach to understanding the recent debates is to attempt to place them in the context of the intellectual currents of the late twentieth century. How does the current conjuncture shape our perceptions of the situation of indigenous "others"?

Obviously, by the 1990s, the processes affecting the Dobe Ju/'hoansi had brought them to becoming clients, laborers, and rural proletarians, subject to and dependent on regional and world economies. Their current predicament is well understood by recourse to theories arising from political economy, dependency theory, or colonial discourse. Current theorizing is much weaker, however, in understanding the antecedent conditions. Part of the inability of contemporary theory to encompass hunters and gatherers as historical subjects is the lack of attention to the *differences* between discourses about hunters and gatherers and the discourses concerning agrarian societies and the emerging world system.

In agrarian discourse the presence of structures of domination are taken as given; it is the *forms* of domination and the modes of exploitation and surplus extraction that are problematic (Amin, 1976; Cliffe, 1982; Wolf 1982; Hindess and Hirst, 1975; Shanin, 1987, etc). In the literature on the agrarian societies of the

Third World, stratification, class and class struggle, patriarchy, accumulation, and immiseration constitute the basic descriptive and analytical vocabulary.

In hunter-gatherer discourse it is not the forms and modes of domination that are at issue; rather the prior question to be asked is whether domination is *present*. I have been struck by the eagerness of otherwise competent analysts to gloss over, sidestep, or ignore this question.

There is no great mystery about what separates hunter-gatherer from agrarian societies. The former usually live lightly on the land at low densities; they can move and still survive, an escape route not available to sedentary farmers. The latter, with high densities and fixed assets, can no longer reproduce themselves outside the system, and are rendered far more vulnerable to domination (Lee, 1979, ch. 15).

In the recent debate some analysts seem to have taken the world systems/political economy position so literally that every culture is seen as nothing more than the sum total of its external relations. But surely there is more to a culture than its links of trade, tribute, domination, and subordination. There is the internal dynamic of the means by which a social group reproduces itself ecologically, socially, and in terms of its collective consciousness (a point taken up by Sahlins in several recent writings; e.g., 1994).

Not all groups have had the same tumultuous history of war, displacement, and destruction as, for example, the nineteenth-century Bushman "raiders" of the Drakensburg chronicled by John Wright (1971). In each case the externalities have to be carefully specified and not glossed over. But we have to strike a balance between the world systems–type of analysis and consideration of the crucial ways in which cultures reproduce themselves. The ethnographic method is uniquely qualified to explore the latter. If Khoisan studies is to benefit from the current debate then it is important for ethnography and political economy to talk to each other and to try to find a common language for airing (and hopefully resolving) differences. (Sue Kent has drawn together recent work emphasizing the diversity of African hunter-gatherers, 1996, in press; see also Kelly, 1995).

An historically informed ethnography can offer an alternative to the totalizing discourses of world systems theory. The unself-conscious sense of their own nineteenth- and early twentieth-century autonomy expressed by Ju/'hoan hunter-gatherers and its corroboration by contemporaneous colonial observers is one example of how these powerful assumptions can be challenged. They bear testimony that in the not very distant past other ways of being were possible.

That said, autonomy should not be taken as an article of faith, nor is it an all-or-nothing proposition. It is, or should be, an empirical question, and each society may exhibit a complex array of more or less autonomy at stages in its history. Even in agrarian societies spaces are opened up, however small, for the expression of autonomous thought and behavior. Thus it need not be the exclusive preserve of non-hierarchical or noncolonized societies (see, for example, Beinart, 1987).

With reference to the latter though, a final point: What is desperately needed is to theorize the communal mode of production and its accompanying world view. Without it there is a theoretical vacuum filled far too facilely by imputing capitalist relations of production, bourgeois subjectivity, or "culture of poverty" frameworks to hunter-gatherer peoples.

ACKNOWLEDGMENTS

Regarding this Appendix, general thanks are due to Rainer Vossen, Tom Patterson, Harriet Rosenberg, Blanca Muratorio, and Julie Cruikshank, as well as to Megan Biesele, Matthias Guenther and Jackie Solway for allowing me to present ideas originally appearing in co-authored papers; thanks as well to Henry Bredekamp, Alison Brooks, Jan-Bart Gewald, Robert Hitchcock, Susan Kent, Barry Morton, Michael Lambek, Robert Ross, Gerald Sider, Andrew Smith, Gavin Smith, Polly Wiessner, and John Wright for useful suggestions and criticisms. Responsibility for errors and interpretations remains my own.

Glossary of Ju/'hoan and Other Non-English Terms

Basarwa (sarwa): the Setswana term for San; includes the !Kung and a number of other San peoples.

bogadi: bride price in Setswana.

chuana: the !Kung leather breechclout.

chu/o: a camp or village.

//gangwa: God.

//gangwasi: ghosts of the dead.

hxaro: traditional system of delayed reciprocal exchange.

Ju/'hoansi: "genuine people," the !Kung term for themselves.

kamasi: gifts exchanged between a prospective groom and his future wife's parents.

kaross: a leather garment and carrying device worn by women.

k"ausi: owners.

kgotla: the Tswana court of law.

!kia: the trance state of the healers.

kraal: corral, an enclosure for keeping cattle and goats.

!kun!a: old name, used for someone with the same name as oneself (man speaking).

mafisa: cattle lent out by Tswana on a sharecropping basis.

molapo: a dry river course, plural *melapo*.

mongongo: a fruit and nut, the main food of the Dobe Ju/'hoansi (*Ricinodendron rautanenii*).

n/um: medicine, energy, power, anything strange or extraordinary.

n/um k"au: owner of *n/um,* a healer.

n≠amasi: roads or paths along which *hxaro* goods travel.

n!ore: an area of land held by a Ju/'hoan camp.

Rads: Remote Area Dwellers, Botswana government term for San.

shoro: tobacco.

swara: the kin term for brother-in-law when members of two different ethnic groups marry.

t'si: the bush, wilderness.

≠tum: father-in-law, son-in-law.

wi: to help, to be older than, important in determining kinship.

za: to sexually insult.

Films on the Ju/'hoansi-!Kung:
An Annotated List

Many high-quality films are available on the Ju/'hoansi–!Kung, making them one of the best-documented foraging peoples on film. Films marked with an asterisk* have an accompanying study guide. Except where noted, all films are in color. Particularly relevant films are keyed into appropriate chapters in this book.

Films by John Marshall
These excellent films are based on footage shot by John Marshall in the 1950s. They are widely available in film libraries throughout North America. They may also be rented or purchased from:

Documentary Educational Resources
Dept. TDK
5 Bridge Street
Watertown, Mass. 02172
[617-926-0491]

Argument about a Marriage. 19 min. Conflict between two !Kung bands concerning the legitimacy of a marriage. Dramatically illustrates how conflicts flare up to the threshold of violence.

(Chapters 6 and 8)

Baobab Play. 8 min. A group of children and teenagers throw toy spears into a tree, trying to make them stick into the bark. Accompanied by 8 pages of film notes.

Bitter Melons. 28½ min. Music of the /Gwi San musician and composer Ukxone, illustrated with documentary material. Animal songs and games are played together with songs of the land that the /Gwi people depend on for their livelihood and social life. (Reviewed by Alan Lomax, *American Anthropologist* 74:1018–1020, 1972.)

(Chapters 2–4)

A Curing Ceremony. 8 min. (b&w) Sa//gai, a young woman about to have a miscarriage, is cured by /Ti!kay, who enters a mild trance without the stimulus of dancing. (Reviewed by Nancie L. Gonzalez *et al., American Anthropologist* 77:175, 1975).

(Chapter 9)

Debe's Tantrum. 8½ min. Di!ai has planned to gather sweet berries with her sister and to leave her five-year-old son, Debe, behind with his half-sister, N!ai. Debe, looking forward to the trip, strongly resists being left. The predicament becomes hopeless and Di!ai struggles off, bearing Debe on her back.

A Group of Women. 5 min. (b&w) !Kung women resting, talking, and nursing a baby while lying under the shade of a baobab tree.

The Hunters. 73 min. Life and culture of a group of !Kung Bushmen in the northern Kalahari Desert, emphasizing the quest for food in the harsh environment. The climax of the film is the epic chase after a giraffe is wounded by a poison arrow. Overemphasizes the dramatic at the expense of the routine and secure nature of !Kung subsistence.

(Chapter 4)

A Joking Relationship. 12½ min. (b&w) For the !Kung, the joking relationship provides opportunities for emotional support. It is an important part of kinship behavior. This film depicts a moment of flirtation in a joking relationship between N!ai, the young wife of /Tontah, and her great-uncle /Ti!kay. N!ai, as an adult, is featured in John Marshall's recent film *N!ai: The Story of a !Kung Woman.*

(Chapter 5)

!Kung Bushmen Hunting Equipment. 37 min.

(Chapter 4)

*Lion Game. 3½ min. /Tontah, a young man, plays a lion and is "hunted" and "killed" by a group of boys.

(Chapter 4)

*The Meat Fight. 14 min. An argument arises between two camps when an antelope killed by a hunter from one band is found and distributed by a man from another band. *The Meat Fight* illustrates dramatically the social structure of conflict and the role of leaders in !Kung society. Accompanied by a 28-page study guide.

(Chapters 4 and 8)

Men Bathing. 14 min. In Nyae Nyae, if the rains have been heavy, water will stay in open pans, like small lakes, all year. One morning five !Kung men went to Nama pan. /Ti!kay came to wash the clothes he had acquired on his trip to rescue his wives from White farmers. The other men came to bathe. The men use the opportunity to launch sexual jokes at each other.

(Chapter 5)

N!owa Tama: The Melon Tossing Game. 14½ min. The melon tossing game is unique in the complexity and stability of its music and in the frequency with which it is played. In this film, women and girls from three separate !Kung bands have gathered at a mongongo grove to play a long and intense game in which undertones of social and personal tension become apparent.

*N/ um Tchai. 20 min. (b&w) An excellent introduction to *n/ um* and the !Kung healing dance. At a dawn healing dance a young trance performer named /Tontah experiences the violent onset of *!kia.* He is helped through the difficult transition by his teacher and other men.

(Chapter 9)

Playing with Scorpions. 4 min. !Kung people, by and large, are not excited by the threat of dangerous encounters with each other or their environment. But !Kung children, tempting fate in small ways, sometimes play with scorpions.

(Chapters 3 and 4)

*A Rite of Passage. 14 min. Hunting has a special importance among the !Kung. The people crave meat; they need skins for clothing and sacks, and sinews to make string for bows and nets. The importance of hunting is symbolized in a small ceremony that takes place when a boy has killed his first antelope. The film depicts such a ceremony from the time /Ti!kay, a young boy, shoots his first wildebeest, through the tracking and finding of the animal, the cooking and eating of the meat, and the symbolic scarification.

(Chapter 4)

Tug of War. 6 min. Twelve or more boys, in two teams, wrestle over a length of rubber hose. Accompanied by six pages of film notes.

The Wasp Nest. 20 min. Gathering wild foods is a basic subsistence activity and is the responsibility of women. This film follows a group of women and children as they gather sweet, fresh ≠*oley* berries and *sha* roots.

(Chapter 4)

The next film was made by John Marshall for the Odyssey Television Series in 1978 and released in 1980.

N!ai: The Story of a !Kung Woman. 53 min. This powerful film is an update on the state of the !Kung 25 years after the Marshalls' first visits. We follow N!ai's life through flashbacks from her hunting and gathering childhood to her contemporary life on a South African settlement station in Namibia. The impact of the cash economy, schools, missionaries, and the recruitment of the San into the South African army are brilliantly explored in this important documentary. A 56-page study guide entitled *The San in Transition,* by Toby A. Volkman, was issued in 1983.

(Chapters 11 and 12)

Later Marshall Films

Pull Ourselves Up or Die. 20 min. (video) After two decades of life at Tjum!kui, the Ju/'hoansi, led by their Farmer's Cooperative, struggle to find solutions to a host of social and economic problems in the face of bureaucratic hostility, ecological setbacks, and their own internal difficulties.

(Chapter 12)

!Kung San Traditional Life. 26 min. (video) A summary statement of the social and economic life of the hunting and gathering !Kung filmed by John Marshall during the 1950s. Includes material on children's games and social interaction. Produced for primary and secondary school use, but suitable for college audiences as well.

(Chapters 1–10)

!Kung San Resettlement. 28 min. (video) Faced with mounting social problems of alcohol consumption, family violence, and youth alienation, the Nyae Nyae Ju/'hoansi, under the auspices of the Farmer's Cooperative, attempt to break out of the cycle of despair by reestablishing themselves on their traditional *n!ores.*

(Chapter 12)

Death By Myth. (1992) 52 min. in three parts. A recap of the history of the Nyae Nyae Ju/'hoansi since 1951, with emphasis on their struggles with the apartheid system as represented by the bureaucracy, the military, and missionaries. Highlights the complex negotiations and events leading up to the eventual liberation of South West Africa and the emergence of an Independent Namibia in March 1990.

(Chapters 12 and 13)

Other Films

Bushmen of the Kalahari. 12 min. Focuses upon the /Gwi San of the central Kalahari Desert of Botswana. Narrated by Dr. George Silberbauer, the film becomes an implied question: "What is Civilization?" /Gwi live in a harmonious self-contained community whose existence is dependent on women finding roots and men tracking and killing game with bow and arrows. Silberbauer speculates on the Bushmen's future as technological society moves closer and closer to his boundaries. (Reviewed by John Marshall, *American Anthropologist* 73:502–503, 1971.)

Bushmen of the Kalahari: Parts 1 and 2. (1974). 50 min. National Geographic Society. Filmmaker-anthropologist John Marshall revisits the same !Kung Bushmen he filmed 15 years earlier. During the years, the !Kung people have changed their subsistence from gathering-hunting to a reliance on water pumps, goats, horses, and work as ranch hands. Though technically sound, the film suffers from a contrived plot line imposed by the National Geographic producers. *N!ai* (see above) is a much better film.

A Human Way of Life. Part 3 of the series *The Making of Mankind.* 50 min. Hosted by Richard Leakey and featuring Richard Lee, this 1980 BBC film is the only film that has been made specifically about the !Kung of the Dobe area. Filmed mainly at Dobe waterhole, it illustrates graphically the main points covered in this book: the security of subsistence, the skill of the hunters, the rich social life, and relations between men and women. The film features many of the Dobe people whose words appear in this book. [Note that the film also highlights the archeological studies of the late Glynn Isaac in Kenya.] Available for rental or purchase in 16mm or videocassette from:

> Time-Life Video Dept. TDK
> P.O. Box 644
> Paramus, N.J. 07652

In Canada:

> British Broadcasting Corp.
> 55 Bloor St. W., Suite 1220
> Toronto, Canada M4W 1A5

or at BBC offices abroad.

(all chapters)

Distant Echoes: Yo Yo Ma and the Kalahari Bushmen. 50 min. Made in 1993 and released in 1994, this film follows the world-famous cellist, Yo Yo Ma, as he explores the music and culture of the Ju/'hoansi. In a rare cross-cultural exchange, Ju musicians perform for Ma and explain their tonal system to him, and he reciprocates by playing for them. The result is a spiritual encounter, bridging cultural distance through the medium of music. Filmed in the villages of Nyae Nyae, Richard Lee accompanies Yo Yo Ma's journey of discovery as interpreter and guide.

WEBSITE

In 2000 The Kalahari Peoples Fund (KPF), based in Austin, Texas, opened a website at www.kalaharipeoples.org. The website, still under development, contains a wealth of information about the Ju/'hoansi and their neighbors, and eventually will maintain links to many other websites about indigenous peoples and their struggles and survival in Africa and the world.

A major purpose of the site is to list organizations, projects, and individuals working on behalf of San communities. Opportunities for contributing to the work of the Fund will be presented in the context of reports on development and environmental issues that impact such projects. The KPF is currently coordinated by a revolving panel of international scholars and activists, assisted by a panel of San facilitators from the various San people's organizations and by an advisory group of experts in various fields. The KPF's website welcomes debate and the exploration of alternative points of view.

> Kalahari Peoples Fund
> P.O. Box 7855
> University Station
> Austin, Texas 78713-7855
> USA

> phone: (512) 453-8935
> fax: (512) 459-1159

Acting Director: Dr. Megan Biesele (kalahari@mail.utexas.edu)

References Cited and
Recommended Readings*

Amin, Samir. 1976. *Unequal Development: An Essay on the Social Formations of Peripheral Capitalism.* Hassocks, UK: Harvester.

Barnard, Alan. 1976. Nharo Bushman kinship and the transformation of Khoi kin categories. Unpublished Ph.D. thesis. University of London.

Barnard, Alan. 1978. Universal systems of kin categorization. *African Studies* 37(1):69–81.

*Barnard, Alan. 1992a. *Hunters and Herders of Southern Africa: A Comparative Ethnography of Khoisan Peoples.* Cambridge: Cambridge University Press.

Barnard, Alan. 1992b. The Kalahari debate: A bibliographic essay. *Occasional Papers, No. 35.* University of Edinburgh: Centre for African Studies.

Beinart, William, ed. 1987. *Hidden Struggles in Rural South Africa: Politics and Popular Movements in the Transkei and Eastern Cape, 1890–1930.* London: J. Currey; Berkeley: University of California Press.

Berreman, Gerald. 1992. The Tasaday: Stone Age survivors or space age fakes? In Tom Headland, ed., *The Tasaday Controversy: Assessing the Evidence.* (Washington, DC: American Anthropological Association Scholarly Series), pp. 21–39.

Bettinger, Robert. 1992. *Hunter-Gatherer Foraging Theory.* New York: Plenum.

Biesele, Megan. 1976. Aspects of !Kung folklore. In Richard B. Lee and Irven DeVore, eds., *Kalahari Hunter-Gatherers: Studies of the !Kung San and their Neighbors* (Cambridge, MA: Harvard University Press), pp. 302–324.

*Biesele, Megan, ed. 1986. *The Past and Future of !Kung Ethnography: Critical Reflections and Symbolic Perspectives* (Lorna Marshall Festschrift). Hamburg: Helmut Busker Verlag.

Biesele, Megan. 1993. *Women Like Meat: The Folklore and Foraging Ideology of the Kalahari Ju/'hoan.* Bloomington: Indiana University Press.

Biesele, Megan, Mathias Guenther, Robert Hitchcock, Richard Lee, and Jean MacGregor. 1989. Hunters, clients and squatters: The contemporary socioeconomic status of the Botswana Basarwa. *Kyoto African Studies Monographs* 9(3):109–151.

Biesele, Megan, and Nancy Howell. 1981. The old people give you life: Aging among !Kung hunter-gatherers. In P. Amoss and S. Harrell, eds., *Other Ways of Growing Old* (Stanford, CA: Stanford University Press).

*Biesele, Megan, and Paul Weinberg. 1990. *Shaken Roots: The Bushmen of Namibia.* Johannesburg: EDA Publications.

Biesele, Megan and Kgau Royal /O/oo. 1997. *San.* New York: Rogen Publishing Group.

Bleek, Dorothea. 1928. *The Naron: A Bushman Tribe of the Kalahari.* Cambridge: Cambridge University Press.

Brooks, Alison, and John Yellen. 1979. Archaeological excavations at ≠Gi: A preliminary report on the first two field sessions. *Botswana Notes and Records* 9:21–30.

Brooks, Alison, and John Yellen. 1992. Decoding the Ju/wasi past. *Symbols* (September): 24–31.

*Readings marked with an asterisk are especially recommended for further study.

Brooks, Alison, Diane E. Gelbrud, and John Yellen. 1981. Food production and culture change among the !Kung San: Implications for prehistoric research. In J. Clark and S. Brandt, eds., *Causes and Consequences of Food Productions in Africa* (Berkeley: University of California Press).

Cashdan, Elizabeth. 1977. Subsistence, mobility, and territories among the G// anakwe of the northeastern Central Kalahari Game Reserve. Mimeograph Report to the Ministry of Local Government and Lands, Gaborone, Botswana.

Cashdan, Elizabeth. 1983. Territoriality among human foragers: Ecological models and an application to four Bushman groups. *Current Anthropology* 24:47–66.

Cashdan, Elizabeth. 1987. Trade and its origins on the Botetli River. *Journal of Anthropological Research* 43:121–138.

Cashdan, Elizabeth, ed. 1990. *Risk and Uncertainty in Tribal and Peasant Economies.* Boulder, CO: Westview.

Chapman, James. 1868 [1971]. *Travels in the Interior of South Africa.* 2 vols. Cape Town: A. A. Balkema.

Cliffe, Lionel. 1982. Class formation as an "articulation" process: East African cases. In H. Alavi and T. Shanin, eds., *Introduction to the Sociology of Developing Countries.* New York: Monthly Review Press.

Darwin, Charles. 1958 (orig. 1859). *The Origin of Species.* New York: New American Library, Mentor.

Davis, Peter. 1996. *In Darkest Hollywood: Exploring the Jungles of Cinema's South Africa.* Athens: University Press.

Denbow, James, and Edwin Wilmsen. 1986. Advent and the course of pastoralism in the Kalahari. *Science* 234:1509–1515.

Dickens, Patrick, and the Ju/'hoan Peoples Literacy Committee. 1990. *Ju/'hoan-English Dictionary.* Windhoek: Nyae Nyae Development Foundation of Namibia.

*Draper, Patricia. 1975. !Kung women: Contrasts in sexual egalitarianism in the foraging and sedentary contexts. In Rayna Reiter, ed., *Toward an Anthropology of Women* (New York: Monthly Review Press), pp. 77–109.

Draper, Patricia. 1976. Social and economic constraints on child life among the !Kung. In Richard B. Lee and Irven DeVore, eds., *Kalahari Hunter-Gatherers: Studies of the !Kung San and their Neighbors* (Cambridge, MA: Harvard University Press), pp. 119–217.

Draper, Patricia, and Henry Harpending. 1994. Cultural considerations in the experience of aging: Two African Cultures. In Bette R. Bonder and Marilyn B. Wagner, eds., *Functional Performance in Older Adults* (Philadelphia: F. A. Davis).

Draper, Patricia, and Jennie Keith. 1992. Cultural contexts of care: Family caregiving for elderly in America and Africa. *Journal of Aging Studies* 6(2):113–134.

Durning, Allan. 1992. *Guardians of the Land: Indigenous People and the Health of the Earth.* Worldwatch Paper No. 112.

Eagleton, Terry. 1983. *Literary Theory: An Introduction.* Oxford: Basil Blackwell.

Eaton, Boyd, Marjorie Shostak, and Melvin Konner. 1988. *The Paleolithic Prescription.* New York: Harper and Row.

Ebert, James. 1979. An ethnoarchaeological approach to reassessing the meaning of variability in stone tool assemblages. In Carol Kramer, ed., *Ethnoarchaeology: Implications of Ethnography for Archaeology* (New York: Columbia University Press), pp. 59–74.

Ebert, James. 1989. *Considerations of Spatial and Temporal Scale in the Study of Contemporary, Historic, and Prehistoric Kalahari San.* Paper presented at the symposium "The Kalahari Forager-Pastoralist Debate," 88th Annual Meetings, American Anthropological Association, Washington, DC, Nov. 1989.

Eibl-Eibesfeldt, I. 1972. Die *!Ko-Buschmanngesellschaft: Gruppenbindung und Aggressions-Kontrolle.* Munich: Piper.

Endicott, Kirk, and Robert Welsch, eds. 2001. *Taking Sides: Clashing Views on Controversial Issues in Anthropology.* Guildford: McGraw-Hill/Dushkin.

Fabian, J. 1965. !Kung Bushman kinship: Componential analysis and alternative interpretations. *Anthropos* 60:663–718.

Fourie, L. M. 1928. The Bushmen of South West Africa. In C. Hahn, H. Vedder, and L. Fourie, eds., *The Native Tribes of South West Africa* (New York: Barnes and Noble), pp. 79–106.

*Gordon, Robert. 1984. The !Kung in the Kalahari exchange: An ethnohistorical perspective. In Carmel Schrire, ed., *Past and Present in Hunter-Gatherer Studies* (Orlando, FL: Academic Press), pp. 195–224.

Gordon, Robert. 1992. *The Bushman Myth.* Boulder, CO: Westview.

Grinker, R. R., and C. Steiner, eds. 1997. *Perspectives on Africa: A Reader in Culture, History, and Representation.* Oxford: Blackwells.

Guenther, Mathias. 1979. *The Farm Bushmen of the Ghanzi District Botswana.* Stuttgart: Hochschul Verlag.

*Guenther, Mathias. 1986. *The Nharo Bushmen of Botswana: Tradition and Change.* Hamburg: Helmut Buske Verlag.

*Guenther, Mathias. 1999. *Tricksters and Trancers: Bushman Religion and Society.* Bloomington: Indiana University Press.

Hansen, J., D. Dunn, R. B. Lee, P. Becker, and T. Jenkins. 1994. Hunter-gatherer to pastoral way of life: Effects of the transition on health, growth and nutritional status. *South African Journal of Science* 89:559–64.

Harpending, Henry. 1976. Regional variations in !Kung populations. In Richard B. Lee and Irven DeVore, eds., *Kalahari Hunter-Gatherers: Studies of the !Kung San and their Neighbors* (Cambridge, MA: Harvard University Press), pp. 152–165.

Heinz, H. J. 1966. Social organization of the !Ko Bushmen. Master's thesis. Department of Anthropology, University of South Africa, Pretoria.

Heinz, H. J. 1972. Territoriality among the Bushmen in general and the !Ko in particular. *Anthropos* 67:405–416.

Hindess, Barry, and Paul Hirst. 1975. *Pre-capitalist Modes of Production.* London: Routledge and Kegan Paul.

Hitchcock, Robert. 1977. *Kalahari Cattle Posts.* Gaborone: Government of Botswana.

Hitchcock, Robert. 1982. Patterns of sedentism among the Basarwa of eastern Botswana. In Eleanor Leacock and Richard Lee, eds., *Politics and History in Band Societies* (Cambridge: Cambridge University Press), pp. 223–267.

Hitchcock, Robert. 1988. *Monitoring Research and Development in the Remote Areas of Botswana.* Gaborone: Government Printer.

*Hitchcock, Robert, and J. D. Holm. 1993. Bureaucratic domination of hunter-gatherer societies: A study of the San in Botswana. *Development and Change* 24:305–338.

*Howell, Nancy. 1979. *Demography of the Dobe !Kung.* New York: Academic Press.

*Howell, Nancy 2000. *Demography of the Dobe !Kung.* Second Edition Hawthorne, NY: Aldine-DeGruyter.

Jacobsen, S. 1990. Comment to Solway and Lee. Foragers, genuine or spurious: Situating the Kalahari San in history. *Current Anthropology* 31:131.

Kapfer, R., W. Petermann, and R. Thoms, eds. 1991. *Jager and Gejagte: John Marshall und seine Filme.* (Festschrift). Munich: Trickster Verlag.

*Katz, Richard. 1982. *Boiling Energy: Community Healing among the Kalahari !Kung.* Cambridge, MA: Harvard University Press.

*Katz, Richard, Megan Biesele, and Verna St. Dennis. 1997. *Healing Makes Our Hearts Happy: Spirituality and Cultural Transformation among the Kalahari Ju/'hoansi.* Rochester, VT: Inner Traditions.

*Kelly, Robert. 1995. *The Foraging Spectrum.* Washington: Smithsonian Institution Press.

Kent, Susan. 1989a. And justice for all: The development of political centralization among newly sedentary foragers. *American Anthropologist* 91:703–712.

Kent, Susan, ed. 1989b. *Farmers as Hunters: The Implications of Sedentism.* Cambridge: Cambridge University Press.

Kent, Susan, ed. 1996. *Cultural Diversity among Twentieth Century Foragers: An African Perspective.* Cambridge, England: Cambridge University Press.

*Kent, Susan, ed. In press. *Ethnicity and Hunter-Gatherers: Association or Assimilation.* Washington: Smithsonian Institution Press.

Kent, Susan, and Richard Lee. 1992. A hematological study of !Kung Kalahari foragers: an eighteen year comparison. In P. Stuart-Macadarn and Susan Kent, eds., *Diet, Demography, and Disease: Changing Perspectives on Anaemia* (Hawthorne, NY: Aldine-DeGruyter), pp. 173–200.

Kent, Susan, and Helga Vierich. 1989. The myth of ecological determinism—Anticipate mobility and site spatial organization. In Susan Kent, ed., *Farmers as Hunters: The Implications of Sedentism* (Cambridge: Cambridge University Press), pp. 96–130.

Kolata, Gina. 1981. !Kung Bushmen join South African army. *Science* 211:562–564.

Konner, Melvin. 1976. Maternal care, infant behavior and development among the !Kung. In Richard B. Lee and Irven DeVore, eds., *Kalahari Hunter-Gatherers: Studies of the !Kung San and their Neighbors* (Cambridge, MA: Harvard University Press), pp. 218–245.

Konner, Melvin. 1983. *The Tangled Wing.* New York: Harper.

*Leacock, Eleanor, and Richard Lee, eds. 1982. *Politics and History in Band Societies.* Cambridge: Cambridge University Press.

Lee, Richard B. 1967. Trance cure of the !Kung Bushmen. *Natural History* (November):30–37.

Lee, Richard B. 1972. !Kung spatial organization: An ecological and historical perspective. *Human Ecology* 1(2):125–147.

Lee, Richard B. 1975. The !Kungs' new culture. In *Science Year 1976* (Chicago: World Book Encyclopedia), pp. 180–195.

*Lee, Richard B. 1979. *The !Kung San: Men, Women, and Work in a Foraging Society.* Cambridge University Press.

Lee, Richard B. 1984. *The Dobe !Kung* (1st edition of *The Dobe Ju/'hoansi*) New York: HBJ-Holt.

Lee, Richard B. 1988. Reflections on primitive Communism. In Tim Ingold, David Riches, and James Woodburn, eds., *Hunters and Gatherers, Vol. 1:Ecology, Evolution, and Social Change* (London: Berg), pp. 252–268.

Lee, Richard B. 1990a. Primitive Communism and the origins of social inequality. In Steadman Upham, ed., *The Evolution of Political Systems: Sociopolitics in Small-scale Sedentary Societies* (Cambridge: Cambridge University Press), pp. 225–246.

Lee, Richard B. 1990b. Comment to Wilmsen and Denbow. Paradigmatic history of San-speaking peoples and current attempts at revision. *Current Anthropology* 31:510–512.

Lee, Richard B. 1991. The !Kung in question: Evidence and context in the Kalahari debate. *Michigan Discussions in Anthropology* 10:9–16.

*Lee, Richard B. 1992a. Art, science or politics? The crisis in hunter-gatherer studies. *American Anthropologist* 90(1):14–34.

Lee, Richard B. 1992b. Making sense of the Tasaday: three discourses. In Tom Headland, ed., *The Tasaday Controversy: Assessing the Evidence* (Washington, DC: American Anthropological Association Scholarly Series), pp. 167–171.

Lee, Richard B. 1992c. Work, sexuality and aging among !Kung women. In V. Kerns and J. Brown, eds., *In Her Prime: New Views of Middle-Aged Women,* 2nd ed. (Urbana, IL: University of Illinois Press), pp. 34–46.

Lee, Richard B. 1998. Gumi kwara: e ba n//a basi o win si !kwana: Oral histories from Nyae Nyae-Dobe and the Khoisan renaissance. In Andrew Bank, ed., *Khoisan Identities and Cultural Heritage Conference* (Institute for Historical Research: University of the Western Cape), pp. 67–73.

Lee, Richard B. 2001. A fatal attraction? AIDS and youth in southern Africa. In Bridging disciplines, cultures and continents: Tenth annual canadian conference on HIV/AIDS Research. *Canadian Journal of Infectious Diseases* 12 (Supplement B): p. 91 (Abstract).

Lee, Richard B., and M. Biesele. 1994. A local culture in the global system: The Ju/'hoansi today. *General Anthropology Newsletter* 1:1–3.

Lee, Richard B., and M. Biesele. In press. Local Cultures and Global Systems: The Ju/'hoansi-!Kung Fifty Years on. In R. Kemper and E. Colson eds. Long-term Fieldwork in Social and Cultural Anthropology 2nd ed., New York: Altamira.

*Lee, Richard B., and R. H. Daly, eds. 1999. *The Cambridge Encyclopedia of Hunters and Gatherers.* Cambridge: Cambridge University Press.

Lee, Richard B., and Irven DeVore, eds. 1968. *Man the Hunter.* Chicago: Aldine.

*Lee, Richard B., and Irven DeVore, eds. 1976. *Kalahari Hunter-Gatherers: Studies of the !Kung San and their Neighbors.* Cambridge, MA: Harvard University Press.

*Lee, Richard B., and Mathias Guenther. 1991. Oxen or onions: The search for trade (and truth) in the Kalahari. *Current Anthropology* 32(5):592–601.

*Lee, Richard B., and Mathias Guenther. 1993. Problems in Kalahari historical ethnography and the tolerance of error. *History in Africa* 20:185–235.

Lee, Richard B., and Susan Hurlich. 1982. From foragers to fighters: South Africa's militarization of the Namibian San. In Eleanor Leacock and Richard Lee, eds., *Politics and History in Band Societies* (Cambridge: Cambridge University Press), pp. 327–346.

Lee, Richard B., and Harriet Rosenberg. 1994. Fragments of the future: Aspects of social reproduction among the Ju/'hoansi. In L. Ellanna, ed., *Papers of the Seventh Conference on Hunting and Gathering Societies, Moscow* (Fairbanks: University of Alaska), pp. 413–424.

Lewin, Roger. 1988. New views emerge on hunters and gatherers. *Science* 240:1146–1147.

*Lewis-Williams, D. 1981. *Believing and Seeing: Symbolic Meanings in Southern San Rock Paintings.* New York: Academic Press.

Liebenberg, Louis. 1990. *The Art of Tracking: The Origin of Science.* Cape Town: David Philip.

Lord, Deane. 1991. Life in the Kalahari Desert. *Harvard Gazette,* Dec. 13.

*Marshall, John. 1980. *N!ai: The Story of a !Kung Woman* (see Film Guide). Watertown, MA: Documentary Educational Resources.

Marshall, John. 1984. Death blow to the Bushmen. *Cultural Survival Quarterly* 8(3):13–16.

Marshall, John and Claire Ritchie. 1984. *Where Are the Bushmen of Nyae Nyae? Changes in a Bushman Society, 1958–1981.* Cape Town: University Center for African Studies, Communication No. 9.

Marshall, Lorna. 1957. The kin terminology system of the !Kung Bushmen. *Africa* 27:1–25.

Marshall, Lorna. 1960. !Kung Bushmen bands. *Africa* 30:325–355.

Marshall, Lorna. 1962. !Kung Bushman religious beliefs. *Africa* 32(3):221–225.

Marshall, Lorna. 1969. The medicine dance of the !Kung Bushmen. *Africa* 39(4):347–381.

*Marshall, Lorna. 1976. *The !Kung of Nyae Nyae.* Cambridge, MA: Harvard University Press.

*Marshall, Lorna. 1999. *Nyae Nyae !Kung: Beliefs and Rites.* Cambridge MA: Peabody Museum Press.

Meissner, M., E. W. Humphries, S. M. Meis, and W. J. Scheu. 1975. No exit for wives: Sexual division of labour and the cumulation of household demands. *Canadian Review of Sociology and Anthropology* 12(4):424–439.

Mogwe, Alice. 1992. *Who Was (T)here First? An Assessment of the Human Rights Situation of Basarwa in Selected Communities in the Gantsi District, Botswana.* Gaborone, Botswana: Botswana Citizens Council, Occasional Paper No. 10.

Morris, C. Patrick, and Robert Hitchcock, eds. 1992. *International Human Rights and Indigenous Peoples.* Iowa City: University of Iowa Press.

Müller, H. 1912. Ein Erkundungsritt in das Kaukau-veld. *Deutsches Kolonialblatt* 23:530–541.

Myerhoff, Barbara. 1978. *Number Our Days.* New York: Simon & Schuster.

Nyae Nyae Farmers Cooperative. 1989. =′Hanu a N!an!a′an: N/ /oag!′ae Farmaskxoasi//Koa//Kae [Statutes of the Nyae Nyae Farmers Cooperative]. /Aotcha, Namibia.

Radcliffe-Brown, A. R. 1930. The social organization of Australian tribes. Part 1. *Oceania* 1:34–63.

Ritchie, Claire. 1989. *The Political Economy of Resource Tenure in the Kalahari.* Master's thesis: Boston University.

*Rosenberg, Harriet G. 1990. Complaint discourse, aging, and caregiving among the !Kung San of Botswana. In Jay Sokolovsky, ed., *The Cultural Context of Aging* (New York: Bergin & Garvey), pp. 19–41.

Sadr, Karim. 1997. Kalahari archaeology and the Bushman debate. *Current Anthropology* 38:104–112.

Sahlins, Marshall. 1994. Cosmologies of capitalism: The trans-Pacific sector of "the World System." In N. Dirks, G. Eley, and S. Ortner, eds., *Culture/Power/History: A Reader in Contemporary Social Theory* (Princeton: Princeton University Press), pp. 412–455.

Sbrzesny, H. 1976. *Die Spiele der !Ko-Buschleute.* Munich: Piper.

Schapera, Isaac. 1930. *The Khoisan People of South Africa: Bushmen and Hottentots.* London: Routledge and Kegan Paul.

Schinz, Hans. 1891. *Deutsch-Sudwest Afrika.* Oldenberg: Schulzescher Hof.

Schrire, Carmel, ed. 1984. *Past and Present in Hunter-Gatherer Studies.* Orlando, FL: Academic Press.

Shanin, Teodor, ed. 1987. *Peasants and Peasant Societies: Selected Readings,* 2nd ed. Oxford and New York: Blackwell.

Shostak, Marjorie. 1976. A !Kung woman's memories of childhood. In Richard B. Lee and Irven DeVore, eds., *Kalahari Hunter-Gatherers: Studies of the !Kung San and their Neighbors* (Cambridge, MA: Harvard University Press), pp. 246–277.

Shostak, Marjorie. 1981. *Nisa: The Life and Words of a !Kung Woman.* Cambridge, MA: Harvard University Press.

*Shostak, Marjorie. 1983. *Nisa: The Life and Words of a !Kung Woman.* New York: Vintage.

*Shostak, Marjorie. 2000. *Return to Nisa.* Cambridge, MA: Harvard University Press.

Silberbauer, George. 1965. *Bushman Survey Report.* Gaborone: Bechuanaland Government.

*Silberbauer, George. 1981. *Hunter and Habitat in the Central Kalahari Desert*. Cambridge: Cambridge University Press.

Sillery, Anthony. 1952. *The Bechuanaland Protectorate*. Cape Town: Oxford University Press.

*Smith, A., and R. B. Lee. 1997. Cho/ana: Archaeologial and ethnohistorical evidence for recent hunter-gatherer/agro-pastoralist contact in northern Bushmanland. *South African Archaeological Bulletin* 52:52–58.

Sokolovsky, Jay ed. 1990. *The Cultural Context of Aging: Worldwide Perspectives*. New York: Bergin and Garvey.

Sokolovsky, Jay ed. 1997. *The Cultural Context of Aging: Worldwide Perspectives*. Westport, CT: Bergin and Garvey, 2nd ed.

Solway, Jacqueline. 1990. Affines and spouses, friends and lovers: The passing of polygyny in Botswana. *Journal of Anthropological Research* 46(1):41–66.

*Solway, Jacqueline, and Richard Lee. 1990. Foragers, genuine or spurious: Situating the Kalahari San in history. *Current Anthropology* 31:109–146.

*Susser, Ida. 2000. Culture, sexuality and women's agency in the prevention of HIV/AIDS in southern Africa. *American Journal of Public Health* 90(7):1042–1048.

*Tanaka, Jiro. (Translated by David W. Hughes.) 1980. *The San, Hunter-Gatherers of the Kalahari: A Study in Ecological Anthropology*. Tokyo: University of Tokyo Press.

Tanaka, Jiro. 1991. Egalitarianism and the cash economy among the central Kalahari San. In N. Peterson and T. Matsuyama, eds., *Cash, Commodization and Contemporary Foragers* (Osaka: Senri Ethnological Studies), 30:117–134.

*Thomas, Elizabeth Marshall. 1959. *The Harmless People*. New York: Alfred A. Knopf.

Tomaselli, Keyan G.; guest editor. 1999. Encounters in the Kalahari. *Visual Anthropology* 12(23):131–364.

Traill, Tony. 1974. *The Compleat Guide to the Koon*. African Studies Institute Communication, No. 2, pp. 1–102. Johannesburg: University of the Witwatersrand.

Truswell, A. S., and J. Hansen. 1976. Medical research among the !Kung. In Richard B. Lee and Irven DeVore, eds., *Kalahari Hunter-Gatherers: Studies of the !Kung San and their Neighbors* (Cambridge, MA: Harvard University Press), pp. 166–194.

Truswell, A. S., B. M. Kennelly, J. D. L. Hansen, and R. B. Lee. 1972. Blood pressures of !Kung Bushmen in northern Botswana. *American Heart Journal* 84:5–12.

Vierich, Helga. 1982. Adaptive flexibility in a multi-ethnic setting: The Basarwa of the Southern Kalahari. In Eleanor Leacock and Richard Lee, eds., *Politics and History in Band Societies* (Cambridge: Cambridge University Press), pp. 213–222.

*Volkman, Toby Alice. 1983. *The San in Transition: Volume I, A Guide to "N!ai: The Story of a !Kung Woman."* Cambridge, MA: Documentary Educational Resources and Cultural Survival.

Volkman, Toby Alice. 1986. The hunter-gatherer myth in southern Africa: preserving nature or culture? *Cultural Survival Quarterly* 10:25–31.

*Widlok, Thomas. 1999. *Living on Mangetti: "Bushman" Autonomy and Namibian Independence*. Oxford and New York: Oxford University Press.

Wiessner, Polly. 1977. *Hxaro: A Regional System of Reciprocity for the !Kung San*. Ph.D. dissertation, University of Michigan, Ann Arbor.

*Wiessner, Polly. 1982. Risk: reciprocity and social influences in !Kung San economics. In Eleanor Leacock and Richard Lee, eds., *Politics and History in Band Societies* (Cambridge: Cambridge University Press), pp. 61–84.

Wiessner, Polly. 1983. Social and ceremonial aspects of death among the !Kung San. *Botswana Notes and Records* 15:1–15.

Wiessner, Polly. 1986. !Kung San networks in a generational perspective. In Megan Biesele, ed., *The Past and Future of !Kung Ethnography: Critical Reflections and Symbolic Perspectives* (Hamburg: Helmut Buske Verlag), pp. 103–136.

Wiessner, Polly. 1990. Comment to Solway and Lee. Foragers, genuine or spurious: Situating the Kalahari San in history. *Current Anthropology* 31(2):135–136.

Wiessner, Polly. 1993. Hxaro. In *Im Spiegel der Anderen: Aus Lebenswerk des Verhaltenforschers Iraenaus Ribl-Eibesfeldt.* Munchen: Realis.

Wiessner, Polly. 1998. Population, Subsistence and Social Relations in the Nyae Nyae area: Three Decades of Change. Unpublished MS Department of Anthropology, University of Utah, Salt Lake City, UT.

Wilmsen, Edwin. 1978a. Prehistoric and historic antecedents of a contemporary Ngamiland community. *Botswana Notes and Records* 10:5–18.

Wilmsen, Edwin. 1978b. Seasonal effects of dietary intake on Kalahari San. *Federation of American Societies for Experimental Biology Proceedings* 37(1):65–72.

Wilmsen, Edwin. 1981. Exchange, interaction and settlement in North Western Botswana: Past and present perspectives. *Working Paper No. 39,* African Studies Center, Boston University.

Wilmsen, Edwin. 1989. *Land Filled with Flies: A Political Economy of the Kalahari.* Chicago: University of Chicago Press.

Wilmsen, Edwin, and James Denbow. 1990. Paradigmatic history of San-speaking peoples and current attempts at revision. *Current Anthropology* 31(5):489–524.

Winterhalder, Bruce, and Eric Smith, eds. 1981. *Hunter-Gatherer Foraging Strategies.* Chicago: Aldine.

Wolf, Eric R. 1982. *Europe and the People without History.* Berkeley and Los Angeles: University of California Press.

Woodburn, James. 1982. Social dimensions of death in four African hunting and gathering societies. In M. Block and J. Parry, eds., *Death and the Regeneration of Life* (London: Athlone), pp. 187–210.

Wright, J. 1971. *Bushman Raiders of the Drakensburg 1840–1870.* Pietermaritzburg: University of Natal Press.

*Yellen, John. 1977. *Archeological Approaches to the Present: Models for Reconstructing the Past.* New York: Academic Press.

Yellen, John. 1990a. Comment to Wilmsen and Denbow. Paradigmatic history of San-speaking peoples and current attempts at revision. *Current Anthropology* 31:516–517.

Yellen, John. 1990b. The present and future of hunter-gatherer studies. In C. C. Lamberg-Karlovsky, ed., *Archaeological Thought in America* (Cambridge: Cambridge University Press), pp. 103–116.

*Yellen, John. 1990c. The transformation of the Kalahari !Kung. *Scientific American* 262(4):96–105.

Yellen, John, and Alison Brooks. 1988. The Late Stone Age archaeology of the !Kangwa and /Xai/ xai valleys. *Botswana Notes and Records* 20:5–27.

Index

Italic letters following a number indicate illustrative material:

f = figure

m = map

p = photograph

t = table